FLORIDA STATE
UNIVERSITY LIBRARIES

JUL 19 1994

TALLAHASSEE, FLORIDA

More Than a Living

Conflict and Social Change Series

Series Editors
Scott Whiteford and William Derman
Michigan State University

More Than a Living: Fishing and the Social Order on a Polynesian Atoll, Michael D. Lieber

"I Am Destroying the Land!" The Political Ecology of Poverty and Environmental Destruction in Honduras, Susan C. Stonich

Computing Myths, Class Realities: An Ethnography of Technology and Working People in Sheffield, England, David Hakken with Barbara Andrews

The Culture of Protest: Religious Activism and the U.S. Sanctuary Movement, Susan Bibler Coutin

Literacy, Power, and Democracy in Mozambique: The Governance of Learning from Colonization to the Present, Judith Marshall

Gender, Sickness, and Healing in Rural Egypt: Ethnography in Historical Context, Soheir A. Morsy

Life Is a Little Better: Redistribution as a Development Strategy in Nadur Village, Kerala, Richard W. Franke

¡Óigame! ¡Óigame! Struggle and Social Change in a Nicaraguan Urban Community, Michael James Higgins and Tanya Leigh Coen

Manufacturing Against the Odds: Small-Scale Producers in an Andean City, Hans C. Buechler and Judith-Maria Buechler

The Bushman Myth: The Making of a Namibian Underclass, Robert J. Gordon

Surviving Drought and Development: Ariaal Pastoralists of Northern Kenya, Elliot Fratkin

Harvest of Want: Hunger and Food Security in Central America and Mexico, edited by Scott Whiteford and Anne E. Ferguson

Singing with Sai Baba: The Politics of Revitalization in Trinidad, Morton Klass

More Than a Living

Fishing and the Social Order on a Polynesian Atoll

Michael D. Lieber

Westview Press
BOULDER • SAN FRANCISCO • OXFORD

Conflict and Social Change Series

This Westview softcover edition is printed on acid-free paper and bound in library-quality, coated covers that carry the highest rating of the National Association of State Textbook Administrators, in consultation with the Association of American Publishers and the Book Manufacturers' Institute.

All rights reserved. No part of this publication may be reproduced or transmitted in any form or by any means, electronic or mechanical, including photocopy, recording, or any information storage and retrieval system, without permission in writing from the publisher.

Copyright © 1994 by Westview Press, Inc.

Published in 1994 in the United States of America by Westview Press, Inc., 5500 Central Avenue, Boulder, Colorado 80301-2877, and in the United Kingdom by Westview Press, 36 Lonsdale Road, Summertown, Oxford OX2 7EW

A CIP catalog record for this book is available from the Library of Congress.
ISBN 0-8133-8780-9

Printed and bound in the United States of America

The paper used in this publication meets the requirements of the American National Standard for Permanence of Paper for Printed Library Materials Z39.48-1984.

10   9   8   7   6   5   4   3   2   1

Dedicated in loving memory to

Fredric Lieber, 1941-1981
and
Timothy Tinoti, 1893-1990

who lived in different worlds, but were cut from the same mould

Contents

List of Illustrations   ix
Foreword, Ward H. Goodenough   xi
Acknowledgments   xix

PART ONE
Researching Traditional Fishing

1   **Getting It Done**   3

    Why Fishing? 12
    Framework of the Research, 19
        Message, Meaning, Context, and Culture, 27
        Cultural Premises: Propositions That Organize Contexts, 33
    Conduct of the Research, 35
    The Scope of the Research, 39
    Notes, 41

PART TWO
Traditional Fishing Activities

2   **Traditional Fishing Activities**   45
3   **Netting**   57
4   **Pole and Line Fishing**   77
5   **Weirs**   87
6   **Collecting**   91
7   **Trapping**   93
8   **Angling**   99

    Lagoon Angling, 100
    Deep Sea Angling, 105

9   **The Ordering of Constraints on Fishing Activity**   113
    Notes, 126

PART THREE
Changing Contexts and the Contexts of Change

10 Coping with a Changing Environment   131

Persons, Groups, and the Location of Authority, 137
Recreating the Social Order, 141
Onotoa, Kapingamarangi, and the Organization
    of Change, 154
Notes, 163

**11 The Americans: Institutionalizing
Differentiation and Uncertainty**   165

The Process of Atomization, 166
Search for Solutions: Looking Outward,
    Looking Inward, 180
Notes, 186

PART FOUR
How It Is, How It Was, How It Might Be

12 Stable Premises in a Changing World   189
Notes, 207

Epilogue   209

Appendix 1: List of Catch Techniques   213
Appendix 2: Native Fishes of Kapingamarangi Atoll   219
References   231

Illustrations

Tables

2.1	Distribution of named activities by category	54

Figures

2.1	Major features of an atoll	46
2.2	Major features of an atoll reef	50
2.3	Reef features near Touhou islet, Kapingamarangi Atoll	50
3.1	Di gubenge iha (netting garfish)	59
3.2	Di gubenge baua (netting spinefoot)	60
3.3	Di gubenge gala i dai (goatfish netting lagoonward)	64
3.4	Di gubenge dunga lloo (netting soldierfish)	65
3.5	Di gubenge lou niu (coconut leaf netting) on the reef	67
3.6	Di gubenge lou niu (coconut leaf netting) in the lagoon	67
3.7	Di gubenge haadolo (netting squirrelfish)	69
3.8	Surrounding fish and driving them to the rock pile	72
3.9	Coir net encircles the rock pile	72
3.10	Building a second pile on a second net	72
3.11	A second pile inside a hand net	72
3.12	Di gubenge tebu (netting by diving)	72
3.13	A triggerfish net	76
4.1	Garfish lure-hook	83
4.2	Ganae (blue spot mullet) hook	85
5.1	Large minnow weir, lagoon to reef	87
5.2	Single chamber and triple chamber minnow weir	88
5.3	Goatfish weir	88
5.4	Di gubenge iha (garfish netting) on the reef	89
9.1	Constraints on catch techniques	115

| 9.2 | Ritual knowledge: its distribution and integration in organizing fishing activity | 120 |
| 9.3 | The organization of regulatory activity in the institutional hierarchy | 125 |

Maps

1	Kapingamarangi Atoll	2
2	Place names on the reef	47
3	Place names of coral heads	48
4	Location of rock piles on the reef	73
5	Location of weirs	90
6	Pohnpei State, Federated States of Micronesia	130

Foreword

Michael Lieber's detailed study of the traditional culture of fishing on Kapingamarangi Atoll has a special place in the history of ethnography. For the first time, an ethnographer has explicitly taken his strategy for data gathering and analysis in a small, nonindustrial society from what is known as systems or operations research. Such a strategy was implicit in Bronislaw Malinowski's classic account (1922) of Trobriand Island culture and the publications of ethnographers influenced by him, but Lieber makes it explicit and develops it methodologically. The only other study by an anthropologist of which I am aware that used a similar approach was of dairy farming in a rural Pennsylvania community (Manolescu 1987).

Using activities (rather than operations) as the significant units, Lieber shows how the methods of fishing were organized and systematically interlinked in their organization and in their performance. He also shows how fishing activities were in themselves tied to the local men's house as an institutionalized standing group, to values relating to manhood, to social standing in the community, and to the office of the high priest and the traditional religion and political organization. These organizational linkages were structured in a way that was entirely consistent with the traditional world view and system of values. Having shown the structural anatomy of these linkages, Lieber is able to trace out the chain effects of change following the advent of Christian missions and colonial rule, showing where and why the points of linkage were broken and what consequentially followed.

After he had gathered his data and was in the process of working it up for publication, Lieber learned of my own interest in the potential utility of a similar approach, using activities as the units of description and analysis. The result was a dialogue that led to his inviting me to write a foreword to this book. I accepted gladly, seeing in the context of this trial of its utility an opportunity to review the conceptual framework I had tried to develop earlier. I was also concerned to consider why anthropologists, prior to the publication of this book, have made so little use of the strategy exemplified here in their ethnographic research. Furthermore, given its obvious utility for forecasting the likely effects of externally introduced change, why has this straightforward approach to data gathering and analysis been ignored as a strategic and tactical tool in economic and social development planning?

It was in the context of "community development," as it was then called, that my attention was first drawn to activities as crucial units of ethnographic research (Goodenough 1963). My concern at the time was that we anthropologists had been telling agents of economic and social development in what were then called "underdeveloped" societies that it was essential to take the local culture into account in order to anticipate whether proposed changes would be constructive or destructive in their ramifying cultural and social effects. But we anthropologists had no method to offer by which to make such assessment of effect. We had done some analyses of such ramifying effects after the fact (e.g., Spicer 1952, Paul 1955), but we had not developed a methodology by which to play out the likely possibilities before the fact. We were telling planners and change agents that it was important to take local culture into account, but we couldn't tell them how to do it other than to learn as much about the culture as they could.

Obviously a conceptual framework was needed that would allow us to see how the fabric of a community's social life is systematically organized. It would serve to highlight the ways various ongoing activities are linked and mutually adjusted so as to promote people's ability optimally to manage their many and often competing concerns. To this end I was drawn to activities. Activities differ enormously both within and across cultures, yet they are all conducted by eligible or qualified people using procedures, tools, and skills to accomplish goals. The goals are either valued intrinsically as ends in themselves, or they are valued extrinsically as prerequisites to the accomplishment of yet other, intrinsically valued goals.

This train of thought reminded me of Malinowski's sketch of the anatomy of what he called "institutions" (Malinowski 1944: 52-54). Apparently, he did not see its utility for the analysis of change--he made reference to it in his posthumously published book on culture change (Malinowski 1945)--but looked on it as a useful frame for collecting and describing ethnographic material. He was much concerned with functional linkages between institutions but did not present his structure of institutions as providing a systematic way for seeing such linkages. He tended to equate institutions with established, standing groups, as did Chapple and Coon (1942). Standing groups may, indeed, be seen as institutionalized groups, but many things other than groups may acquire institutional fixity, becoming publicly established as the beliefs to profess, the food taboos to observe, or the ways to do things. In the United

States, for instance, people are continually getting together in voluntary associations to deal with local community concerns. Though they begin as *ad hoc* groups with no institutional standing, they tend to conduct their meetings in accordance with the highly institutionalized procedures known as "Robert's Rules of Order."

Malinowski (1944: 52-53) saw an institution as a traditional or newly instituted group whose members engage in "an organized system of purposeful activities." He saw an institution as consisting of "charter," "personnel," "norms," "material apparatus," "activities," and "functions." By charter, he meant "the system of values for the pursuit of which human beings organize or enter into organizations already existing." He defined personnel as "the group organized on definite principles of authority, division of functions, and distribution of privileges and duties." "The rules or norms of an institution, " he said, "are the technical acquired skills, habits, legal norms, and ethical commands which are accepted by members or imposed upon them." He called attention to the necessity of distinguishing between activities and the rules or norms for their performance, noting that norms represent ideals from which actual performance often deviates. The activities, he said, "are embodied in actual behavior; the rules are very often in precepts, texts, and regulations." Function referred to "the integral result of organized activities, as distinguished from charter, that is, the traditional or new end to be obtained."

This content of an institution, as Malinowski outlined it, seemed to me to be fully applicable to the analysis of activities. Activities, moreover, are clearly the natural units or contexts in terms of which much ethnographic data are collected and informants readily provide information. In all societies, human behavior is purposive, and an activity can be understood as comprising the behaviors and events governed by what is considered appropriate to achieving a goal or accomplishing a purpose.

Elaborating a little on Malinowski's outline, I suggested looking at activities as having the following structural features (Goodenough 1963: 330-331).

1. Purpose
    a. stated goals and their justifications
    b. other gratifications accruing to participants
2. Procedures
    a. operations performed
    b. media used, including raw materials
    c. instruments employed
    d. skills
3. Time and Space Requirements
    a. time required for each operation

       b. time as affected by numbers of participants and their skills
       c. minimum and maximum time requirements
       d. space requirements such as work areas and storage facilities
4. Personnel Requirements
       a. minimal and optimal division of tasks
       b. minimal and optimal number of persons for each
       c. specialists, if any
5. Social Organization
       a. categories of personnel
       b. rights, duties, privileges, and powers and their allocation
       c. management and direction
       d. sanctions
       e. permanence of organization (*ad hoc* vs. standing groups)
6. Occasions for Performance
       a. occasions when mandatory, permitted, or prohibited
       b. processes by which activity initiated
       c. locus of privilege, power, or duty to initiate
       d. relation of initiation to direction
       e. availability of media, instruments, personnel

Orderly living necessitates that each activity in which people engage be organized with due regard to the requirements of other activities. Activities whose purposes are highly valued but that allow little latitude in procedure and personnel become the ones to which the organization of other activities is adapted, especially those with more latitude in how they are conducted. The overall efficacy with which people can manage their many and often competing purposes depends on the mutual adjustment of the various features of their many activities.

Such mutual adjustment is accomplished in several ways. One is by *feature overlap*, such as when two or more activities can be accomplished with the same tools, in the same place, or with the same personnel. Different groupings of personnel may be organized in terms of the same principles for allocating authority and making decisions. Such overlap of features provides an important channel through which the effects of change in one activity spread to others.

Activities may be systematically related by *feature complementation*, as when one activity exploits one set of raw materials and another activity avoids them, using other materials instead. Such complementation is important in determining how activities are scheduled in relation to one another. Some can occur simultaneously and others cannot. Divisions of labor serve to implement feature complementation.

When the purpose of one activity is to provide conditions necessary to the conduct of another, the two activities are *instrumentally linked*. Activities may be valued both as ends in themselves and as necessary means to the accomplishment of others. Fishing, as we see in Kapingamarangi, may be instrumental to eating but may be enjoyed for its own sake as well, having both *extrinsic* and *intrinsic* value. Many activities may be instrumental to the performance of one, and one activity may be instrumental to several others at once. We see the ultimate outcome of such multiple instrumentality in working for money. Activities that have only extrinsic value are more likely to be seen as tedious or onerous by comparison with those whose conduct provides intrinsic satisfactions. Making a social occasion of otherwise tedious work is one way of turning onerous tasks into fun. People can visit with friends and still knit at the same time.

As the last example suggests, where their features allow it, people will *fuse* the conduct of activities, making the occasion of one the occasion for the other as well, as when two activities require mobilizing people with the same skills, gearing up the same equipment, or going to the same places. Incidentally, doing a job while engaging in another one appears to be a universal human proclivity.

All of these linkages promote scheduling, establishing standing groups, preferring one way of doing things over another, and stockpiling resources, knowledge, and skills. They promote, that is, the institutionalization of activities, groups, and professed values in a form that caught Malinowski's attention. They promote the making of special tools requiring peculiar skills for activities frequently undertaken in a place set aside for their performance; and they promote making multi-purpose tools and acquiring widely applicable skills for activities that occur less frequently or whose occasions and places of conduct are not readily controlled. The result is that, insofar as their circumstances permit, societies tend toward a balance of institutionalization of groups and procedures, on the one hand, and the ability to remain flexible and to adjust to changing circumstances on the other. This balance is reflected in the multi-faceted linkages between and the complementarities among the many activities in which a society's members engage. These linkages and complementarities reveal the points at which they are likely to be resistant to change. It also reveals the pathways along which changes they do make (or are forced to make) will have their ramifying effects.

Routinely focussing on activities as the units for gathering data and for analysis in ethnography can be helpful in other ways as well, as when one wishes to mine ethnographic data in relation to a question that had not motivated its gathering. Thus, when Ann Chowning and I were invited to write a paper on the political organization of the "stateless"

Lakalai (Chowning and Goodenough 1966), a topic we had not had as a primary focus of our field work, we decided to examine every activity for which we had data and that was not done by individuals working alone. For each activity, we looked at who the people were who took part and how they were socially connected with one another. We looked at who initiated the activity, who directed or managed it, and what their social relationships were to other participants. This exercise revealed a limited set of cultural principles governing participation, organization, and management of activities generally. These principles, when projected against data on channels of authority in kinship relations, rights in land, and the custodianship of moveable wealth, gave us an understanding of political processes in Lakalai society that we could not have had otherwise.

What helped us in the Lakalai case was our having undertaken to do an old-fashioned, "general" ethnography while also pursuing more specific ethnographic concerns. We did not manage to make a full inventory of all Lakalai activities and their representative features, but we gathered data in the context of activities and were interested in the entire range of activities that came to our attention and on which we could get information. Incomplete as our record was, it was full enough to make our look at the organization of activities a highly productive exercise.

In the light of our experience there, I estimate that a team of two or three ethnographers of different ages and genders could have made a comprehensive inventory of all Lakalai activities, their respective features, scheduling, and other systematic interconnections in about a year's field work time and written a description of it all within another year's time, if that had been the team's assigned mission.

The scale of such an effort in a large, complex, industrial society would obviously be enormous. Yet activities and interconnected systems of activities remain the appropriate units of ethnographic research even there. The study of dairy farming in Montgomery County, Pennsylvania, mentioned above (Manolescu 1987), could be linked to a study of the milk collecting and processing industry to which those farmers are under contract and with another study of how the products of that processing plant are distributed through wholesalers and retailers. The result would be an ethnography of how a complex part of the economy of the northeastern United States is actually conducted. A search of the literature by Manolescu indicated that no such studies have ever been done.

It is remarkable that such an undertaking has not been the mission of ethnography. Comprehensive coverage of activities productive of food and goods can be found in a few ethnographies (e.g., Conklin 1957, Buck 1930, 1950); but the vast majority of ethnographers have not undertaken

Foreword xvii

to make a complete inventory of activities engaged in by a society's members, even within restricted spheres of activity, nor have they systematically gathered the kinds of information regarding each of those activities suggested by Malinowski's outline or my later expansion of it. Indeed, anyone making a systematic study of activities would necessarily arrive at the same schedule of relevant kinds of information as Malinowski did. Such a schedule has, indeed, been recommended to ethnographers as far back as the Royal Anthropological Institute's *Notes and Queries* (1951), but we anthropologists have not taken it as seriously as we ought to have.

This neglect of activities results, I think, from several things. Once the kind of social anthropology advocated by Radcliffe-Brown became fashionable right after World War II, ethnographers tended to give short shrift to activities *per se*, largely ignoring such things as tool manufacture and the exploitation and use of natural resources. The interests of those who call themselves symbolic anthropologists are similarly one-sided, being concerned with the meaning of things in the environment and material goods as symbols but not with the organization of activities. Cultural ecologists have paid more attention to activities, but have not dealt systematically with those activity features that they did not consider relevant to their immediate research goals. Furthermore, most ethnography is undertaken in the context of research for doctoral dissertations. The social sciences' fashion of requiring doctoral research to be focussed on a problem or testing an hypothesis has not encouraged the systematic account of activities in interconnected systems. Nor has the length of time spent in field work by ethnographers working alone made such accounts practicable.

As for development planners, to use inventories of a society's activities to forecast or game out the effects of their proposals for economic or social change, they must undertake precisely the kind of systematic ethnographic study that I have proposed and that is illustrated here by Lieber's study of fishing. To do this is a major undertaking, requiring the services of anthropologists and other social scientists well in advance of the time when change programs are to be implemented. In industry, careful preliminary study of this kind is given to the effects of proposed changes in equipment and procedures, because managers are accountable for the cost of failure. A state's highway department is careful to have engineers and other scientists study the geological features of the area where a bridge is to be built over a major river before designing the bridge. Collapse of the bridge can be a political disaster. Social and economic projects, by contrast, are designed for people who live in other parts of the world or who lack political clout. Development program designers and planners need only draw up programs that look good on paper to funding agencies. When they have decided that something needs to be done, funding agencies tend to be impatient about taking the time for appropriate preliminary research, nor do they understand the need for it. Once funds are made available, what matters is that they get spent. A program's failure can be glossed over, and its costs do not come back to haunt the developers and their funders. Those costs are borne by people without redress, people who have learned by experience to have low expectations. Under present systems of accountability in social and economic development, there is little incentive to take the time to do the job well.

It seems, then, that failure to make the kind of systematic ethnographic study of activities illustrated here and advocated by myself, following Malinowski, can be attributed to what have been the fashionable agendas within anthropology and to the lack of pressure on anthropologists for such studies by development agencies, who remain largely immune from being accountable for the human results of their programs.

Lieber's account of Kapingamarangi fishing activities serves, therefore, as a timely reminder that we have much to lose in advancing our understanding of cultural and social systems as long as we fail to make the systematic study of activities a standard part of what we expect of competent ethnography.

Ward H. Goodenough

Acknowledgments

I am indebted to many people for the wherewithal that has made both the research and the production of this monograph possible. It was the interest and the material help of Dr. Tom King, the first director of the TTPI Office of Historic Preservation that resulted in the archaeological survey on Kapingamarangi by Drs. Foss Leach and Graeme Ward in 1980. When Dr. Leach had made it obvious that a study of traditional fishing would be a necessary supplement to the archaeological work, Dr. King's successors, Ross Cordy and Scott Russell, provided the encouragement, advice, and resources to make the research possible. Scott Russell and Dr. Ward have since been most generous with the needed advice and resources to produce the present manuscript.

My wife, Esther, has contributed substantially to this manuscript both in her own work on Kapingamarangi and Pohnpei and in her invaluable commentary and editorial skills. Her calm patience with my often misplaced exuberance is partially responsible for whatever scientific caution is evident herein. I am also grateful to Rehao, to Heweireu, to Kuaiharara, to Timothy Tinoti, to Linson Headu, to Elwik Amida, to Dawiti Madagi, to Apinel Mateaki, and to the late Leo Monopi for their patience and knowledge, gracefully shared and gratefully accepted. I must make special mention of Koro Monopi, Kapingamarangi's first elementary school teacher and the school's first principal. His knack for cautious sifting of information, his keen sense of logical connection, and a dedication to getting it right have indelibly shaped my own orientation to posing questions. He remains first and foremost a teacher long after his retirement from that profession.

The maps included here were produced by Dr. Ray Brod, Department of Geography, University of Illinois at Chicago. The illustrations for this monograph were drawn by Melanie Herzog, University of Wisconsin. Her patience has made clarity of depiction possible for nearly extinct practices. The cover illustration is the work of Pavla Hanzlikova.

I am grateful to Eve Pinsker, Ward Goodenough, Susan Tax Freeman, M. Estelli Smith, and Kellie Masterson for their critiques of the manuscript, to Judith Grobe-Sachs for enabling me to produce the manuscript, and to Martin G. Silverman, who is partly responsible for the breadth of perspective that this research took. Finally, I want to thank Richard Markow, Daniel O'Donnell, and Trudi Zelko for helping to provide a major part of the infrastructure that made the field research possible. Trudi in particular made this research happen as she makes so many important things happen--with style and grace all her own.

Michael D. Lieber

PART ONE

Researching Traditional Fishing

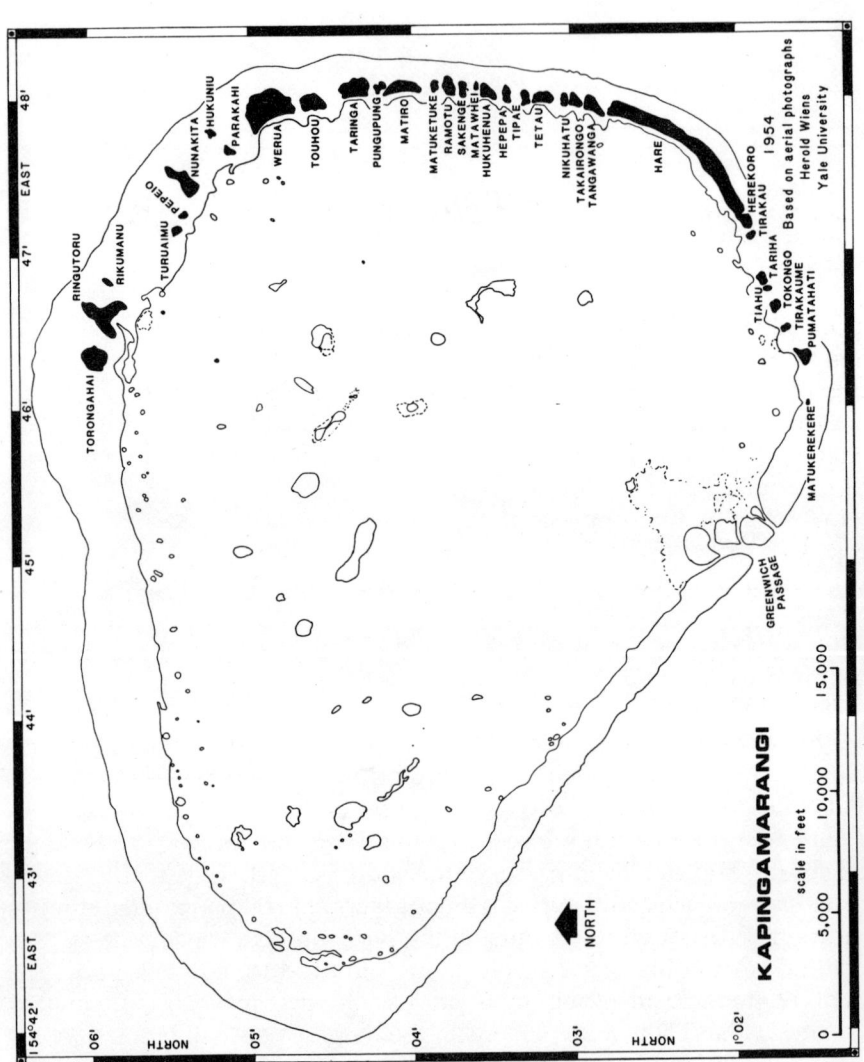

MAP 1 Kapingamarangi Atoll (after Emory 1965)

1

Getting It Done

Approaching Kapingamarangi Atoll on a ship from the north, you really have to hit 154 degrees, 46 minutes east longitude dead on. If you pass three miles east or west of it, you'll never see the place. Its first appearance from about two miles away struck me as if I was seeing a low, green hedge growing out of the ocean. The hedge gets taller as you get closer until, about a mile off, you can distinguish trees and reef. High islanders seeing it for the first time are always struck by the lack of a mountain to keep it from being washed away by the first big wave. From the first time I entered that lagoon and approached the while beaches, tall tress, and the canoe houses and crystal clear waters that line the islets' shores in 1966--and every time since--the sight of this place has never failed to take my breath away.

The atoll's 0.42 square miles of land area is spread as a semi-circle over the northern half of an egg shaped reef in thirty-three flat islets (see Map 1). The lagoon is 6 to 8 miles in diameter with depths to about 180 feet (Wiens 1956). It is a productive lagoon for fish in its deep waters, at its many coral heads, on the reef margins, reef flats, inter-islet channels, islet shores, and two deep passes at the southern end of the reef.

This tiny place could support a population of 600 people in optimum conditions. Although it lies outside the typhoon belt, it has been subject to periodic droughts, some severe enough to produce famines, and occasional epidemics, resulting in a population that probably fluctuated between 200 and 500 or so persons in the past. This small land area produced not only all the vegetable diet for the population--coconuts, taro, breadfruit, pandanus fruit, and nitrogen fixing creepers--but also all of the materials for constructing houses, canoes, utensils and fishing gear (Buck 1950, Emory 1965). Aside from coconut and breadfruit trees, other trees used for construction, *Guettarda speciosa*, *Calophyllum*, *Premna obtusifolia*, *Cordia subcordata*, and *Morinda* were harvested judiciously, but not propagated. People planted hibiscus and breadfruit saplings near their houses, mainly for their inner bark, which they used to make clothing, fishing lines, and leaders for heavy lines. Pandanus trees provided not only a nutritious fruit that could be preserved for long periods of time, but its leaves also provided plaiting material for mats and for canoe sails.

What you see when you go inland from the beach is not much different from what the first ship captains saw in the 19th century. The population is concentrated on the three central islets--Werua, Touhou, and Talinga--in adjoining family compounds, making it easy for people to see and hear their neighbors, fish-bowl style. From early morning until late at night, women and men carry on their daily routines separate from one another. You find women cooking, cleaning, caring for children, and making mats and baskets together on the family compound. They leave their compounds to help relatives on other compounds, to run errands, and to work in their taro plots. Women occasionally travel to one of the uninhabited islets to collect food or leaves, usually accompanied by their spouses, male relatives, or by other women. You find men working together making or repairing fishing gear in men's houses or in canoe houses, fishing in deep water or in groups on the reef, or working on an outer islet planting, climbing trees for food and leaves, or clearing underbrush from coconut groves. The only time you'd find men in the compounds during the day would be for house construction or repair. Men and women are together only at mealtimes, to sleep, or at ceremonies.

The islets on either side of these three central ones are mostly uninhabited, though people say that some of them used to be populated. Hale, the largest islet, not only had a resident population in the early 19th century, but was the site of the cult house in ancient times. There are still houses here and there on Hale, where people stay while they are working on their land and in taro patches. The outer islets are divided into bounded plots, each one owned either by an individual or by a family group composed of descendants of a former owner. Since Kapinga trace descent through both parents, each person is a member of two or more of these land owning groups (Lieber 1970, 1974).

Because the population size fluctuated with droughts, epidemics, and other occasional disasters, the proportion of land owned by individuals and by groups varied over time. Nowadays, all land is owned by groups, each one having a male steward who controls land use and a female steward who is responsible for organizing feasts for group members. Even individual land owners depended on membership in family groups for organizing weddings, funerals, canoe building and house thatching, and other ceremonies requiring group effort. Economic organization, in other words, was and is indentical with family organization.

If you walk inland on Touhou, the only strictly residential islet, you'll come to a central square called a *malae*. A church now stands on the spot that used to be the ancient temple or cult house until it was torn down in 1917. The smaller ceremonial houses that flanked the old temple are also gone now. Just seaward of the church stands a stone slab marking the grave of the founder of the community, Utamatua, and his wife, Roua, goddess of women who, like herself, died in childbirth. It was Roua who sent whales to beach on the reef whenever a pregnant woman died. It was to this sacred area that the gods came each evening to sleep on mats the high priest laid out for them in the temple. The old people told me that they could sometimes hear the gods chanting late at night. The gods would leave the island each morning for their daily journey over the horizon, returning each evening.

The ancient gods represented pure, unbridled power. They could bring rain, fish, and drift logs or they could withhold them at their whim. They could unleash violent storms or high waves if they were feeling particularly vengeful or simply mischievous. No one could control them, but certain people--the high priests--could communicate with them to ascertain their wishes and the reasons for their displeasure. The original Kapinga ancestor, Utamatua, was a priest who had brought gods with him from his homeland. They helped him to defeat the sorcerer Korae (who was already living on the island when Utamatua and his two servants arrived) in a test of magical power. They also helped him transform Touhou from a small sand bar into a habitable islet and the final site of the temple. The priests since that time formed an unbroken line of descent from Utamatua, and many of them became, like Utamatua, gods themselves. Each high priest, then, had at least the advantage of potentially sympathetic relatives among the gods who might listen to his pleas and tell him what was necessary to appease the powers that be.

Because the community's very survival depended on the relationship between gods and priests, political authority was vested in the organization of the priesthood, the cement that held this community together as a single entity. Those who were eligible to be high priests (by descent through women) formed a sacred class called *dau donu*, those who 'count truely.' They were distinguished from the secular class, the *dau ihala*, those who 'count wrongly.' Men of the priestly class were usually trained for several of the thirteen possible positions in the priesthood open only to that class. Priestly class people had priority in participating in and directing groups organized for ritual occasions. Households of the priestly class provided the core of crews for tuna fishing, and so had control over the tuna, which they smoked and dried. There were occasions when no canoe could go without a member of the priestly class.

Men of the priestly class had priority of access to new canoes and to bonito (skipjack) fishing, the most prestigeous sort of fishing on the atoll before Christianity.

The priesthood was organized into two ranked sets, one headed by the high priest, called *di aligi hagamadago*, and the other headed by *di aligi hagalulu*, 'the calling priest,' who summoned people to ritual gatherings.[1] Under each of these men were four lesser priests, five sergeants-at-arms, and a priestess responsible for care of the mats that covered the outside walls of the temple (Emory 1965: 223-228).

The high priest had a good deal of control over the conduct of daily life on the atoll. He controlled all mature breadfruit trees and all drift logs that came onto the reef. Since these were the basic materials for canoe hulls, the high priest, in effect, controlled the number and the distribution of canoes in the population. He also controlled the timing of ritual and ritual fishing expeditions, and he could, if necessary, restrict fishing to certain areas and/or to certain people, such as the sacred class. He could taboo certain lands for use in ritual. He also controlled the disposal of all turtles, giving him control of the turtle shell from which certain sorts of fish hooks were made. The high priest could call down the wrath of the gods on the community. It is said that it was a high priest who appealed to the gods for retaliation when two priestesses (or, in another version, island women) neglected their tasks at the cult house. The result was a flotilla of Marshallese castaways (between 1860 and 1865), who slaughtered more than half the Kapinga population. Lay people avoided contact with the high priest, speaking very circumspectly and always lowering themselves before him when contact could not be avoided.

Among the high gods were six who had come to the atoll with Utamatua. Each of these six inhabited his own sector of the deep sea, two of them also controlling a sand bar (called Korae) and an islet (Bumadahadi). Not only did the priest direct prayers to these gods, but the older men would have to address them whenever a canoe went fishing in their areas. It was, in general, the ability to communicate with the gods that was the basis of power positions on the atoll, not only for the priesthood, but for age divisions among men. It was the older men who 'knew' the ritual formulae for communicating with the gods on the deep sea, for example, so only they could fish in the deep sea by themselves and lead the annual tuna fishing expeditions. There could only be as many tuna fishing canoes as there were old men to lead them in a given year.

Between the priesthood and the family was an organization that cross-cut each of them--the men's house. Every man belonged to one of them, and their numbers varied between two and five, depending on variations in population size and distribution. The men's house was, first, a place, a large communal house where men gathered to work on fishing gear, to talk, and to plan and organize group fishing expeditions. Teenage boys and unmarried men slept there at night. Each men's house had its own canoes, nets, and traps that were its property. Each had its headman, called the *dagi teledaane*, 'leader (of the) men's house,' and an elder sponsor, called a *tomono*. The headman was responsible for organizing group fishing expeditions and for care of men's house property. The *tomono* was responsible for maintenance of the men's house and for provisioning its feasts.

A boy was ceremonially 'introduced' to the men's house by his father or uncle at age seven, and by puberty, he moved his sleeping mat into the men's house to join other adolescent boys. A boy ordinarily joined the men's house that his father belonged to, but if he married a woman from another islet, he ordinarily became a member of the men's house there (since men usually lived with their wives' families). A men's house membership, then, contained a mix of men from both ritual classes and from different families. The significant distinctions among men's house members was one of relative age. The oldest men sat at the lagoonward end of the house with younger men seated progressively inland. The youngest members sat at the end of the house facing the islet interior, and they were at the beck and call of their elders.

Because of its size, the men's house was an ideal place to work on net manufacture and repair. The net could be hung from a post or rafter, exposing that end of it that required attention. The ample rafters provided storage space for sleeping mats and gear. The canoe house that fronted the lagoon end held the men's house canoes, nets, traps, and other gear. The men's house provided an ideal meeting space, where men got together each evening to discuss the next day's fishing plans. Here, men who had been fishing with hook and line that day could relay information about where they had seen large concentrations of fish on the reef and what the tide looked like. This sort of information allowed the men to assess what sorts of fishing would be most likely to produce large catches for the next day. It also allowed the headman to coordinate the use of nets and traps, particularly if more than one expedition was being planned.

Men's houses competed with one another in a number of ways. One was in song composition, conducted by the young men of two men's houses and judged by their elders in formal gatherings called *hagamada*, 'try and see.' There was also competition in the relative size of catches, knowledge of fishing sites, and the reputed prowess of their members as fishermen. The general tenor of competition sometimes resulted in brawls between men's houses. Given that much, if not most of the fishing done on the atoll was organized through the men's house, this was the proving ground for young men, their opportunity to distinguish themselves and to become desireable crew members on canoes going out to do angling. This meant that there was also a good deal of competition among the young men within a single men's house.

The men's house located just lagoonward of the cult house on Touhou islet was called *Madangi* 'wind'. It was closely connected with the cult house through its proximity and through one of its leaders, an old man called the *tomono* who acted as an assistant to the high priest, particularly for organizing the provisioning of work parties and feasts for cult house construction and repair. It was in community meetings in this men's house that a new high priest was elected (Emory 1965: 41-42). Its *tomono* also participated in the ritual initiation of work on a new canoe, so canoe construction required both his and the high priest's permission.[2] Clear evidence shows that these two men limited the number of individually owned canoes (and thereby the frequency of deep water fishing) to about a third of the number in use today for the same size population. Old people said that these two men reserved the privilege of canoe ownership to mainly sacred class people and to their friends. What this meant for fishermen was that most fishing activity was group fishing and that men would have to compete for membership in canoe crews by demonstrating superior ability and by forming good relations with canoe owners. A fisherman's intimate knowledge of the reef and its features depended as much on his ritual position and his relationships with the high priest, *tomono*, and canoe owners as it did on his own preferences for particular kinds of fishing.

Clearly, fishing activity was a part of the larger environmental, social, and ritual order that constituted the community. But it was more than that. Fishing was an expression of that order. You can see this in the general term for fishing, which means, literally, 'surfacing of the sacred,' expressing the relation between people and the gods who control the fish. You can see it in the activity, which brought the relationship to life in everyday experience, as played out in a fisherman's career.

A fisherman's career was marked as a series of ever larger circles, one inside another, that radiate out from the islet to the horizon, and a career step consists of a man's being able to cross the boundary between a smaller one and the next larger one. Beginning with a coconut shell trap placed on the lagoon beach, a boy's next step was to the channels between islets, where he caught small fish with a hook and line attached to a pole. The next step was onto the seaward reef by the islet shore, where he and his friends caught flounder in shallow depressions in the reef. From there he moved to small coral heads at the lagoon beach, where he caught small fish from a canoe with a baited hook and hand held line. By age ten or so, the boy had fished a circle around the islet.

Once a boy joined the men's house, his circle expanded to include the bases of the channels between islets, small channels and reef depressions of the outer reef where the waves break, the exposed reef out beyond the islets, and the deep lagoon--all in the company of older men. His initiation took him to the deep sea just beyond the breakers for flying fish and gets him his first loincloth. If he worked hard and kept his mouth shut, he might be taken along on angling expeditions in the lagoon or deep sea to paddle the canoe, help with the bait, and untangle lines. He might even be given a baited line to handle. These circles were not really his, though. He was there under an elder's direction. Not until he was in his late thirties or forties could he take a canoe to the deep lagoon or outer reef by himself. He would be even older before he could take a canoe outside the reef by himself, and even then, he would have to stay close to the breakers. Once outside the reef, you see, he had a very different sort of environment to cope with.

The deep sea was divided into six concentric cylinders that began where the waves break and extended to the horizon. Each one housed a god who controlled the fish in his domain. Each god required men to get his permission before fishing in his sector, and the man had to be of the requisite age and experience before the god would listen to his appeals. The minimum age got older from the reef to the horizon. So having your own canoe didn't necessarily mean that you were your own boss. Getting your own canoe was enough of a trick--since you needed to have a father-in-law that was happy enough with you to have one made for you. This assumes, however, that the father-in-law had enough clout with the high priest and the *tomono* to get permission to fell the breadfruit tree and to get those two men to initiate the canoe construction ritual. After all of that, you could take that canoe only as far as your age category allows--on your own, that is. If you wanted to use a sixty fathom line and you were only forty years old, you needed a friend in his sixties willing to go with you, because no line touched water until that man sang the chant of appeasement to the god of that sector.

This age grading meant, among other things, that most canoes going much beyond the outer reef slope had a crew of two or three men. One of them had to be a man old enough to get access to the area fished. Another partner might be the canoe owner or a friend or a relative. A third could be a young apprentice brought along to help with the scut work like paddling and baling. The crew not only handled the details of fishing, sharing the catch, but also the maintenance of the canoe and its gear. For an older canoe owner, the crew was a convenience, but for a younger one, it was a necessity. Because so few fishermen owned canoes, each had a wide choice of crewmen, making for a lot of subtle competition for open places on a canoe as men competed to curry favor among canoe owners, using friendship and kinship links to strengthen mutual ties.

Without his own canoe or a place in someone's crew, a man's only other options were occasional fishing with a pole, line and hook (pole and line), hand netting on the reef, and group fishing with men's house colleagues. With hard work, he could acquire an intimate knowledge of the reef and its fishing sites, and with subtle diplomacy, he could get himself chosen as one of the headman's lieutenants and lead an occasional expedition himself. If he showed good leadership capabilities, he might be elected headman eventually, but he would have stiff competition all along the way. It was, then, a man's place in the social order and how he manipulated his social relationships within that order that determined the shape of his career.

It should surprise no one to learn that colonial contact served to introduce some major changes in fishing technology and method to the atoll. What might be surprising, however, is the time that it took to induce really fundamental changes in the organization of fishing. The first contact with Europeans did not begin until 1877, and it was not until the the 1880's that trading ships visited Kapingamarangi on a regular basis (Emory 1965:12-18). Germany had taken control of Micronesia from the Spanish by that time, and ships came to the atoll from New Britain collecting copra, provisions, and sometimes crewmen. By the time that the first anthropological investigation was conducted on Kapingamarangi in 1910 by members of the Thilenius Expedition, Kapinga people had become familiar with such items as tables and chairs, chests, cooking utensils, steel axes, knives, and other tools, sewing machines, bedsteads, and the like. Kapinga were interested in European fishing lines and hooks, but these were not dependably available, and the barbs on the metal hooks made it difficult to get the fish off the hooks. Kapinga used only native hooks and lines for tuna and bonito fishing until they converted to Christianity in 1917.

German colonial control over Micronesia was ceded to Japan in 1914, and the administrative center of control shifted from New Britain to Kolonia Town on Pohnpei. It was during the Japanese administration that fundamental structural changes began to reshape Kapinga society. The changes were hastened by a two year drought and famine on the atoll between 1916 and 1918. Besides accounting for many deaths, the drought also led to the collapse of the ancient religion and its cult house organization, the introduction of Christianity and the rapid conversion of the populace, and the establishment of a permanent Kapinga colony on Pohnpei (Emory 1965: 20, Lieber 1968: 1-6). The emergence of a secular authority, which had already begun by the 1890's, was completed when conversion to Christianity obliterated the sacred/secular class distinction and its attendant distribution of privileges. A well established village on Pohnpei, called Porakied and located just outside the administrative center of Kolonia Town, made possible a regular flow of people between Pohnpei and the atoll. This flow was interrupted briefly by World War II, but has actually increased in frequency as the number of ship trips to and from the atoll have increased year by year (e.g., four trips in 1966, twelve per year by 1978).

Since about 1954, the atoll population has remained relatively stable at between 450 and 485 persons (see Wiens 1956, Lieber 1968, 1984). The population of Porakied, the Kapinga village on Pohnpei, has grown from about 80 persons in 1947 to 600 in 1982 (Lieber 1984). The American administration, unlike its Japanese predecessor, has been very aggressive about introducing social, economic, and political change to the atoll in the form of educational, medical, political, and economic development programs. The atoll now has an elementary school that goes from first to eighth grade, a chief magistrate with a legislative council and two local court judges, a cooperative store that is part of a federation of cooperatives, a Protestant and a Catholic church, a weather station, and a government radio.

The regularity of contacts with Japanese, Americans, and other islanders has been particularly important in changing the fishing practices of the Kapinga people. The introduction from Nukuoro of their light, maneuverable canoe and of spear fishing, trolling, and *Cyrtosperma* taro were of fundamental importance (along with diving goggles from the Germans and Japanese). The Japanese throwing net, for example, replaced many traditional netting techniques. By the 1970s, outboard engines were being affixed to outrigger booms on the canoes, and spear guns and snorckling gear had supplanted the throwing net. These items are bought on Pohnpei and arrive on the atoll on the government field trip ship.

By the time I began my research in 1980, fishing, the 'surfacing of the sacred,' was still a tangible manifestation of the the community's integrity. But by then, it had come to stand for disintegration and chaos. Only twenty five years earlier, the ecologist, Harold Weins (1954) observed that Kapinga fishermen had managed to maintain an ecological balance between human and fish populations. By 1980 there were several species rapidly declining in numbers, and the list of endangered species was growing. Cooperation among fishermen had deteriorated, and the repertoire of fishing techniques in use had declined to less than a third of its former numbers. People saw all this as a manifestation of what was happening to their community, a slow but apparent disintegration that they felt powerless to stop.

It would be comforting to see this transformation as one more example of primeval innocence lost to the ravages of colonial masters intent only on their own interests, but the reality is far more complex than that. There is no way to make the complexity simple. The best anyone can do is to make it clear. I attempt to do this by showing how Kapinga fishing practices, ecology, the Kapinga polity, religion, cosmology, and Kapinga conceptions of knowledge and personhood combine as parts of a single system, change and recombine, then change and recombine once again during the tumultuous 20th century. Lurking in the background is one fact whose significance only becomes clear once we grasp the complexities of the organization and reorganization of this community's universe. Throughout most of its history, Kapingamarangi was one of the most isolated communities on this earth and in profound ways, its isolation continues despite over a century of contact with a variety of outsiders. One payoff of grasping the complexities of change and stability of this tiny community is an understanding of what monoculturalism really is, what it means, and how it shapes the experience of people suddenly thrust into a multicultural universe.

The task of making clear the systemic complexity of this island and its history begins with an account of how I came to do this research, how it was conducted, and why in this way and not some other. In other words, this account begins by making clear how I have come to know what I know.

Why Fishing?

I have conducted field research in the Kapingamarangi communities on Kapingamarangi Atoll and on Pohnpei Island during several field stays since 1965, reporting on such topics as adoption (Lieber 1970), land tenure (Lieber 1974), the resettled community on Pohnpei (Lieber 1968, 1977a), the Kapingamarangi lexicon (Lieber and Dikepa 1974), and ethnicity (1984, 1990). None of my previous research has been as totally absorbing or has afforded the pure pleasure and satisfaction at every stage--from the planning to the field work to the analysis and writing--as this that I report to you in these pages.

The subject matter is only part it. I enjoy fishing, but am certainly not an avid fisherman. More to the point is that fishing is so central, ecologically and symbolically, to Kapingamarangi people themselves, and at long last I had the opportunity to study it. My total absorption in this project owes to the fact that it is, for me, the complete anthropological experience. The work from its very outset has combined the theoretical with the substantive, the ideological with the practical, induction with deduction, and interview with participant observation. The data, during and since their collection, have presented mazes of intriguing detail with its host of false starts, blind alleys, and, best of all, discoveries of pattern that have punctuated each stage of the research. But to be honest, it all happened by accident.

In my own defense I suppose that I could point out that sometimes the hardest thing to see is the obvious--and what could be more obvious than the critical importance of fishing to atoll people inhabiting less than half a square mile of land? That's a pretty lame excuse, and my other one--that I was busy doing other things that seemed important at the time--is even worse. It was a bit of luck and some very peculiar circumstances that led me, stumbling, into traditional fishing.

In a conversation with the school principal on Kapingamarangi, a man intensely interested in the atoll's history and an oral historian himself, he whimsically mentioned that it would be nice to have some archaeology done on the atoll. So the two of us hatched a conspiracy to make it happen by getting current chief magistrate to write a letter to the Office of Historic Preservation of the Trust Territory of the Pacific Islands requesting an archaeological survey. We gilded the lily a bit, making the request look urgent, noting that the progress of soil erosion on some islets was threatening potential archaeological sites. This wasn't complete perjury, mind you. There was soil erosion on the ocean side of Souhou, the main inhabited islet, due to a recently built pier on the lagoon side that was blocking the normal circulation of sand around the islet. Whatever, it worked. The Historic Preservation officer contracted with Dr. Foss Leach of the University of Otago (New Zealand) to conduct the survey in November and December of 1979. We had no way of knowing at the time how portentous our claim of urgency was to be.

My wife and I were on Pohnpei for the summer of 1979, where I was working in Porakied, the Kapinga village. My wife was finishing a reading and writing curriculum in the Kapinga language for first through third grades and getting ready to have our first baby. Over the summer, I worked out a research plan with the Historic Preservation Office to prepare for Dr. Leach's arrival by working out site histories for every discrete plot of land on the atoll. Ten days after our son was born in October, we boarded the field trip ship for Kapingamarangi for what was supposed to be one month's work.

First, the field trip ship broke down, and it took the bureaucrats on Pohnpei seven weeks to get the parts to fix it. As October wore into November, the ship did not move, and Dr. Leach and his colleague, Graehm Ward, waited helplessly on Pohnpei. Then, the morning of November 19, the vulnerability of atoll living became frightfully clear to all of us.

A strong surf coming over the reef edge began to pound at the ocean sides of the islets. No one had ever seen anything like it. Usually the surf broke at the coral rocks at the outer reef edge, sending a gentle current to the islets. But the surf was breaking at the islets, and it got stronger as the morning wore on. The ocean currents hitting the outer reef were sending sprays twenty feet high, the sprays becoming the swift, hard, incoming surf. The outhouses standing on stilts on the reef quickly collapsed, their thatched roofs carried by the current to the inter-islet channel and on into the lagoon where they bobbed like corks in the choppy waters. The sea walls inland of the outhouses seemed to melt away like butter, and as the surf quickened, it broke in twelve foot waves against the ocean side of Werua, the next islet north of Souhou (where I stayed), carrying boulders and houses inland and washing them into nearby taro patches.

It was a fast surf generated by a very strong westward current, which in turn had been generated by high winds. By mid-afternoon, the surf had shattered an ancient rock formation on the seaward reef, called 'the anchor of the island,' and when the 'anchor' went, we were all terrified. Frantic calls on the government radio to the weather service and the governor produced no aid or advice. We lost houses, trees, taro patches, and land on the ocean sides of the islets, eaten away as much as seven feet inland in some places. Ancient burials were unearthed, and human bones were scattered over the reef flat, where a few of us collected them to save for Foss Leach and eventual reburial.

That fast, destructive surf continued for three more days, doing most of its damage during the first two. As the surf subsided, the wind picked up. We heard on the radio that we were in for a possible typhoon coming from the west. We were all pretty burnt out by then, and people calmly went about getting their canoes and pigs inland and tying them down. Household goods were moved inland, and some tied their house and canoe house cornerposts to trees so as not to lose them. The winds hit us the day after the surf subsided, but they only reached gale force for three days. Aside from toppling a few trees, the threat was a lot worse than the damage.

I continued to work through this and was nearly finished when the ship arrived on December 24, bringing passengers, officials, mail, and two archaeologists with their equipment. Foss Leach and Graehm Ward moved into our house, which we thought was large until it had to hold five of us and our stuff. Then the fun began.

Please understand that I mean no disrespect when I tell you that Foss Leach is the kind of man who can fall off the roof at a party at a ten-story building, hit the ground running and talking at the same time, never spill a drop of his drink, and then stop, look around, and ask disgustedly where everyone went. The man is a human dynamo who combines a quick, alert intelligence, a vast store of knowledge, unlimited self-confidence, and true grit in a compact frame that never seems to stop moving. When it became clear to him that he would not be able to begin work for two whole days, his frustration knew no bounds. He had only about a month to work, and the Kapinga were busy unloading cargo, greeting incoming relatives, and getting ready for the Christmas celebration the next day. Foss's gloom lifted a bit when the island's generator broke down, and he could unpack his tools and fix it. Otherwise he was left to his own devices, which mostly meant arguing with me. His natural intellectual combativeness is matched only by my own, and his frustration over inactivity was matched by my desperate need to finish typing the report--for him--before the ship left. Foss was not even mollified by the goodies, even the halvah, that my mother-in-law had sent (to the great relief of my Kapinga family, who coveted the stuff). But our arguments were lively, intense, and interesting. I also like Foss Leach a lot.

Almost any subject we hit on produced a tirade of words, but the subject Foss was most adamant about was fishing. Had it been done? Well, Peter Buck (1950) had studied fishing technology. No, no, dammit! The whole system, man, what have you done? Well, not very much, I'm afraid. Why the hell not, aren't there people who still know about the traditional methods? Yes. Well then, what are you going to do about it? Not just the damned fish hooks, mind you...why are they shaped that way? What are they going to do with them? To hell with the catch sizes, to hell with mindless counting. What is fishing about? How do they do it? An ethnography, man, a damned ethnography! And that was my introduction to the subject.

Next day, after the huge Christmas feast, Foss cornered two old men, my best informants, and pulled out from his satchel two books, one of fishes of New Zealand and another of Polynesian fish hooks. Quickly, he elicited identifications of fish, getting Kapinga names for species pictured in the book. With an efficiency I found staggering, he paged through the fish hooks, with the Kapinga men identifying Kapinga style hooks and their near equivalents and hooks they'd seen from other islands. Then, with equal facility, he had the two men giving detailed accounts of how Kapinga fishermen at the turn of the century modified imported metal hooks to suit particular fish and to suit traditional methods of controlling the fish while pulling in hand lines. I realized as I listened that I had neither tape recorder nor notebook with me. Foss noticed, too, but he had the decency not to comment on it. He'd made his point. An ethnography it would be.

Once we got back to Pohnpei, the Trust Territory Historic Preservation Officer, Ross Cordy, assured me that traditional fishing was of great interest to his program and that a contract for the next summer's work would be forthcoming, depending on what the proposal looked like. If there was money and the research was promising, another summer might be possible, but resources were limited. So here was the problem. I knew next to nothing about fish or fishing, and I had three months, six at the most, to collect enough data to do the ethnography of traditional fishing. All I had at hand was an incomplete list of fish names, collected and uncertainly identified for the *Kapingamarangi Lexicon* (Lieber and Tikepa 1974), and bits and pieces in my notes. Whatever method I chose to organize this research would have to be very, very efficient.

My only experience collecting detailed data with a severe time limit came while I was a graduate student at the University of Pittsburgh. I was hired with two other students by the Commonwealth of Pennsylvania Department of Sanitation to test a new field research method in the summer of 1963.

Many of the small communities in western Pennsylvania were using antiquated and unsafe sewage treatment plants. Although the state had the authority to force them to construct new ones, experience showed that this was counterproductive. Leaders of those communities, forced to shell out thousands of dollars, were angry enough to retaliate by bringing suit and by refusing to cooperate with (and in some cases sabotaging) other state projects, such as environmental and wildlife programs. The Department of Sanitation hired Dr. Thomas McCorckle, an anthropologist, to figure out a way to get the communities to cooperate with the state.

McCorckle reasoned that any state agency with a program to sell would be successful only to the extent that the community leadership adopted the program as its own. To ensure adoption, one would have to know what the power structure of the community was--who were the movers and shakers, what were their relationships, and how did they usually get things done? The quickest way to answer these questions was to look at community projects that had been undertaken in the recent past, finding out who suggested them, who pushed them, who organized them, who got the financing, etc.. Using these considerations, McCorckle worked out a research strategy that he called "event analysis," and the three of us were hired to field-test it (McCorckle 1963).

The method was very straightforward. Each of us had two communities to study in six weeks. For each community, we spent two weeks in the community collecting data and one week analyzing and writing up the results. We began by making contacts with individuals in the community and eliciting from them a list of community projects that had been undertaken over the past five years and names of people involved in each of them. We then contacted those people to get more detailed lists of projects and a detailed history of each one. Each interview gave us more detail and more names for further contacts. Two weeks later, we each had a tremendous amount of detailed information. Of course, the same names kept showing up in project after project, and analysis of the roles of each seemed consistent enough to show clear patterns of influence, relations between influentials, their specialties, and the like. By the time our reports were finished, we had a clear idea of what the power structure of these communities looked like.

What made this method so effective was that the abstract levels of "community organization" and "power structure" were arrived at as obvious generalizations from a *series* of concrete events. The complexities of the events emerged from people's narrations about their specifics. By concentrating on the event, the specific issues that participants confronted and the ways that they handled them became instances of organization, influence, and power. Comparing these instances yielded patterns of organization, influence, and power peculiar to specific communities.

As efficient a field method as event analysis was, its application to traditional fishing would require some modification. After all, there is a big difference between three or four once-in-a-lifetime projects over a five year period and an unknown number of repetitive events occuring on a more or less daily basis over much longer time periods. Fishing, moreover, is not an event. It is a category of activity. Alternatively, viewing each fishing expedition as an event (with its context to be discovered) made sense but seemed a bit atomistic to me, something on the order of filling out index cards and sorting them into piles. I'd have to do something like that anyway, but I wouldn't call it a research direction. The compromise I hit on was to view fishing as a kind of activity, a category with members that were specific activities. The activity would be the unit of analysis, and the focus of inquiry would be understanding what gives the activity its shape. With the activity as the analytical unit, a framework for research fell rapidly into place because of what is entailed by the properties of an activity.

Any activity can be more or less random or more or less organized. A random activity, like wandering around aimlessly waiting for something to happen (Kapinga call this *madamada*) may involve patterned activity, such as scanning one's surroundings, but its outcomes tend to be random. That is, it is as likely that nothing much will happen as it is that something will happen to involve the person. In the latter case, it is impossible to predict with better than random success what kind of situation might involve our wanderer in non-random activity. An injury or a sexual encounter or a contribution of labor to a project are all equally possible outcomes.

Organized human activity, however, involves a goal, an end result that it is supposed to achieve. Then, there are participants, one or more people who agree to and/or must engage in the activity to achieve the goal. The participants usually have some idea of how to achieve the goal--a set of strategies and tactics to be deployed. The strategies and tactics often require that certain resources be brought to the activity--like tools, templates, and the like to implement the strategies. The participants often have a good idea of the order in which strategies, techniques, resources, and their own efforts are to be deployed. Moreover, there may be alternative strategies for achieving the goal requiring participants to choose among them, and some participants may have a greater say in the choice than others. These considerations may, in turn, be part of some yet larger context and larger goal. The activity, moreover, may be possible at some times and impossible at others, requiring participants to take their environment into account. Properties of activities, in other words, read like the properties of a system.

I had already learned from event analysis that data collected on a series of events are generalizeable to levels of relationship that organize the entire series. But it was far more than community power structure that I was after this time. I wanted the field collection procedure to yield information rich enough to permit obvious inferences about how traditional fishing activity was organized and how that organization articulated with the larger community and the atoll environment. It was a human ecosystem that I was after, and for that reason it made sense to use a research framework designed for an understanding of whole systems. Cybernetics was an obvious choice, and I used it first to conceptualize "activity" and then to design the field collection. I did all this with an eye on the kinds of inferences about the organization of the larger human ecosystem that the collected data would facilitate.

Cybernetics is popularly associated with computers, robots, and engineering design, but these are only a couple spin-offs of a broad framework for thinking about phenomena that are organized as information processing, self-regulating systems. Cybernetics has been an interdisciplinary enterprise from the outset, its proponents coming from biology (e.g., McCulloch 1965), psychology (e.g., Miller 1975), anthropology (e.g., Bateson 1972), and sociology (e.g., Berrien 1976) as well as from mathematics and engineering (e.g., Wiener 1965, Ashby 1956). Applications of cybernetics include issues in communication theory, psychiatry, sociology, anthropology, philosophy, biology, theories of play and drug addiction, and epistemology to name only a few. What workers in these various fields find appealing about cybernetics is that it is designed to deal with any phenomena that show purposeful behavior in response to some environment and the capacity to correct errors resulting from purposeful (goal oriented) behavior. Man-made machines have these properties, but so do organisms, ecosystems, and human and non-human communities. It is no accident that the list of properties of an activity reads like a list of variables that comprise a system.

I have no intention to present a thesis or even a thumbnail sketch of cybernetics. There are a few basic ideas that help in understanding four concepts that I will be using throughout this report: information, context, culture, and cultural premis. How these concepts fit together in relation to activities as part of a single research framework shaped the sorts of data I collected, how I got them, and how I used them to construct a model of the organization of traditional fishing activity. Information is essential to understanding how any system works and serves to define what constitutes constraints on any activity. The idea of context is particularly important in understanding how traditional fishing activities were regulated (Chapter Nine) and, in Part Three, how fishing activity has changed in this century. The relation between context and cultural premis is critical to understanding Part Four, which is about how an unchanging set of assumptions Kapinga people make about the world shape their responses to rapidly changing events that profoundly affect their lives. The account of change in fishing activity and its contexts in Part Three is influenced and shaped by Ward Goodenough's approach to activity as an analytical unit, and I will briefly compare our results.

Framework of the Research

The concern with describing and understanding whole systems is nothing new for anthropologists. The functionalist theories of Malinowski and Radcliffe-Brown and their students were designed to comprehend a whole community through careful description of its parts, how each worked, what its functioning contributed to other parts, and how the parts of a community fit together to form and maintain the whole. These scholars saw themselves as observers of systems. Their work has profoundly shaped the ways in which anthropologists approach the observation, description, and comparison of human communities. So if a cybernetic approach appears reminiscent of functionalist method, this is as it should be.[3] What functionalist scholars meant by system, however, was a mechanism like a clock or an engine, and their analyses were shaped by the metaphor of energy conversion that mechanisms presuppose. Social systems, in this view, were "dynamic" and subject to "forces" and "impacts," such that social change represented "disequilibrium." The social system was a Newtonian world of objects in motion.

Cyberneticists view systems in communicational terms, as organized processes of information transfer and transformation. In cybernetic thinking, a system is defined as a set of components and relationships between those components inside a boundary that filters inputs from the environment and serves as an exit for outputs to the environment, all *in relation to some observer*. Inputs (anything in the environment that can impinge on the system) are typically transformed at the boundary into forms that the components can handle. So, for example, food is transformed by chewing, salivation, and by bacteria that line the gullet. The boundary's output is the components' input, which is transformed by the components into an output that may go to yet other components (as, say, the stomach's output becomes input to the small intestine) or to the environment through the boundary (say as activity or as wastes like urine). The sequence of transformations depends on the particular system under study. These transformations are the activities by which the system maintains itself. Taking activity as the analytical unit focusses attention on transformation processes, such as the sequence of acts, each representing a change in the current state of the fisherman, his equipment, the fish, the contents of his cooking fire, etc., that comprise specific instances of fishing activity. To the extent that these sequences of transformations are repetitive, we can assume that they are organized and that our task is to specify how they are organized. Thus, activity as an analytical unit concentrates our attention on systemic *processes* and how those processes are regulated.

The larger and more complex a system is, the more likely it is that its activities are hierarchically organized. The components of a system, for example, may themselves be systems (called subsystems in relation to the whole system) with their own components, which are also systems. The human body is typical of this sort of hierarchy. The gene system is a component of the nucleus, which is a component of the cell, which is a component of the tissue, and so on up to the whole organism, which may be a component of a yet larger system, like a family. The term "level" is used to refer to the difference between a system and its subsystems. Typical of hierarchical systems is the fact that the higher level of system has properties that its components do not have. The cell, for example, can synthesize proteins while the nucleus cannot. Water can dissolve at least small amounts of almost any substance, a property that neither of its components, hydrogen nor oxygen, has. The higher level of system also typically regulates its components by coordinating their activities in a process called negative feedback.

Because the systems that concern cyberneticists are "open" to their environments, they are subject to changes in the kinds and magnitudes of their inputs. In order for a system to maintain its stability--to keep the relations among its components at a more or less steady state--the system must have a way of tracking and responding to changes in both its inputs and in its components' states, particularly when such changes can threaten irreversible changes in the components' relations. For example, when air temperature rises, it warms the human body surface, and once past a certain temperature, this warming may raise the temperature of the blood. For humans and other mammals, whose organs operate efficiently only within a narrow range of blood temperatures, a rise (or fall) beyond these limits threatens the entire organism. The typical human response to this situation is to perspire. The evaporation of perspiration at the skin surface tends to cool the skin and the blood at the capillaries just underneath the skin surface, eventually bringing blood temperature down. This example illustrates the general principle of self-regulation of a system's components through negative feedback. Negative feedback is a process whereby the system gets information about its current state, compares it with its goal state, and acts automatically to reduce any mismatch between the two. The system, in other words, is able to use information about its own behavior in relation to some internal variable (at a lower level of the system) or in relation to some environmental variable (at a higher level of the system) in order to correct its own errors. One way a system regulates its components is by transmitting to each a signal that specifies for each the goal state to which its current state can be compared for any mismatch. By this means, the higher level of system can regulate the component's output. A complex system has a large number of feedback mechanisms at each level of the system to maintain component and subcomponent relationships at more or less constant values. Apologizing for a *faux pas* is, thus, no different in principle from perspiring in the heat.

While negative feedback is a process whereby the system automatically reduces any deviation from a goal state, some transformations can amplify deviation. Using the blood temperature example, once that temperature rises above tolerable limits, there is an accelerating, irreversible process of transformation that follows. Rising blood temperature speeds up metabolism, which generates more heat and a further rise in blood temperature, which further speeds up metabolism, and so on until the organism dies. This is an example of positive feedback, which can manifest itself in vicious cycles at both the organismic and population levels (e.g., an arms race). But the same process at a population level over a long period of time may also result in what we call evolution (Maruyama 1963). Cybernetic theory is not limited to the study of static organizations, but is also concerned with change in systems and in their relationships with their environments.

Whether we focus attention on system maintenance through regulation (reducing a system's or component's deviation from a goal state) or systemic change (amplification of deviation from an initial state), it is communication processes that we deal with: the processing of *information*. Phenomena ordinarily considered categorically distinct become comparable in this framework. Immune systems, gene systems, machines with feedback, ecosystems, and social systems can all be compared as communication systems of various sorts.

Social scientists were initially excited about and eventually frustrated by the concept of information. What excited social scientists in the 1950s and 1960s were the research possibilities stemming from the formal demonstration that information and order are identical (Shannan and Weaver 1949). What frustrated social scientists was that information and meaning are not identical.

Information is defined as any event or thing whose occurrence eliminates other events or things that might have occurred at that time and place instead. Information is, therefore, not itself a thing or event but a property of things and events--their probability of occurrence. That probability is computed in comparison to the set of other things or events that might have occurred. Take a set of ten equally likely events. The probability of occurrence of each one of them is one in ten or 0.1. But then let us say that once event A from that set occurs, event C has a probability of 0.99 of following it, that is, that event C is contingent on A. The occurrence of C, then, did not eliminate nine other alternatives. Once A has occurred, the occurrence of C is almost certain, so its actual occurrence gives us practically no information at all.

The first instance of ten equally likely events showed no apparent order in the set. But the second instance, C almost always following A, does show order, and the measure of information reflects this in that the occurrence of A carries much more information than that of C. To be precise about it, the actual measure (Log to the base 2 of the probability of the event) has a minus sign in front of it. This is important, because this formula for measuring information is the negative of the formula for measuring entropy, randomness or disorder in a system. That means that information, the negative of entropy, is formally identical to order. Thus, by measuring the amount of information in a system or subsystem, one measures the order in the system. There is another way of looking at information that requires making the system and its relationship to the observer explicit.

Gregory Bateson (1972: 451-453) characterizes information as a "difference that makes a difference." Any system is subject to variety, to differences in its kinds and magnitudes of possible input and in its possible internal states. Given the many different events or things in its environment that might impinge on the system and convey information that the system must somehow respond to, some of them carry information and some do not. That is, given the structure and organization of a particular system's boundary and components, some events that appear different to the observer carry information (are perceived and responded to as different) and some are not. Take, for example, a thermostat in a house whose goal state is set for 68 degrees F. The observer can see the room temperature recorded by the thermometer fluctuating between 65 degrees and 73 degrees as the furnace switches on and off over time. The observer looking at the thermometer sees a difference between 67 and 68 degrees, but the system does not respond to that difference. In fact the thermostat responds only to the difference between 66 and 65 degrees and to the difference between 72 and 73 degrees. All of the temperature differences between 66 and 72 degrees are not differences that make a difference to the system.

The less probable an event that makes a difference is, the more information it carries. Given a set of possible events, each of them is equally likely to occur unless some *constraint* is applied to the set, making some of the events more probable than others. Indeed, it is in the application of constraints that we see how hierarchical organization works.

Take a situation in which 26 slips of paper, each with a four letter English word and each beginning with a different letter of the alphabet, are shuffled in a box. We are asked to guess each of the four letters in the slip that one of our number has drawn from the box. Now, say we guess that "a" is the first letter on the slip. The chances of drawing an "a" for a first letter are 1 in 26. Having drawn the slip with the first letter "a", the chances of the second letter on that slip being "a" are zero. Our chances of finding "o" as the second letter are also very small. The chances of finding a "b" as the second letter are better, but they are not 1 in 26, since "a" and "o" (at the very least) are not possible. Given "a" and "b" as the first two letters, the chances of finding "u" to be the third letter are not 1 in 26, because v, z, w, x, f, k, m, p, and q cannot occur after "b" in any word. Other letters, such as "c" do not occur after "b" in a four letter word. So the chances of drawing a "u" are less than 1 in 17. Given "a," "b," and "u" as the first three letters of the word, the chance that "t" will be the fourth letter are 1 of 2, since "d" is the only other possibility. The amount of information carried by each letter does not decrease by regular intervals. Instead, the alternatives at each position in the word depend on linguistic rules of how sounds and letters can be combined. These rules *constrain* the occurrence of any letter *in relation to* other letters of the alphabet, producing, for example, combinations that occur across many words, such as -ble, qu-, str-, etc., giving English orthography recognizable patterns of combination.

Now, language, like most other complex communication systems, is hierarchically organized. Particular phonological and orthographic combinations are constrained by higher levels of organization such as syntax, which is in turn constrained by the level of semantics. So we can see the amount of information carried by the four letters "a," "b," "u," and "t" change radically when they are contextualized by the sentence

> The north side of the garage is designed to ____ [a four letter word] a sidewalk that leads east to the alley.

The letter "a" no longer has a 1 in 26 probability of being the initial letter of the missing word. Its occurrence carries less information than in the slip of paper in a hat, since there are so few possible syntactic classes of words that can occur at that position in the sentence, and of the few that can occur, very few are semantically appropriate. Given the letter "a" as occurring, "b," "u," and "t" carry no information whatever. There is far more information in the sequence of words than in the sequence of letters in this case. Both sequences are ordered by patterns of combination--of words and of letters--but in this case the difference that makes a difference is at the higher level of patterning, making the pattern at the lower level more predictable.

Now, working from this systemic perspective, the first question to answer is whether fishing activity is more or less random or more or less ordered. If traditional fishing activity was more or less random, then it follows that any fish available in Kapingamarangi waters is as likely to end up on someone's cooking fire on any given day as any other fish. So, for example, any given person was as likely to be cooking a tuna or a triggerfish as he or she would be a squirrelfish on any randomly selected day. Even the fragmentary data I had was enough to tell me that this was false. First, I already knew that tuna are are seasonal. Second, I knew from my own and Emory's (1965) work that priestly control of canoe wood limited private canoe ownership to about a third of the fishing population, thus limiting the catch of deep sea fish such as triggerfish. Third, I learned early on in my research that access to the lagoon, the reef, and sectors of the deep sea were restricted to people of appropriate age categories, so that what fish ended up where depended on the fisherman's age or on the ages of his fishing partners. Tuna and triggerfish would be a more likely meal in households of older fishermen and squirrelfish in those of younger fishermen. So traditional fishing activity was, obviously, ordered. There were at least constraints on canoe ownership, on the presence of certain age categories in certain fishing places, and on seasonal availability of fish.

Given that fishing activity was ordered, there were still two possibilities of ordering. The constraints that order fishing activity could be unordered with respect to one another or they could be internally ordered in one or more sets. Even if constraints were ordered in sets, there were still many possible ways in which those sets might be arranged. Therefore, data collecting procedures would have to ensure enough detail in people's descriptions of specific fishing activities either to record their statements about ordering of constraints or to enable testable inferences about their ordering.

The questions to be answered by field research were two--what are the variables that constrain fishing activity and how are these constraints related to one another? The task of field collection was primarily that of developing an exhaustive list of conditions that Kapinga fishermen had to take into account in order to determine whether (a) fishing was possible at all and (b) if fishing was possible, then the sort of fishing that was possible, and (c) if there was more than one sort of fishing possible at a given moment, then what conditions constrained the choices people actually made.

One could justifiably argue that any ethnographer could figure this out without reference to cybernetic theory but for the fact that the theory is embedded in the operational definition of constraint. Given that fishing activity is a relation between the fish and fishermen, and the goal of observation is understanding what orders fishing activity for the fishermen, then any variable can be said to be a constraint if and only if it encodes information. That is, a constraint must eliminate other alternatives such that some activities are more probable than others. The constraint must be a difference that makes a difference to the fishermen. A constraint on fishing activity, therefore, is any condition or set of conditions that a fisherman *must take account of* in deciding whether he can fish and/or what kind of fishing he can do.

So, for example, one's relationship with the high priest determines the probability of one's owning a canoe and, therefore determines the frequency with which one is likely to be angling (relative to the frequency with which one is likely to be fishing with a net, a trap, pole and line, and so on). If we shift our focus to the level of the entire male fishing population, the relationships of all males to the high priest, taken together, determines the range of frequency of angling (over a period of time) relative the frequency ranges of other catch techniques. If we shift our focus to the level of the atoll ecosystem, the collective relations of fishermen to the high priest imply that the relative percentage of older to younger standing breadfruit trees should be higher than would be the case if canoe construction were constrained only by fishermen's wants and the availability of suitable trees. That this implication was probably correct is suggested not only by informants' statements but also by Emory's observations in 1947, thirty years after Kapinga abandoned their traditional cult house and converted to Christianity.

> The number of canoes possessed by the people of Kapingamarangi is amazing, considering that each canoe represents a giant breadfruit tree and that the number of trees which can grow on the islets is very limited. A few canoes, it is true, are made from logs which have drifted in, probably from the New Guinea or Melanesian area. Whereas the Germans counted 47 canoes in 1910, we counted 122 in service, and also 122 canoe hulls, most of them old and totally unfit for use, stored away in canoe sheds or houses (Emory 1965: 127)

> Twenty five years seems to be the minimum time for a tree to grow large enough for a canoe hull. It is doubtful that the atoll can supply enough timber for a continuous supply of more canoes than are being used at present (Emory 1965: 128).

If we use a conservative estimate of there being two thirds more canoes in 1947 than there were before 1917, then it follows that the relationship of fishermen to the high priest made it twice as probable that we would find a standing breadfruit tree older than 25 years than would be the case without this relationship constraining breadfruit use. Clearly, any condition that constrains fishing activity is information, and it is at least theoretically possible, depending on how rich our data are, to measure just how much information is carried by the constraint. While this approach might make an engineer or a mathematician happy (if it's done well), it tells a social scientist very little that he or she needs to know.

For the social scientist, there is clearly a difference between, say, the seasonal availability of fish and the relation between a fisherman and the high priest. Seeing both as information blurs the obvious differences between them, and their quantitative differences tell us nothing about them as sources or kinds of constraint. The mathematician might be equally wary about the arbitrary limitation of constraints to those that the fishermen perceive as such. For example, I was told by fisheries managers on Pohnpei about recent research showing that yellow fin tuna occupy a very narrow water temperature range and that this range can move to higher or lower depths with changing water currents over a day. This would explain why Kapinga fishermen have to employ a trial-and-error depth test each time they go out for yellow fin tuna, starting with a sixty fathom line and moving down until the fish bite. Clearly, the observed facts of the ecozone of the tuna can be seen to influence what Kapinga fishermen have to do during their fishing activity. Mustn't water temperature count as a constraint on fishing activity?

If the purpose of observation is to determine what makes Kapinga fishermen's universe more predictable, then we include only those variables that Kapinga fishermen attend to. If the purpose of observation is to make the observer's universe more orderly, then we must include variables that Kapinga might not perceive as such. We may even have to exclude from consideration some variables that Kapinga recognize as constraints on their fishing activity. Although I am phrasing this matter as one of point of view, it is also clear that we are dealing with what constitutes a difference that makes a difference.

Message, Meaning, Context, and Culture

The filtering of signal inputs at the boundary is common to all systems. But since it is human perceptual subsystems, specifically Kapinga fishermen, who are interpreting and responding to constraining variables, we must come head to head with the problem of meaning--what kinds of difference make a difference, and what kinds of differences do they make? These are questions about what is meaningful to Kapinga fishermen.

Information is a quantity, a ratio of probability of occurrence of an event relative to other events, a difference that makes a difference. Meaning is (at the very least) a relationship between a sign and its referents. Meaning may be conveyed in the virtual or total absence of information, as exemplified in "peak" religious experiences such as "cosmic consciousness," the experience of "oneness with the universe." Rappaport (1986) refers to these experiences as "informationless states," since differences that would constitute information disappear in the sense of unity. Athletes report similar experiences variously called the "runner's high" or the "sweet spot," e.g., in cycling, where the rider experiences a unity of him- or herself with the bicycle, the road, the surroundings, and other cyclists (Kita 1987, Jerome 1980). Yet these states are the very essence of meaning to those who experience or attempt to achieve them.

The concept that bridges information and meaning is "message," an event or object acting as a signal (of measureable information content) whose internal structure, referent(s), and relationships with other signals are observable or inferable from what one can observe. Information refers to the probability of a signal; message refers to its form and to what it is about, i.e., its referent. Messages can be encoded in any conceivable form, e.g., a hormone, an electric pulse, the wink of an eye, or even a sequence of events as complex as the practice of adoption in Oceanic societies (see Carroll 1970, Levy 1970).

The concept of "message," as used by scholars influenced by the cybernetic paradigm, is hierarchically ordered. Besides the text, its context also encodes information. The *context* of a message is the relationship between the communicating parties (systems, subsystems, etc.). The relationship consists of the *pattern* of messages exchanged. For example, when Tom calls Bill a son of a bitch, he may be using an epithet of gross insult or a term of endearment. Depending on where and how "son of a bitch" fits into the sequence of messages exchanged and the tone of voice, body movements, and facial expression that mark its expression, we understand the relation between Tom and Bill as one of conflict or one of friendly banter. The message occurs as part of a context (Bateson 1972: 257-258), this part-to-whole relation lending the construct of message its hierarchical character. Different patternings of message material constitute different kinds of relationships. Change the pattern, and you change the relationship (and, thus, the context of the message). Any relationship, moreover, may be (and usually is) part of some more encompassing relation or set of relations that contextualizes it, yielding a context of a context of a message, and so on in a theoretically infinite regress.

Human communication typically employs verbal symbols to encode messages and paralinguistic symbols such as tone of voice, facial expression, body posture and movement, and the like to classify messages as one or another kind of message. Since they convey messages about the linguistic message, they are metamessages, referring to the relationship between the communicating parties, serving to clarify the relationship between speaker and listener (Reusch and Bateson 1951) or to ambiguate it (Watzlawick 1977). A says to B, "You're a nice person," and that may be a message of reassurance or of sarcasm, depending on its metamessage. The setting in which the message is conveyed, including previous messages exchanged, provides the context of the metamessage, as, for example, the stage of a theater conveys the metametamessage "this is a play." Now, take the "nice person" message conveyed by a man to a woman in a restaurant, followed by his inviting her back to his apartment for a drink. We might guess with better than random success that the metamessage is one of invitation to further intimacy. But if the "nice person" message is conveyed as part of the woman's response to the man's invitation to his apartment, conciliation is a more likely metamessage. The informational aspect of the message (eliminating alternatives) is surely present here. But how many bits of information the text carries is a lot less interesting to social scientists than what meanings are conveyed and how and by what means they are encoded.

The cybernetic concept of message and the anthropological concept of cultural symbol (Schneider 1968, Geertz 1972) are synonymous, at least as I understand them. Message and symbol are synonymous, not identical, because the two concepts share some but not all of their properties. Information measurement is inherent in the concept of message, while it is not in the concept of symbol. It is also the case that not every sign functioning as a message can be considered a symbol. There are messages whose meanings (referents) are not arbitrarily assigned conventions, such as cries of pain, onomotopoea, animal danger calls, animal signals of intent to fight or court, and most other non-human forms of communication.[4] A symbol, in anthropological parlance, is a sign whose relation to its referent is assigned by convention. For example, there is nothing inherent in the phonemes "p," "a," and "i" or in their combination that would indicate something to eat. In this sense the relation between the sound and its referent is arbitrary. In Greek, that sound combination denotes a number, and in Kapingamarangi, it refers to a wall.

The synonymy of message and symbol makes a cultural analysis of human communication and its organizational contexts amenable to a systems approach and *vice versa*. How amenable, how compatible, and how useful the wedding of the two approaches are depends in large measure on what "culture" means and on how it is used.[5] I use the term, culture, to denote a class of explanations (Bateson 1972), a theory about why people do what they do in the more or less predictable ways that they do them and why the canons of predictability in one community can vary so radically from those of other communities. Like economics, politics, intelligence, personality, etc., culture is a construct social scientists use to explain an aspect of human variability. We seek to explain variability in human action and interaction and the ways they are organized as outcomes of the various ways that people in different communities define, perceive, and respond to the perceived realities of the universe they inhabit. People confer reality on the things, persons, and their relations that comprise their universe by conferring meaning on them. These meanings are encoded on symbols--linguistic and paralinguistic signs and icons, like crucifixes, art objects, buildings, paths, spatial design, and the like--that people share through learning. Even such "natural" events as, say, menstruation are subject to great variation in meaning. In many Melanesian societies, for example, menstruation defines women as a category, associating them with attributes of pollution, debilitation through contact, and even death (for example, see Poole 1985, Herdt 1987). Relations between men and women are framed by these "facts" of menstruation. That is, menstruation as a symbol combines with other symbols, such as pollution, debilitation, danger, death, and sexual acts to form a pattern of messages and metamessages that contextualize male-female interaction, that mark the boundaries of male and female activities, and that shape the conduct of activities in which both participate. On Kapingamarangi, people see menstruation as a sign of a woman's physical maturity and an indication that she is not pregnant. It is referred to as the 'monthly illness' and associated as illness with reduced levels of strenuous activity and spatial mobility, not from debilitation but from considerations of modesty, since days of heavy flow are messy. Menstruation does not mark the boundaries of male and female activity nor contextualize male-female relations. It does mark the category of women, i.e., anyone who menstruates is a woman, but it does not define the category. Melanesians load much more (and different) meaning into menstruation than Kapinga do. These differences make menstruation a very different sort of symbol in Melanesia than that on Kapingamarangi, combineable with very different symbols to form very different kinds of contexts of human interaction in these places.

Culture, because it is a theory about human perception, has a special place in the study of human communities as systems. One of the nice things about systems theories for looking at human communities is that there is no specific model of a system that the community has to look like. Where and how an observer draws a boundary, what will be called a component--say a discreet person, groups that people form, networks of people, and the like--depends on what is convenient for the observer to make an accurate description of the specific case. In observing a human social system, culture is included inside the boundary that the observer must draw between him- or herself and the system observed.[6] This is an important boundary, since it is the order in the universe of the people observed, rather than that of the observer's universe, to which observation and inference are initially directed. Culture as part of this boundary is critical for two reasons. First, culture as an operational construct serves to direct the way in which observation is conducted, and how boundaries are drawn, components designated, and relationships between components described and inferred. It does so by focussing attention on how the people observed construe messages of relationship with one another and with their non-human environment. Second, the observer needs to be careful not to contaminate observations by importing meanings into the description that are not shared with the people observed. The boundary between observer and observed can always be redrawn when necessary, e.g., introducing fish breeding seasons, which Kapinga do not recognize, to help the observer (and the reader) understand why some fish species are endangered.

Because the observation of the Kapingamarangi social system begins with traditional Kapinga fishing activity from the point of view of how the fishermen's universe is ordered, the initial boundary we draw is around fish and fishermen as components of the system under study. The islets, reef, lagoon, deep sea and other people are its environment. We examine how specific fishing activities are conducted to identify the specific variables that constrain each activity. With this initial system under study, the analytical advantage of being able to demonstrate that an identified constraint is information is the reasonable certainty that all variables listed as constraints are "system relevant." That is, all constraints are differences that make a difference to Kapinga fishermen and are not spurious variables intruded (or imported) into the system from the observer's universe. Water temperature mentioned above as a possible constraint on Kapinga fishing activity exemplifies this point.

Subsurface water temperatures are differences that may make the observer's universe more predictable, but it clearly made no difference to Kapinga trial-and-error procedures for locating tuna. Water temperature differences would qualify as constraints if and only if those differences elicited altered responses in fishermen's activity, e.g., if they used water thermometers tied to their leaders to locate the proper fishing depth. That water temperature is a difference is demonstrable, at least by western standards, but it never was a difference that Kapinga fishermen took account of. For this reason, it is not a constraint, and thus not information of any sort within the system of Kapinga fishing activity. A constraint on fishing activity eliminates alternative activities because of the kind of difference it makes to fishermen, human beings who are capable of being explicit about the kind of difference a constraint makes. They can tell us how they decode the messages that constraints convey by telling us what the messages mean and how and why they respond to them in the ways that they do.

We can observe, for instance, that strong winds from the southeast make the lagoon too choppy to be navigable by outrigger canoes, preventing fishing anywhere in the lagoon. But in calm waters with groupers known to be entering the lagoon in large numbers, the observation that men are doing no fishing at all would be inexplicable. It becomes explicable when a fisherman tells us that a spirit has been sited in the deep sea, and the high priest has tabooed fishing of any sort until the proper ritual of appeasement has been performed. The observation of men (improbably) eschewing fishing activity on an ideal day for it and the obvious questions about why they refrain from fishing elicits yet one more constraint for our list.

But surely anyone can see that there is a difference between wind and spirits, no? Indeed there is. Any Kapinga familiar with traditional fishing activity can tell you that wind is on top of the water and spirits under it. Winds come and go, but the spirits are always there. One does not have to pray to the wind, while one must pray to the spirits, and so on. That the existence of spirits is not demonstrable by any methods within the bounds of western, scientific discovery procedures is every bit as irrelevant to understanding the systemic nature of Kapinga fishing activity as the demonstrability of water temperature ranges within which yellow fin tuna operate. From a cybernetic point of view, all that is necessary (and relevant) to the inquiry is the demonstration that Kapinga fishermen recognized differences between spirits, people, and fish, and that they regulated their own activities in terms of those differences (cf. Schneider 1968: 6).

What possible analytical advantage can there be in ignoring the obvious fact that wind is a variable external to the island and its people, while spirits are clearly an invention of Kapinga people? The wind will blow, after all, whether or not people are around to be inconvenienced by it. Yet, what reason is there to suppose that Kapinga fishermen experience wind in the same way Americans (or Chinese, for that matter) do? Such an assertion would presuppose that that the experience of wind is no more than raw sense data, innocent of any such contamination as meaning or interpretation. This is demonstrably false. To Kapinga fishermen, strong northeasterly winds carry the metamessage of hunger. Wind as a symbol is combined with rough waters, fast currents, and altered tidal patterns, all in association with canoes that are easily swamped in choppy water. Strong winds, thus, connote reduced access to fish, dependence on fewer species, and lower probabilities of catches. To fishermen in the same waters on a one thousand ton purse seiner boat, strong northeast winds mean something quite different. Not only is access to fish relatively unaffected by the winds and rough seas, but the likelihood of large catches is increased with higher frequencies of drift logs coming from high islands to the south (especially from New Guinea). Enormous numbers of fish congregate around these logs, each of which can yield well over a hundred tons per catch. The experience of wind in each case is shaped by a pattern of meaning, a relationship among symbols (and their referents) that forms the context of the experience of wind. The two contexts are different and, thus, the experiences are different. Wind is no more natural nor any less cultural than canoe technology or spirits. It follows that every one of the constraints on Kapinga fishing activity is not only information, but also a cultural constraint.

Given that the constraints on fishing activity are information encoded on symbolic messages, the ordering of those messages form patterns, which are contexts of fishing activity. Because the coding of these messages are in the form of conventionally understood symbols, the messages are cultural messages and the contexts of fishing activity are cultural contexts. Because contexts are hierarchically ordered, then the patterns of symbols that comprise them are also hierarchically ordered. This logical ordering is important, because it makes possible logical inferences about why the contexts of fishing activity are ordered in the ways that they are.[7]

A hierarchy of symbols is a hierarchy of logical levels of generality. Following this ladder, we often find that several different contexts of activity share the same pattern of symbols. You will see, for example, that the relationship between the high priest and the spirits, the headman of the men's communal house and the high priest, and the men's house and its members all share the same configuring of contextual ordering. Thus, these contexts all form a single class. We can take this class as a given, or we can try to explain it. Cultural anthropologists typically pursue the explanation of patterns that are distributed through more than one specific context using much the same inference procedure--what are the minimal assumptions that we would have to make in order to generate this pattern? The inference that answers this question is a model of the assumptions the people we observe make, and we look for ways to test the validity of our logical model.

Cultural Premises: Propositions That Organize Contexts

The assumptions people make and share about the nature of the relations that connect their universe are so abstract as to be unconscious--things that people know but do not know that they know. They are implicit in people's expectations and evaluations of situations and of one another. These implicit assumptions have been variously termed "configurations" (Benedict 1934), "themes" (Opler 1946), "implicit culture," and "covert culture." Following Carroll (1988), I think of these implicit assumptions as cultural *premises*. That is, the assumptions people make about the general nature of the relations between people, non-human beings, things, and the like are propositions (or stateable as propositions) about relationships. Looking at implicit assumptions as premises keeps explicit the connection between these propositions and the logic by which people draw specific conclusions about specific contexts.

A familiar example of a cultural premis is how American popularly conceptualize human nature, human careers, and human attributes. No American ever states explicitly that people, like everything else in the universe, are objects in motion (albeit with thought, will, and speech) and, as such, are describable in terms of position, trajectories, and functions of the two. But Americans talk and act as if they assume that this is true. Someone is on his way up, on his way down, has made it to the top, is over the hill, bottomed out, getting ahead, getting nowhere (fast), on target, off the wall, falling in love, falling flat (on his or her face), high as a kite, low man on the totem pole, flat broke, gone bust, etc., to name only a few. Functions of motion, particularly those of kinetic energy, are particularly popular for describing personal attributes and relations, such as energetic, forceful, powerful, having an impact, making an impression, bouncing off people, and being dynamic, attractive, repulsive, and compelling. The reader can come up with many more of these, not just in popular speech, but from academic literature in the humanities, sciences, and social sciences. One might argue that these are "merely" words, metaphors, but that is belied by the fact that the way Americans use these terms is so patterned and consistent. It is the patterning and consistency of use, not any individual term of speech, that makes this inference valid. If a test of this inference is necessary, then try figuring out why we call all knowledge other than our inner, personal perceptions *objective*.

The importance of the cultural premis is its potential for explaining why the symbolic messages that form contexts are patterned in the ways that they are. These unconscious assumptions function as rules for putting messages together into sequences, i.e., they generate the patterning of messages that constitute a relationship.[8]

This entire theoretical framework can be summarized in one word: *context*. The goal of this research is understanding the organization of traditional fishing on Kapingamarangi in terms of the contexts and the ordering of contexts of specific fishing activities. The reason for choosing a cybernetic approach to this subject matter is that it provides a clear, useful way of understanding context that is applicable to any purposeful activity in any conceivable sort of system--electronic, chemical, social or what have you. A theory of culture is necessary when it is contexts of human activity that have to be explained, since people construe and respond to the the relationships that constitute their contexts of activity in terms of the patterns of meaning they confer on them. Inferring the premises that generate these patterns of meaning not only explains the organization of the contexts of the activities we observe, but also provides a set of criteria for understanding how new information is combined with what people already know (since any rule limits the possible combinations of messages). This is a lot to ask from field research as compressed as mine had to be, making the focus on constraints on fishing activity as much a practical as a theoretical matter.

Conduct of the Research

The initial research design hadn't formulated this theoretical background nearly as explicitly as presented here. In fact, the connections between information, meaning, and culture emerged during the field research and subsequent analysis of the data. But the pieces were clear enough to guide the directions of data collection. The centerpiece of collection was obvious--the fishing expedition from start to finish. An exhaustive list of constraints on fishing activity would minimally require an exhaustive list of kinds of expeditions.

I could have simply asked older fishermen to list every catch method from the 'old time' or, more explicitly, for every netting, angling, trapping, etc., expedition practiced before Christianity (1917). This would have provided a quick list to start, but there was no assurance that it would be a complete list. Seventeen years' work in the same community was enough to know that Kapinga do their best to answer any question as clearly as possible, but they usually will not volunteer facts related to the question if its phrasing did not specifically call for them. For this short field stint, I didn't want to be in a position of having to stumble on important data by luck.

The solution was to take a necessary but tedious task and to use it to both generate new data and to cross-check lists of fishing expedition (catch) types gotten from direct questioning. The task that initiated field research was the identification of all named varieties of fish and other marine animals, matching Kapinga names as closely as possible with common names and scientific names (see Appendix 2).

Identifying fish was a nasty job, but somebody had to do it. Luckily, part of Foss Leach's project included the scientific identification of one hundred different varieties of fish. Foss kindly sent copies of all of his identifications. For the remainder, using several books of Pacific fish, fishermen in both the Pohnpei and atoll communities identified Kapinga varieties from photographs. The work was slow, and the older men were more patient than the younger ones. In fact, one could easily tell when the younger men were getting bored, because the names they gave the fish got ever more colorful, as did my sincere expressions of gratitude. Good taste precludes giving examples. Working with a dozen fishermen, it took two weeks to develop a list of 257 named varieties of fish in the Kapinga community on Pohnpei. Several more names were added as work proceeded.

An alphabetical sorting of the list of fish effectively randomized them from a Kapinga point of view. Each fish name went on a separate index card to be filled in with the answers to the following questions.

(1) What specific catch techniques are used to get this fish?

Then for each catch technique (read type of expedition) listed, the following:

(2) What other fish are likely to be caught along with it?
(3) Is it this fish you are after, another fish caught with it, or any fish in the area?
(4) Where is this fish usually caught?
(5) When (season, month, week, time of day) is this fish caught?
(6) Is this fish seasonal or always available?
(7) If seasonal, then what determines the catch season?
(8) What equipment is used?
(9) Who could (or had to) participate in the expedition and who could not and why?
(10) What does this fish eat, and how does it breed?

This work proceeded slowly with barely time to complete questioning of one fisherman and train a young Kapinga assistant to work with another man before being called home by serious illness in my family. I made arrangements with a man on Kapinga who had worked with me and with Foss Leach to complete the questioning of two men on the atoll and mail the tapes back to me upon completion. These two men completed their field tapes in March, 1981. Analysis of these tapes compared to mine was fascinating. The younger man working in the Pohnpei community was almost as naive as I; we both tended to stick to the question format, asking questions about new or unclear materials in much the same ways. The atoll assistant, a fisherman in his forties, used my question format, but he already shared knowledge about many of the details in the answers. The sorts of clarifications he asked for were much more subtle and elicited fine points of technique, equipment, timing, fish habits, and the like that would have taken me weeks or months to discover on my own. The first phase of collection was, thus, completed partially in my absence. The second phase, again sponsored by the Office of Historic Preservation, was completed during the summer of 1982.

Analysis of the interview tapes yielded forty-five different, named fishing expeditions (or catch techniques) and hints that there were more of them. The data, even in this atomistic form, also indicated patterns of circulation of fish with tide, current, and lunar phases, as well as seasons. Wind and tide patterns were clearly determinative of catch technique selection, and there was a clear distinction between fish gotten in daytime and those caught at night. The next phase of the project built on these data when field research resumed in 1982.

Getting It Done

Two of the three men I had worked with on Pohnpei had moved to the atoll by 1982, while one of the atoll informants had died. Most of my formal interviews were with those two and a third man that my atoll assistant had questioned. Their information was supplemented by cross-checking with eight other men, four in their seventies and four between forty and sixty years of age. Three older women provided details about fish preparation, fishing crews, distribution of catches, and fishing chants.

The collection procedure with each of the three major informants was as follows. Using Kapinga categories, I divided up fish catching activity by time and space. The first distinction was between windy and calm seasons. The next was between fish caught in the lagoon, the reef, in the channels between islets, and in the deep sea, each of which was further bisected by day catch and night catch. For each of the resulting classes, e.g., calm season-reef-night, each man listed all fish caught with each list checked against my index cards, noting which fish did not appear on their lists and asking each man to complete the lists by adding the missing fish where they belonged. These revised lists were then compared to account for the very few discrepancies that I found.

When these lists were completed, I turned to catch techniques, simply asking each of the three men to list every catch technique used for each season-space-time category. For each item listed, I asked which fish were caught using it. The only important discrepancies were between the lists of fish in the area-season-time list and those in the catch technique list each man had given me. Asking about these produced a few more catch techniques, but it was clear that the set of discrete fishing expeditions was as complete as it would get using a listing procedure. It was time to move on to the details of the fishing expeditions.

For each fishing expedition type (or catch technique), I asked the following questions:

(1) How was it initiated and who initiated it?
(2) The number of participants and how they were selected.
(3) How and by whom was it managed?
(4) What equipment was used and why?
(5) When and under what conditions was it done?
(6) What was the typical procedure, were there alternatives to it, and under what conditions would the alternative be selected?
(7) What would threaten or abort it?
(8) What other catch techniques could be used at the same time?

While this might sound like a pretty dry interview structure, it was really where the fun began. This is what a fisherman lives for, the stuff that they talk to each other about. These are the things that engender and embroider the anecdotes, the cautionary tales, and the chants. Most of all, on this tiny atoll where a sense of manhood was so intimately bound up with fishing, these sorts of details were the raw materials on which personal reputations were built.

All of the work preceding the inquiry into the catch types was like filling in data base entries at the computer. The older fishermen understood why I was spending all those hours on such elementary stuff and even approved of it. So they were very patient with my questions, and I could see at times that they were bearing down to get it done. The work on catch techniques had a totally different character, however.

If these sessions with fishermen could be called interviews--they had the external structure of interviews and all my questions got answered--then they were interviews that I never really controlled. That much was clear from very first day. Better them than me, as it turned out, for our sessions had a rhythm to them, a sort of conversational dance where they led and I followed.[9]

For years, these men had endured my questions about kinship, land, adoption, ritual, political structure, history, ethnicity, mobility, household structure, and all those other categories of inquiry that my discipline demands. They had done so with patience and good humor, though all except land tenure was everyday stuff that didn't much excite the imagination. Since there is so little land to go around for an exploding population, and control of it confers influence and prestige, land tenure involves partisan interest emotionally charged situations (Lieber 1970, 1974). But fishing was something else again.

To be a man is to be a fisherman, and to be a good fisherman is to be a *real* man. People are memorialized in chants, for example, and when their names appear, men or women, it is always connected somehow with fishing. If land tenure is emotionally charged, then fishing is symbolically charged. So when I began to work on fishing (not the fish, but fishing) with these men, I was finally and squarely on their turf and talking about things that really mattered. It was natural that they should take the lead and that I should follow. To do that required me to be attentive to the messages and metamessages of this discourse, and it required of them that they provide me the wherewithal to follow properly and keep the conversation going. I had not only become privy to a discourse, but in a sense had become part of it. Because this was so, pursuing the minutia of techniques, of tide patterns, of reef forms, etc., and participating in fishing activities at every opportunity became as much a matter of personal hunger as of professional obligation.

Short of reproducing these conversations, I have tried to keep the tone of descriptions of fishing activity in Part Two informal enough to communicate my fascination with their details and what makes them so fascinating. As masters of their art, Kapinga managed to accumulate a wide repertoire of effective catch techniques without damaging their ecosystem or the species on which they depended. I will argue in Part Three that they had the technology to wipe out any number of species long before colonial contact. That they did not do so then and appear to be doing so now requires explanation, for which their catch repertoire and its organization are the *sine qua non*.

The Scope of the Research

My original plan for this report was to work out the organization of traditional fishing activity, using data on change during the 20th century to test hypotheses derived from the analysis, e.g., about the maintenance of ecological balance between fishing activity and fish populations. Two things forced me to change that plan. One was my encounter with Ward Goodenough's work, which used activity as an analytical unit to understand systemic change in the social order of Onotoa Atoll (in the Gilbert Islands) generated by changes in Onotoan fishing activities. The other was the painfully obvious fact that fishing activities had become, for Kapinga people, a metaphor for the disintegration of their community, and that fact demanded explanation.

Goodenough's work is critical to understanding the Kapinga case in two ways. First, the details of our two cases are strikingly similar in some ways and strikingly different in others, and I use the comparison between them to understand both the traditional Kapinga system of fishing activities and the historical changes in that system. Second, the comparison of an otherwise puzzling mix of similarities and differences is made clear by a combination of Goodenough's connection between activities and institutions with a cybernetic approach to historical transformation.

As Goodenough notes in the Foreword, activities may be related by feature overlap, feature complementation, instrumental linkage (with intrinsic and/or extrinsic value of linked activities) by having the the same or similar procedural requirements, or (e) by the inherent conflict between maintaining efficiency in the performance of a single activity and the need to maintain overall flexibility in performing all activities taken together (net efficacy). Change in any of these relations will affect two or more activities simultaneously. How activities are related determines whether they can be implemeted by individuals on their own initiative, by *ad hoc* groups formed on the spot, or by standing groups, each with its own prerogatives. The organization of a community's social order, in other words, can be seen as an outcome of exigencies of the relations between activities. Goodenough (1963) uses the term "institution" to label the standing groups that manage related activities. This is very different from looking at groups as given units of social structure. There is nothing "given" about them in Goodenough's framework; human institutions emerge as a community's adaptive responses to the organizational necessities of coordinating activities.

After presenting the details of Kapinga fishing activities in Part Two (Chapters 2 through 8), I take advantage of Goodenough's concept of institution to show how the constraints on fishing activities are filtered through two institutions--the cult house, whose activities regulated men's house activities, which regulated fishermen's activities. This demonstration adds one important feature to Goodenough's list--what enables any institution to regulate activity is its control of the flow of information, and different institutions often process and communicate information in very different ways.

The comparison between Onotoa and Kapingamarangi shapes the first half of Part Three, which details the historical changes in Kapinga fishing activities and their larger institutional contexts in a setting of domination by three different colonial regimes since 1900. The comparison follows an account of the reorganization of the Kapinga community and of its fishing activity consequent on the abandonment of the traditional religion and wholesale conversion to Christianity (during Japanese colonial hegemony between 1914 and 1946). If one looks at the organization of these two communities as social structures and their changes as structural changes, Onotoa and Kapingamarangi appear to be quite different. But comparing them in terms of institutions and processes of institutional change, they appear to be identical. This conclusion is arrived at, however, by viewing the historic events that constitute institutional change from an information-theoretic perspective (following the strategy outlined in Carroll 1977). That is, rather than searching for causal connections in a linear sequence of events--event A caused event B, which caused event C--a significant event or sequence of events is seen as one of a set of possible events or sequence of events that might have occurred. Understanding and comparing particular patterns of historical transformation forces us to focus on the constraints that made the events that actually occurred more probable than the other possible events that did not.

Kapinga fishing activity and its institutional contexts undergo a much more drastic change under the American colonial regime and the beginnings of political independence from that regime. It is during this period that Kapinga focus on fishing as the tangible evidence of and the metaphor for community disintegration and chaos. Yet atoll affairs seemed to hum along without any major conflicts, and the community did not appear to be in any danger of immanent dissolution. In what sense, then, could these statements be true? The answer lies in Kapinga conceptions of community, which I examine in Part Four.

In Part Four, I explain the patterns of change described in Part Three by showing how they are shaped by unchanging assumptions that Kapinga make about the world--cultural premises about the meaning of 'community' that structure people's historical experience--assumptions indelibly shaped by the experience of centuries of isolation. I use evidence of historical patterning of structural transformations of the Kapinga community to generate predictions about the next most likely organizational change in the present post-colonial era, and I'll tell you how they turned out.

Notes

1. This organization is similar to that of the ritual chief-talking chief pairing of Samoa (Shore 1983) and Pohnpei (Riesenberg 1966).

2. It was this *tomono* position that evolved into the secular chieftainship by the end of the 19th century.

3. I find it ironic that even while anthropologists continue to be concerned with how social systems are put together, how the parts work, both singly and together, and how their interactions maintain or change the system, and though we continue to employ much of the functionalist method to find out these things, one of the easiest ways to dismiss a scholar's work is to label it "functionalist." As if anthropologists ever abandoned teleology as a necessary part of any description or explanation. This has less to do with how anthropologists do their work than with how they present themselves to their colleagues.

4. I reluctantly exclude from consideration here the problem of non-referential meaning, particularly indexical meaning, where a sign or some property of a sign indicates, by conventional understanding, the context or some property of the context of observed interaction. For example, regardless of the particular referent of someone's speech act, one's accent may indicate that he or she is from the South (or New York or Boston, etc.). The relationship of indexical meaning to problems of context, the structure of metamessages, and the like remain to be worked out, and this, unfortunately, is not the place to do it. I mention this here because we encounter indexical meaning in fishing activity, e.g., lunar phase as an index of tide pattern. An excellent account of indexical meaning and its rela-

tion to referential meaning can be found in Silverstein (1976).

5. While anthropologists agree on the central importance of meaning (encoded on symbols) that people use to construct what community members take to be reality, they don't agree on much else when it comes to a definition of culture. Generally speaking, anthropologists subscribe to either of two sorts of definition: one takes culture as an entity, as a kind of thing that people "have", and the other takes culture as an abstraction (of one kind or another) that observers use to order and to compare their observations. Culture taken as an entity is thought to do things like mould people's perception and thought or to maintain itself or to change. Culture can also vary, so the culture that one community has is different from the one that another has. This view of culture is the one popularly accepted by the general public as well as by many social scientists. The facticity of culture relies, however, on one's willingness to take a way of understanding the organization of thought and action in human communities and to transform it into a thing that is inside people. This transformation process is logically fallacious and referred to as "reification" or the "fallacy of misplaced concreteness" (Bidney 1967: 114-119).

6. Since it is human beings who report observations of systems, culture would have to be included in the boundary between the observer and the system in any observation of any system, given that it is the meanings the observer has learned through enculturation that constrain the observer's interpretations. When it is an exotic social system that is observed, the observer's own premises for interpreting experience need to be consciously and consistently distinguished from those of the people observed.

7. Keep in mind that the hierarchy of contexts of activities is a logical hierarchy used by the observer to explain a set of observations. This logical hierarchy is not the same as the activities that people organize. The activities, constraints that order them, and the groups that mount them may turn out to be hierarchically ordered or they may not. That depends on what people do, not on what the observer does.

8. Those familiar with Gregory Bateson's work will notice that what I've done here is to link culture to his theory of context, first by using message to connect information and meaning and, second, by showing how cultural premises are what Bateson (1972: 338) calls "contextual structure." The explanatory and predictive power of this linkage becomes evident in Part Four.

9. I owe my belated understanding of this experience to Helen Schwartzman (1981), who has developed this apt metaphor in the context of play in serious encounters.

PART TWO

Traditional Fishing Activities

2

Traditional Fishing Activities

What makes the details of traditional fishing so intriguing to someone who is not a totally committed, canoe-hugging fisherperson (or marine biologist, or fisheries expert) is what they bespeak of the sheer ingenuity of people who inhabit one of the earth's most marginal environments. Using an admittedly sketchy description of the atoll, try putting yourselves in their place for a moment.

Here you are on less than half a square mile of land, surrounded by ocean with no contact with other islands, and a population of 500 people to feed. And these people aren't exactly your delicate flower types, either. They are Polynesians, the stuff of which National Football League linemen are made--and they *like* to eat. All you Jewish or Italian grandsons who think you can get away from grandma's "Eat! Eat!" by running off to an exotic atoll can forget it. *Hanimoi miami*! may be a different code, but it's the same message, and, just like grandma (your own, your spouse's, your friend's), "But I'm not hungry" is not an acceptable response. We are not talking subsistence here; we're talking *food*, with everything that means--it's not imminent starvation that grandma is worried about (even if she says it is). There are families to be fed, but there are also feasts of all kinds to be provisioned, not just enough to feed the guests, but also enough for each of them to take home for their family's meal--not a snack, mind you, but a meal.

Provisioning this population from an atoll's resources is a formidable task. The wherewithal to do it is only what is at hand, and it isn't much. Coconut husk and the bark of breadfruit and hibiscus trees provide the cordage. Tree trunks and branches from five or six varieties are the material for canoes, outrigger assemblies, poles, masts, paddles, clubs, balers, tool boxes, handles, hafts, and frames for nets. Shell provides all the cutting tools, awls, chisels, scrapers, drills, hammers, abrasives, and fish hooks. Coral rock does the pounding, cracking, and breaking, while limestone (baked and watered) is putty and calk. Pandanus leaf, stripped and plaited, made a workable sail. That and coconut, breadfruit, pandanus, taro, and one creeper vine for vegetable food. The rest is what is in people's heads: what they know about what they can do with what they have. Even a casual glance at Peter Buck's *Material Culture of Kapingamarangi* will tell you that it was plenty. But fabricating tools, canoes, and gear is only part of what you'd need to know. You also need to know how, when, and where to use your hardware. I'll start with where and when.

Figure 2.1 is a schematic drawing to help you to visualize what a typical atoll looks like. Every one of the labelled features is a place where you can get fish, so the labels are useful in describing fishing activity.

Kapingamarangi has all of the features in Figure 2.1, but in its own peculiar combinations. To be a consistently successful fisherman, you'd need to know every one of them, and in a way that is easily communicable to others. Your knowledge of your environment, in other words, would have to be reasonably complete, well organized, and common knowledge. The way that people in this part of the world do that is by parsing their environment into bounded places and naming each one. So, for example, if you flew over Kapingamarangi in a plane and looked down, what you'd see is pretty much what is in Map 1, except that it's in living color minus the islet names. If you were a Kapinga person flying over the atoll and looking down, what you'd see is more like what is in Maps 2 and 3 (except that the names would be in your head).

Without knowing a word of Kapinga, you can still figure out something about the way they organized their environment from a casual inspection of Map 2. Starting from the right side of the page where the islets are, run your eyes counterclockwise along the reef. Look at two or three names on the ocean side and then look across the reef to the lagoon side names. Not only are they mostly different names, but the boundary lines on the seaward reef don't match those on the lagoon side. The line

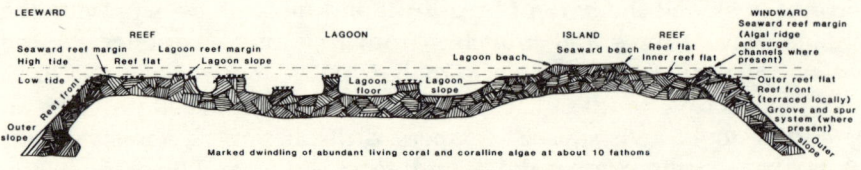

FIGURE 2.1 Major features of an atoll (after Weins 1962)

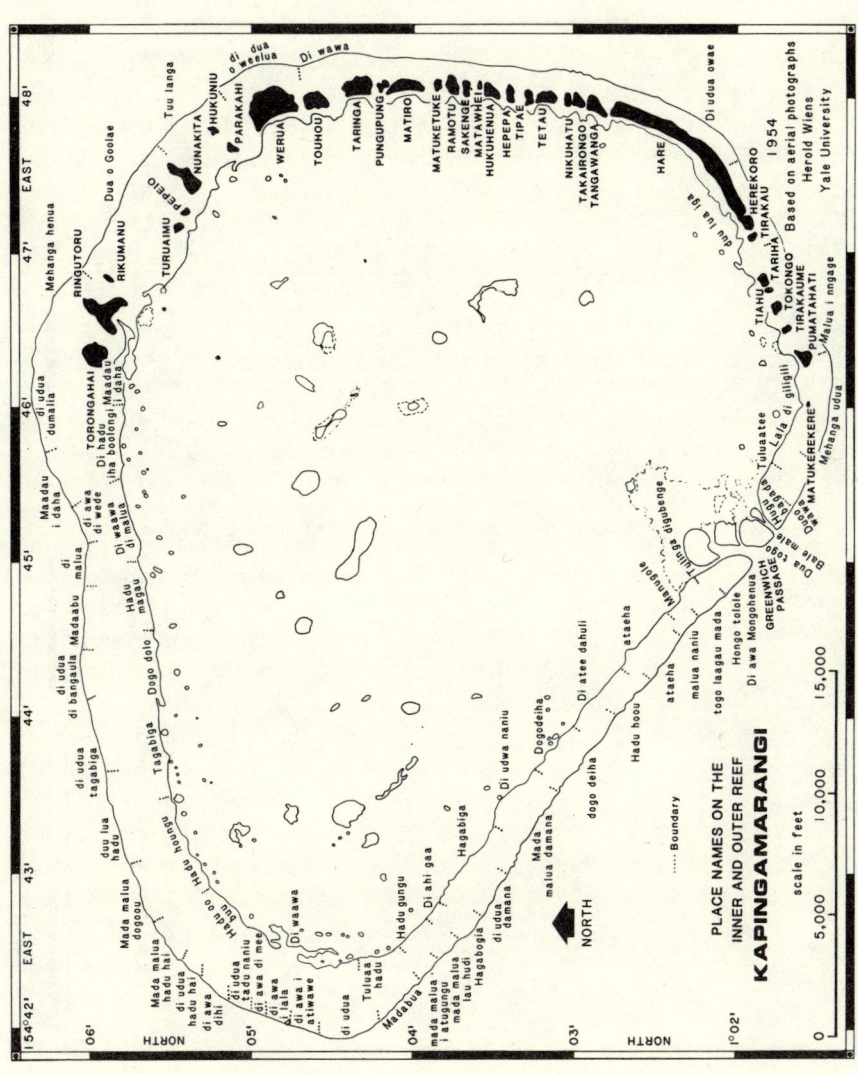

MAP 2 Place names on the reef

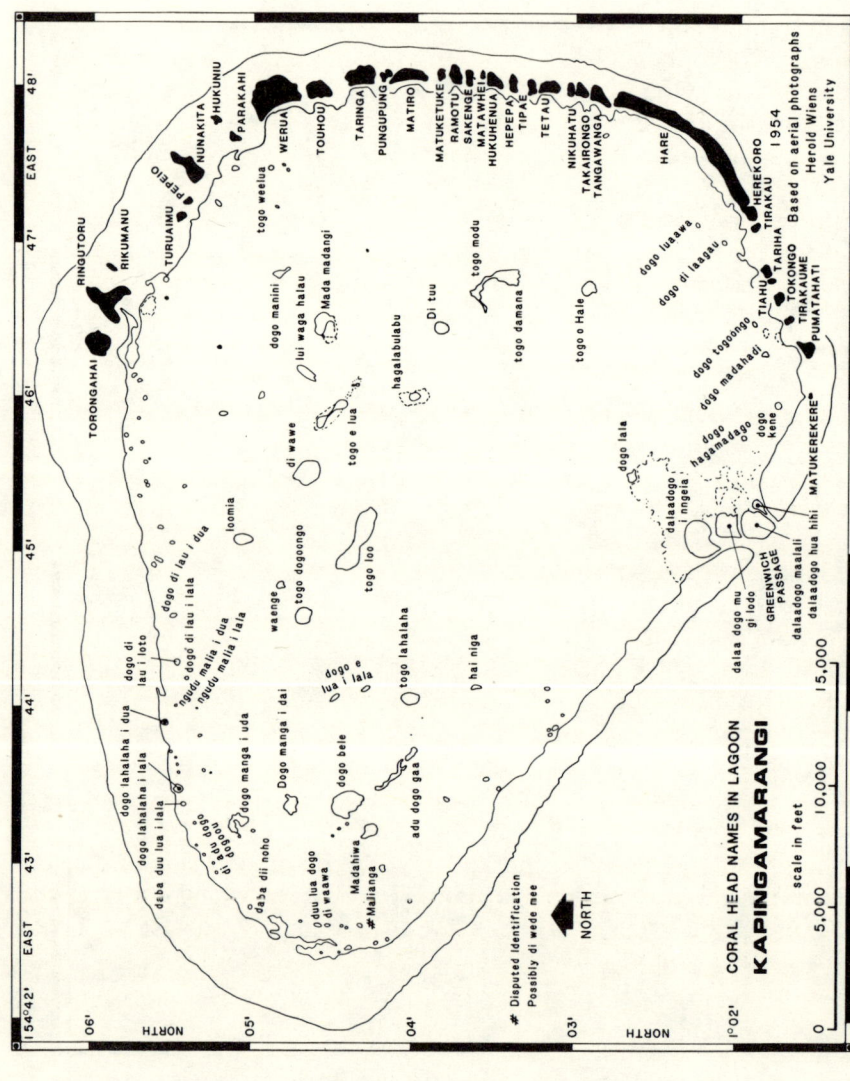

MAP 3 Place names of coral heads

doesn't just start on one side and run directly to the other. Lagoon side and seaward side areas are different places, in other words. This makes a certain kind of sense, since those places are different geologically, and they accommodate very different kinds of fish. The name not only locates a place, but encodes something of what kind of place it is relative to other places. One place has a sand beach clear of big rocks and coral formations; another is strewn with them; another has a sharp bend in the reef, and so on. You can see that most of the coral heads are also named (Map 3), as should be the case given that these are good places to get fish with traps, hook and line, nets, and even small sleeping mats. The ones that don't have names can be located using the ones that do: "just seaward of *adu dogo gaa*," or "the one between *dogo togongo* and *dogo madahati*." But the names do more than just designate (kinds of) places on the reef. They are reference points for locating places in the lagoon and ocean.

Say you've happened on a spot in the ocean just 50 yards or so off the reef between Torongohai islet and *di malua*, where the reef curves sharply. You've run out of bait, and you'd like to come back tomorrow, so you need a way of marking the spot. The way you do it is by triangulating your canoe between two significant features that you know: with *Madabuu* on your right, Bumadahadi islet across the lagoon should be to the left of and almost touching the groove and spur at the boundary between *di malua* and *di awa di wede*. Whether it's marking a spot, or returning to a well known place, whether a fisherman is looking for a spot to place his net or his trap or his line, he recognizes the spot from a feature of a named place, and he heads for that place first.

So between the reef areas, coral heads, passes, and islets, there is no important place inside or outside the reef that is not known and mapped. The general details are common knowledge; but the more different kinds of fishing a man does, the more detailed the map becomes. The details link features of places with particular fish gotten at particular times.

Knowing the map like the back of your hand goes a long way toward getting you good catches, but it doesn't guarantee them. There are a couple of reasons for this. One of them is luck--and Kapinga fishermen are very explicit about this. Some fishermen just seem to attract fish, while others can do everything right and still go out on the water with a black cloud over their heads. Everyone empathizes with such men, but no one wants them on his canoe. The other reason for the difference between consistently good and consistently bad catches is timing. Timing has its gross and its subtle aspects, so let's approach it by looking at a specific kind of place, illustrated in Figure 2.2.

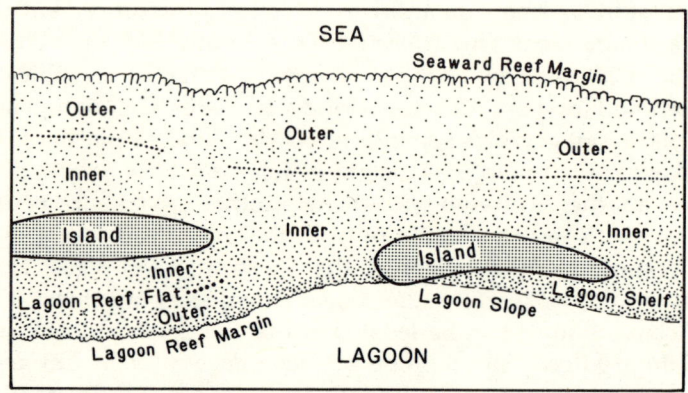

FIGURE 2.2 Major features of an atoll reef (after Weins 1962).

In this figure, you get a bird's eye view of what an atoll reef looks like. On the ocean side of the islets is the reef flat, divided into the inner and outer reef flat, which merges with the outer reef margin, where the waves break. All of these labelled features are fishing places. Now, let's go right from this general view to how it looks on Kapingamarangi (in Figure 2.3).

In this figure, you see a close-up of the three central islets, Touhou, Werua, and Taringa, where most Kapinga reside. You see labelled some important details of the lagoon beaches, the channel between the islets, and the form it takes as it fans out to the deeper lagoon. Now this area is one sort of place under a four foot high tide and quite another under a

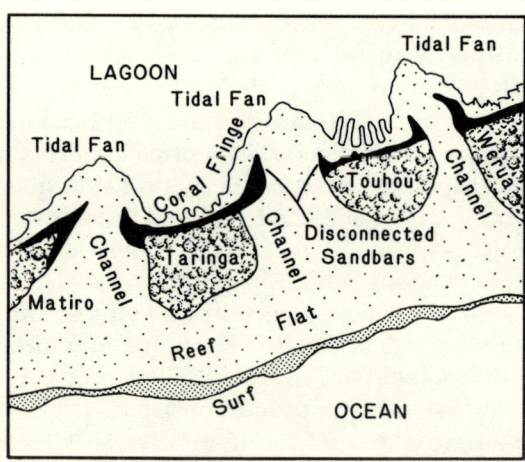

FIGURE 2.3 Reef features near Touhou Islet, Kapingamarangi Atoll (after Weins, 1962).

Traditional Fishing Activities

fourteen inch high tide. A four foot high tide makes this a lousy place to fish, while a fourteen incher makes it a great place to fish, but only during the day when people can see. The tidal fan is another place that produces good catches, but only when the tide is slowly rising. The outer reef margin is also productive, but only when the wave action is low and gentle. If you happen to be at these places with a few friends and the right gear at these times, then your next big decision is whether to fry, bake, or barbecue. Show up an hour or so later and you'll just be sightseeing.

If you had to learn all these things by trial-and-error, you'd soon be frustrated and skinny. Luckily, the important features of timing are all non-random, so if you could eke out a living for a year or so, you'd learn some of the more important ones on your own. With someone to show you the ropes, you'd have most of the important stuff down in a year or so. I say a year, because it takes that long just for the gross aspects of timing to play themselves out. It's a lot like being in business, where there are only two seasons--the busy and the dull. On Kapingamarangi there is calm season (the busy) and windy season (the dull). Each one transforms the marine ecosystem from one sort of environment into another.

Calm season, from mid-May through early September, is a time of gentle breezes when the lagoon is as smooth and clear as glass on a sunny day. Even the ocean waves lap rather than break. This is the stuff of which tourist photos are made. If you're there to fish, then you'll have all you can handle, because every fish habitat is accessible to you even with the simplest of water craft. This is the time of year Kapinga call 'fish season,' because they can use nearly every technique in their repertoire. Windy season, from late September through mid-May, is another story. Southeast trade winds blow strong and steady enough to make the ocean rough and the lagoon choppy and murky. Unless you're in a New England whale boat (or something larger), your craft gets swamped quickly. This means that all of those wonderful spots in the lagoon are out of reach. You can still fish, but you have far fewer options. Kapinga call this the 'hungry season,' not because people always starve then, but because of the reduction in the variety of available fish and the uncertainty of catch sizes that comes with having fewer options. A bad day of deep sea fishing during calm season is not that big a deal, because there are at least two other kinds of fishing being done on a given day that will produce a catch. A bad day of deep sea fishing during windy season is a bigger deal, because there may be no other option on that day. Three days later may not be so bad, since an in-shore option may be available then. There is more to timing than just seasons, in other words.

Each season has its own sorts of tides. Calm season has two high tides and two low tides per day, and high water marks are much lower than windy season tides. Windy season, with its generally higher tides, has only one low tide per day, usually in the evening or night. You don't need to know a lot about fish to figure out the kinds of difference these tide variations make. Take that reef flat seaward of Werua (in Figure 2.3) again. Because it's so relatively flat and smooth without any big boulders, smaller fish who feed on the reef have nowhere to hide from their bigger predators. This means that the only time they're relatively safe is when the high tide is still too low for those bigger predators to negotiate. That's why a fourteen inch high tide makes that reef flat a good place to fish and a four foot high tide doesn't. That same four foot tide on a section of reef with good size coral rocks brings out the reef feeders and their predators, and that can be a good place to fish. You get those four foot high tides during windy season, so there are some options then. What you need to remember is that there is a relationship between the physical form of the reef or beach area, the kind of tide, and the kinds and numbers of fish that you're likely to find. The trick is knowing when conditions in that area are right for fishing. Fortunately, it's not much of a trick, since these conditions vary with the regularity of clockwork, but only if you're willing to forget the seven day week and reckon time by the lunar month, from new moon to new moon.

Tides vary in a highly patterned way. The elements of the pattern are: (1) the time of the lowest and highest tide during the day,
(2) the rapidity of the rise and ebb,
(3)   how high the high water mark is at the highest tide and how low the low water mark is at the lowest tide, and
(4)   how long the tide remains steady at its high water and at its low water marks.

These four elements do not vary in every conceivable combination in a given month, however. In fact, a particular combination doesn't even vary all that much from day to day. On Kapingamarangi, a particular combination of elements--which I call a tide pattern--changes very gradually over a three day period.

Take calm season, say the new moon in June. The night high tide stays steady for a couple of hours until about 4:00 am., and the ebb thereafter is very rapid, so that the reef is dry by about 5:30 or so. The lagoon fish that have been feeding on the reef flat seaward of Touhou and Werua often fail to notice how low the tide is until there is barely enough water for them to swim in. At that point, the channel between Touhou and Werua leading to the lagoon looks like the New York City subway at rush hour. The same thing happens the next night but about an hour or so later with a slightly longer ebb. The night after that, you still get the same pattern but another hour later with a longer ebb. By this time, the fish have a longer time and more daylight to notice what's happening. By the next day, you get a different tide pattern bringing different combinations of fish at different times in different numbers for the next three days. With that kind of regularity, you can plan your forays with a much better than even chance of success. It should surprise no one that Kapinga fishermen divide the lunar month into successive three day periods from new moon to two days after the full moon, followed by one four day period, followed by three more three day periods--a twenty eight day month. They use lunar phases to index conditions of fish habitats from the coral heads to the lagoon beaches, the channels between the islets, the inner reef and outer reef flats, and the outer reef margin (since tide pattern is a good predictor of wave action).

One of the beauties of this way of systematizing what you know about your environment (at least for us non-specialists) is that it works well on nothing more than correlations (each of which has both a verbal and an arithmetic signal--you know what tide it is even if it's been cloudy, just counting from the last new or full moon). You also don't need to be a marine biologist to make the system work. It can't hurt to know why the fish are there, what they eat, how they reproduce, etc.. All you minimally have to know is when the fish are there, for how long, and how they move when they're disturbed.

Once you move outside the reef into deep water, you're dealing with different fish, different timing patterns, and different catch techniques. But the way you know all this is still correlational, particularly since you can't see most of the fish you're after until you get them up to the surface. But between personal experience and scuttlebutt, there is a lot of information to be had. These are mostly carnivorous fish, and you may not know precisely what they usually eat, but you can get a good idea from what bait each variety takes and what it passes up. From where you catch them over a month, and at what depths during what times of day or night, you can get a reasonably clear picture of their range of daily movement over a lunar month. Some deep water fish move in clusters, so you get a good catch just by getting your hook down in the right place. Others are more spread out, so you have to collect them together by chumming before offering a baited hook.

Calm and windy seasons affect ocean fishing in two ways. Although the seas are usually rough during windy season, they are not evenly so. A strong wind coming up from the south, for example, will make for choppy water in the southern, eastern, and western quadrants, but once the wind hits the islets, the trees block most of it, so the waters in the northern quadrant are relatively calm. As long as the current is not too strong, you can take a canoe out for some angling. The other major seasonal effect is access to bait, most of which comes from inside the reef. Since the lagoon is not navigable, the only available bait is what can be gotten on or near the islets.

Now, with some idea of the where and when, we can make a start on how. The older Kapinga men named eighty-four different fishing expeditions that comprised their fathers' and grandfathers' repertoire. The oldest men I talked with had done most of them. Men in the next generation had participated in 70% of them, while men in their 50s had done about half of them (mostly when they were kids).

Eighty-four different named expeditions doesn't mean there were eighty-four totally different procedures. That total consisted of variations on seven or eight categories of technique. "Seven or eight" is not very precise, but I'm interested in making some reasonably complex material understandable, not in establishing a scientific classification. Basically, Kapinga caught fish with nets, with weirs, with traps, by collecting on the reef, with pole and line, by diving (claming), and with a hand held line and hook (angling). That's seven, but netting could be divided into use of big nets to surround fish and hand netting. Netting can also overlap with trapping, but these are just academic quibbles. Table 1 summarizes the numbers of named fishing expeditions under each category, each divided into those designed to exploit a particular area and those designed to exploit particular fish. I am going to use the details of these eighty-four expeditions to show how variations on procedural themes meet the demands of particular environments and cope with or take advantage of the peculiarities of particular fish. It is in these accounts that you can get an idea of the ingenuity of Kapinga fishermen and of the interplay between the organization of knowledge and the organization of activity. What I want to make very clear in these accounts is that in Kapinga fishing activity, what we see is a relatively simple technology that is complexly calibrated

TABLE 2.1 Distribution of named activities by category

name of	netting	angling	pole & line	trap	weir	collecting	claming
area	12	13	4	1	0	0	0
species	15	16	11	4	3	4	1
total	27	29	15	5	3	4	1

Traditional Fishing Activities

to the variations of the atoll's environment. What I mean by technology and by environment will be my rendering of what Kapinga mean by those constructs. I'll summarize and reorganize these expeditions in coded form in Appendix 1, integrating them into the list of Kapinga fish names and their scientific equivalents (in Appendix 2) as a quick reference.

I'll conclude this presentation of the expeditions with a section of analysis that takes the constraints on fishing activity emerging from the descriptions and shows how those constraints are ordered relative to one another. I'm going use that ordering of constraints to construct a model of how Kapinga organized their universe and their activities within that universe. Constructing these sorts of models is an important part of what anthropologists do with our ethnographic data. What makes this more than just abstract play is the fact that the model can be wrong. If it can be tested against evidence that could falsify it (Part Three) and found to be reasonably sound, then it can be useful in explaining the subsequent history of the community.

Now on to fishing, starting with netting, followed by pole and line fishing, weirs, collecting on the reef, trapping, and angling. I'll include diving for clams with collecting. The first four categories all take fish at or near the surface of the water. Diving, trapping, and angling take fish at progressively greater depths beneath the surface.

3
Netting

If fishing activity were a skeleton, then netting would be the backbone. Comprising only a third of the catch repertoire, netting accounted for well over half of the fish people ate. Of all the active fishermen working over a year's time, two-thirds of them were involved in netting. What makes the backbone analogy so apt is not the numbers, but the fact that most netting activity is done by groups of from two to fifty men. Netting is rivaled only by the family in its requirements of sustained organizational effort in this community. It was in netting expeditions that men learned what organization was and what discipline, rapid co-ordinated response, and leadership meant. From the beach to the fishing spot and back, the men's house headman and his assistants were the law. Giving instructions quietly before the expedition, they communicated with hand signals thereafter until the fish were ready to be secured in the net or trap. Then they spoke quickly and expected immediate obedience. It was netting that institutionalized group endeavor in the form of the men's house, the only secular, non-kin standing group in this society and the work force for its major ritual activities. Because the essence of masculinity is defined by fishing activity, it was netting--as an activity and as an ambience--that defined for every fisherman what it meant to be a man among men. Yet there is an irony here.

Netting never had the prestige of angling. Given the choice, any fisherman would rather have been out on a canoe in deep water, even if he caught no fish. The man hard at work making a new canoe was accorded more admiration than the man making a new net, and both would agree that the canoe maker deserved it. But prestige is one thing and practicality another.

There are two reasons for a fisherman to use a net rather than some other implement to catch fish. First, a very large number of fish, all the non-carnivorous fish that inhabit the reef, the lagoon, the coral heads, and the outer reef margins, plus those like flying fish that appear periodically, cannot be gotten any other way. Second, there are fish that could be gotten with hook and line but are caught more efficiently with nets, such as triggerfish and Waigeu drummers (rudderfish).

Kapinga use two kinds of nets--big, long ones called *gubenge* and smaller, hand held nets with various names. The big *gubenge* nets are several feet long and about four feet high with floats attached at the top and weights at the bottom. One of them, the coir net, is made from coconut husk sennit cord, and it is used like a wall to funnel fish toward another net or trap. The other net is a purse net, made of breadfruit bast cord with a thick cord threaded through the bottom mesh, closing it and securing the fish once they are driven into it. The idea is simple and very effective. A group of men fans out in a semi-circle over a wide area of reef or shallow beach, driving the fish into a smaller area inside the semi-circle. It's like tightening a noose around the fish, because the men drive them toward a V-shaped net assembly with a coir net attached to each end of the purse net, like a dead-end alley. Once the fish go far enough, the two ends of the coir nets can be pulled together preventing escape. Then the fish are pushed into the purse net, which the men hoist into a canoe to dump the fish. For smaller fish, a trap is substituted for the purse net. This procedure, called a surround, is used not only by fisherfolk, but also by hunting and gathering people all over the world. Shoshone Indian friends of mine remember rabbit and antelope surrounds, for example.

Hand held nets are all attached to wooden frames, and they come in four varieties. There are two kinds of nets that have long handles, called *tae*, one for netting flying fish and the other for trapping minnows. There is an all-purpose net with a short handle, more like a hand grip on a pistol, called a *hulihuli*, literally 'keeps turning.' It comes in wide mesh and narrow mesh for bigger and smaller fish, and it can be set like a trap, twisted to cover a running fish (like a butterfly net), used as a scoop for transferring fish to another container, and more. The other net is called a triggerfish net, since it gets only triggerfish. Only the flying fish net takes fish one-by-one, but unlike angling or pole-and-line, it gets them very fast. A man with a flying fish net will have thirty fish in the canoe by the time an angler gets his first bite. Netting, in other words, is designed to get fish in big bunches quickly.

Because my prodigious appetite is in inverse proportion to my fishing skills, my ideal fishing method is as follows. Have the fish line up (by species) about 150 yards from the lagoon shore and, at the sound of the starter's gun, race like hell to the beach, ending with a flying leap out of the water to see which ones hit the sand first. Collecting and cooking them is more than sufficient effort for someone with my busy schedule. Failing this, the next best alternative would be to set up a container and

Netting

simply let the fish swim into it. That Kapinga fishermen have found several ways to do just that is, for me, adequate evidence to prove that we are dealing with true genius here.

I'll start with my favorite because (a) it's the one requiring least effort and (b) I've already set it up. Remember the new moon in June, the early morning high tide with the rapid ebb that catches fish in a last moment rush back to the lagoon? All that's needed to get them is a long coir net that spans the channel. Kapinga men set it just before the big rush starts and then wait for an hour or so until the reef is dry before collecting the fish. The method is called *bono di ae hanga*, 'plugging the channel,' which picks up different species like goatfish, rabbitfish, and other lagoon fish that feed on the reef at night. The same method works in the windy season: *di gubenge iha*, 'netting garfish.' During late November or early December, garfish appear in large numbers in the interislet channels, e.g., between Touhou and Werua and between Touhou and Dalinga. During the last week of the lunar month, high tide is at night (between 2 and 4 am.), and the tide ebbs slowly. Before first light of the morning, four or five men stretch a small mesh coir net between the islets away from the deep water in the channel, blocking off the return of the garfish from the reef flat to the lagoon, as illustrated in Figure 3.1. Once it is light, the garfish are trapped with no water to swim back to. A goatfish trap is placed on one sand spit of an islet in the shallow water. Several men take the edge of the net on the sand spit opposite the trap, pulling it across the channel behind the fish, driving them into the trap. The method can be used for three or four days until the tide changes. It can net literally thousands of the small fish per catch.

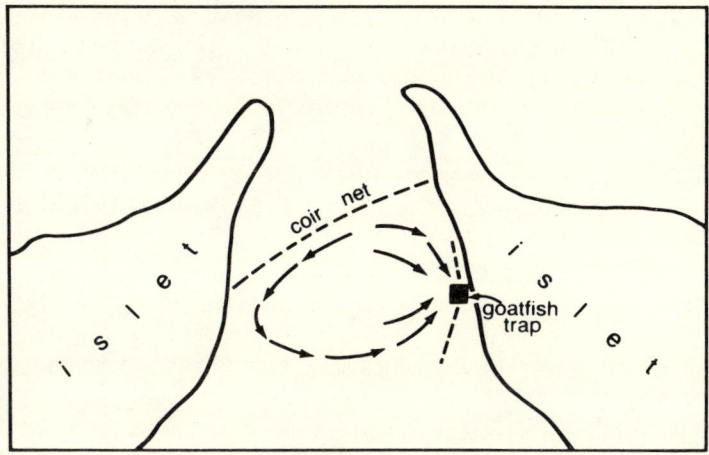

FIGURE 3.1 Di gubenge iha (netting garfish)

Elegant, but it won't work everywhere. For example, in Figure 2.3, note particularly the difference between the channel between Talinga and Touhou on the left and the one spanning Touhou and Werua to the right. The method works for Touhou-Werua because it's a narrow channel, but not between Touhou and Talinga, where you'd need a coir net the length of two football fields and would still lose fish because the reef there is so uneven.

Now, back to our June new moon. Even if a hungry fisherman missed the morning rush hour, there is more to come, but with a bit more work. Beginning about May and continuing through August, fishermen can take advantage of eight consecutive days worth of fish schooling, beginning with coral trout two days before a new moon and followed by rabbitfaced spinefoot and then vermiculated spinefoot, called *baua*, and *bongongo*. They school at the northeast quadrant of the outer reef and move in a clockwise direction toward the main pass. The coral trout run lasts two days and spinefoot migrations three each. By the time the fish pass the southern islets, they are schooled on the outer reef flat. The men's house group sets up a purse net whose near edge is at the inner reef margin with the other edge of the V-shape flared out toward the outer reef margin. The outer edge of the purse net is extended across the outer reef by the attachment of a coir net; this blocks the path of the fish (see Figure 3.2). Some of the men stand with the net while others spread out on the outer reef flat. They wait for the waves of fish to pass, beating the water with poles to frighten them toward the inner reef margin, then moving behind the fish to drive them into the purse net. The fish tend to stay between the men (on the outer reef flat) and the inner reef margin for fear of their predators in the deeper lagoon. As each wave reaches the purse net, men close the net behind them, dump them into canoes, and reset the nets for the next wave. About 700 fish is good morning's work.

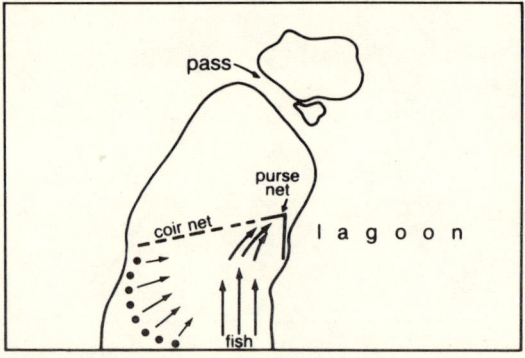

FIGURE 3.2 Di gubenge baua (netting spinefoot)

No sooner do the rabbitfaced spinefoot run out, when vermiculated spinefoot, called, *bongongo*, show up for the next three days. These spinefoot move slower than their cousins, so that instead of waiting for them at a designated spot, the men's house group waits until the tide reaches about a foot and then proceeds out as a group of canoes toward the southern reef to look for the school. Once spotted, the canoes move ahead of the school to set up the purse and coir net to block its path. The men not at the net spread out at the outer reef flat with a few men at the inner reef margins. They use punting poles to make gentle waves, 'pushing' the fish toward the net. About 400 to 500 fish constitute a large catch.

The final installment of the lazy man's guide to reef fishing, *di gubenge buu awa*, 'netting at the end of the channel,' is a wonderful example of the happy marriage of geography and timing. The groove-and-spur form of the outer reef slope (in Figure 2.1) helps to create small channels that run from the outer reef margin to the outer reef flat. The channels are a foot to two feet wide, up to eighteen inches deep, and several feet long. At low tide, you can see them fill up with water that waves carry in and empty out again with the undertow. They are called surge channels, and they can be fished throughout the year at end of the lunar month in the evening at low tide. One man sets a *hulihuli* net at the lagoonward end of a surge channel awaiting fish coming into the channel on a wave. Another closes in behind the fish to prevent them from escaping back to the breakers. Between 40 to 60 fish (sea perch, red emperor, and parrotfish) are a good night's catch.

So that you appreciate how efficient these methods really are, try one at the bottom of my list of favorites, *heehee agau*, 'walking the reef,' which is hot, tedious, and tiresome, but still effective. This method of capture (of small fish like goatfish, rabbitfish, and small reef dwelling white eels) was important during tuna season. As the tide began to rise and cover the reef flat during the morning, one to four men would set out together over the reef flat seaward of the islets. Whoever spotted small fish would chase them to rocks on the reef, where the fish would hide. A man would set a *hulihuli* net on one side of the rock and lift that side of it, driving the fish into the net. This could be done at any time of day, and sixty or more fish could be caught per person or per group during the day.

I asked several of the older men why people wouldn't prefer this method to others, given its obvious productivity (per person fishing). They all said the same thing. 'Walking the reef' might be productive, but it wasn't much fun. It was a repetitious and boring, and the catch was unimportant fish ('only food'). Most of a big catch would be given away to relatives, and, most important, fishermen got nothing in the way of excitement or prestige among other fishermen. A large catch from 'walking the reef' meant only that there were lots of fish around that day and that the fisherman had the initiative and endurance to get them. Expeditions, in other words, were about more than fish. They were about skill, strength, daring and competition, in the context of cooperative activity with other men. Each expedition offered men an opportunity to prove themselves as competent fishermen and valuable partners. These were powerful incentives to maintaining fishing as a group endeavor, constraining men's choices about how they allocated their time and effort. This theme runs through the rest of the techniques you're about to see.

Except for two bait fishing methods (for flying fish and for small *Apogon* species), all the other netting techniques are variations of the surround. This isn't as cut and dried as you might think, however. Different fish require different approaches. With some kinds of fish, a sledge hammer approach works well; you can chase them or raise a ruckus to scare them. Other fish require finesse; they have to be coaxed or gently herded along. The area fished will always make a difference, because at the very least, both approaches take time to set up. The men have to position themselves without disturbing the fish. The difference between them is what happens after the group is positioned. We'll start with two examples of the pure sledge hammer approach.

Di gubenge taile laa dua, 'netting (while) strolling seaward,' was as much competitive sport as getting fish. During July and early August, when late afternoon high tides are a foot or so on the outer reef flat, a group of twelve to fourteen men set out on foot to the seaward reef margin at surge channels oceanward of the islets. While one or two men hold the *hulihuli* net at the base of the surge channel, the rest fan out oceanward of the breakers on the seaward reef margin. Here is where the sea bass, several varieties of surgeonfish, trevally, triggerfish, and emperors come in to feed. In this tide, you can see the tails of these fish sticking out of the water as they feed. Once in position, the men scream and pound the surf, racing to the net as they chase the fish. The last one to reach the net, or anyone unfortunate enough to have fallen while running, was hazed on the spot by having to don a woman's sarong and do a women's dance for the amusement of his peers. In a reef area where surge channels are close enough to one another, three or four could be fished in an afternoon, so a lucky dancer had company.

The other sport netting is called *di gubenge tila aga*, 'netting (while) glancing up.' The men's house headman selects twenty or so young men to compete and two or three men to hold the purse net. The group sails out to the outer reef areas that are clear of big rocks and have large tide pools--depressions in the reef that hold water when the rest of the reef is dry. At mid-month in calm season, a high tide reaches a foot and stays steady, ebbing only slightly during the day. The tide pools have lots of fish in them. When the fish on the surrounding reef get spooked, they head for the tide pool. Two men set up the net at the edge of a tide pool on the inner reef. The headman then selects six to ten men who compete. They spread out seaward of the tide pool, and at the headman's signal, they race for the net, running through the tide pool and driving the frightened fish (sea bass, emperor, bream, surgeonfish, etc.) in front of them. The group can make four passes in an afternoon, and the headman chooses different combinations of men for each one. The slow-of-foot didn't have to dance; they were simply the objects of quiet ridicule back at the men's house as participants recounted (read embellished) the events of the day.

Interislet channels are good places to net fish all year, but their geography and the fish around them demand speed rather than finesse. A good channel to fish is one that isn't too wide and has a deep slope in mid-channel between the sand spits of the islets. This gives the lagoonward end of the channel a pocket of deeper water with a reasonably strong current running from seaward to lagoon. Smaller fish avoid this pocket both for the current and for the larger fish who prey on them, creating two alleys of shallow water for them. Starting at the edges of the tidal fan, say the one between Touhou and Werua in Figure 2.3, fish can be driven to one or both alleys by beating the water behind them with paddles or poles. The idea is for the fish to see only a wall of turbulence around them with only one clear, calm place in front of them. The next four methods work on this principle.

Di gubenge gala i dai, 'netting goatfish lagoonward,' is one of three methods used to catch goatfish. It takes advantage of low tides that bring lagoon fish to the tidal fan to feed. The Touhou-Werua channel is a good one that's close to home, but there are others, and if one gets finished quickly enough, the men can fish them.

Twenty men form two groups, one at the edges of the tidal fan and another spread out along a channel edge in shallow water opposite to the sand spit where the net and trap are placed to receive the fish (Figure 3.3). The men surrounding the edge of the tidal fan beat the water with poles, frightening the fish toward the channel. As the fish move into the channel, they are driven toward the second group (say on the Touhou side). This group uses poles to narrow the space between the fish and deep water. They beat the water just ahead of the oncoming fish, who are forced in a counter-clockwise direction toward the sand spit where the goatfish trap is set in shallow water (see Buck 1950: 257 for details about the trap). The trap itself has a low coir net attached to it called *di ngudu uu* 'the mouth of the trap.' One length of the coir net is stretched

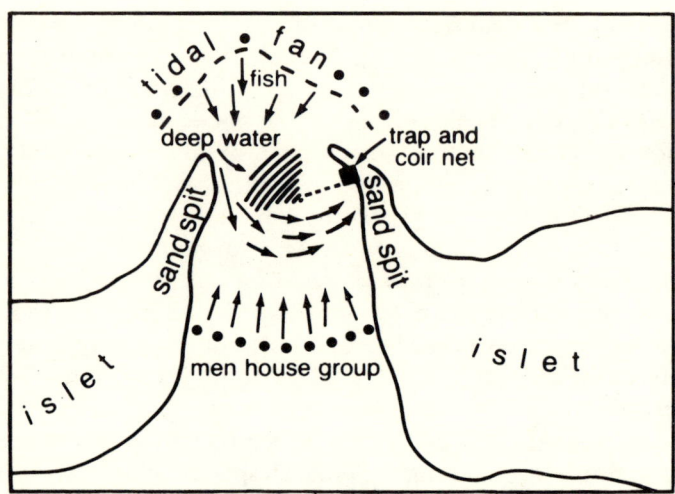

FIGURE 3.3. Di gubenge gala i dai (goatfish netting lagoonward)

between the sand spit and the deep water in the channel; the other end is stretched along the shallow water of the sand spit, as seen in Figure 3.3. If there are too many fish to get in one trap, then the coir nets are loosened to allow two men to pick up the trap and empty its contents on the beach. Meanwhile, two other men close the ends of the coir nets to keep the fish from escaping until the trap can be reset.

A variation of this method is used during the middle of calm season when the reef is dry in the morning following a full moon. Called *di gubenge holoholo aga i dai*, 'netting by spreading out toward the beach,' it takes advantage of the shallow water in the channel that leaves goatfish and rabbitfish unable to get to the inner reef flat (and looking for places to hide). Fifteen to twenty men surround the tidal fan with poles, beating the water to drive the fish toward the sand spits at the islet beaches. Meanwhile several men build small rock piles, and when the fish come up to the sand spits, they hide in these rock piles, which the rest of the men proceed to surround with a coir net. Two men enter the circle of the net, and while one discards rocks from the pile, the other holds a *hulihuli* net for the fish to escape to. This is one of two methods using rock piles, so I won't go into detail about their use now.

This last method is not strictly netting, but it uses every surround technique except a net. Called *Modoholo*, from the word, *doholo*, meaning 'reef flat,' this method is used throughout the year to take advantage of night low tides just before the new moon. In fact, it precedes that rush hour technique I talked about by a day or two and coincides with it at the new moon by about an hour. Taking advantage of the rapid ebb of the tide, as many as thirty men and women spread out at a tidal fan with poles, paddles, and torches, driving the sea perch, squirrelfish, and soldierfish onto the reef flat. The tide is so low that the fish are easily driven into tide pools on the reef, where they are clubbed and stabbed. Then the group moves on to the reef flat where the same fish varieties have been trapped simply by lingering too long during the ebb tide. A group can do two or three channels in a night, catching between 200 to 300 fish.

Finally, there is one method in the Kapinga repertoire that takes advantage of fish congregating at coral heads. It can be used throughout the year on any evening when the tide is low enough for men to stand comfortably in the lagoon. Called *di gubenge dunga lloo*, 'netting soldierfish,' it gets both soldierfish and squirrelfish feeding at the coral heads near the islets. Eight to ten men set up a coir net in a long V shape beside one of the coral heads facing toward the lagoon beach. Then, using canoe paddles, the men beat the water around the lagoonward sides of the coral head, driving the fish into shallow water. They block off the side of the coral head opposite to the net by splashing their paddles there, forcing the fish to circle back toward the net. Then two more men splash the water behind them to prevent them from turning back to the beach (Figure 3.4). Once they enter the V of the coir net, the ends of the net are closed behind them, driving them into the goatfish trap that has been set at the crotch of the V. Two or three coral heads can be fished in a single evening.

The rest of the netting methods take a bit more finesse, a bit more skill, and a few tricks. Most are variations of the surround, so I'll describe them first, beginning with an ancient technique for netting on the outer reef flat. Called *hohoologi aga i dai*, '(netting by) pushing up to the lagoon beach,' it is done away from the islets, selecting reef areas with small rock piles and coral heads. This method needs a high tide of about three feet, so you find it being used during the very early and the

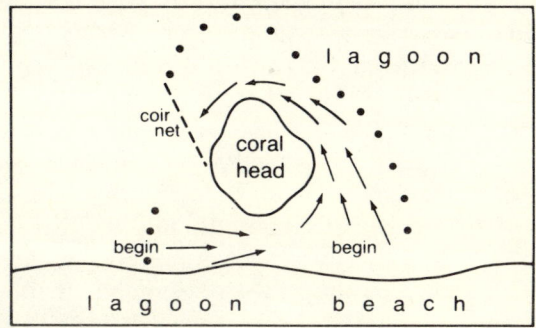

FIGURE 3.4 Di gubenge dunga lloo (netting soldierfish)

later parts of calm season. As many as thirty or more men fan out over a half mile of lagoon margin and reef, using punting poles to frighten the fish. They don't beat the water, though. They drag the pole just under the water in a wide, sweeping motion, so this method takes a lot longer to collect the fish than driving them. The fish, meanwhile, run for the safety of the rock piles and coral heads as the semi-circle of poles closes in. One end of the semi-circle is the purse net flanked with the coir nets in the standard V shape. As the men near the rocks and coral heads, the larger fish tend to run from them while the smaller fish, such as angelfish, stay hidden in the rocks. The only place for those larger fish (wrasses, groupers, parrotfish, pufferfish, box fish, etc.) to run is into the alley formed by the coir nets. As they approach the purse net, the men at each end of the coir nets close the ends to prevent any escape. This method, then, selects larger fish. Because of the time it takes, one or two passes is an afternoon's work.

Di gubenge lou niu, 'netting (with) coconut leaves' gets its name from the leaves that are tied at five to ten foot intervals along the length of a rope that is used to surround fish. While 'pushing up to the lagoon beach' selects for larger fish, 'coconut leaf netting' clears the reef. This method can be used at any time of year when the high tide is three feet or more on a section of reef that is clear of large rocks and coral heads. If the tide is lower than three feet, the rope used to surround the fish is taken into the deeper water of the lagoon and suspended several feet under water by strings. The men swimming at the surface actually drag the lagoon bottom, pushing the fish up the beach and onto the reef flat. With a higher tide, the men can spread out on the beach in the half mile semi-circle with the rope to sweep the fish toward the waiting nets. Besides men at the purse net and the ends of the coir nets, two other men stand at each end of the coir net hauling in the rope. It is literally like tightening a noose. The surround rope can be used without the coconut leaves, but experience shows that the fish are really frightened by the leaves. The fish are slowly pushed toward the coir nets. As they approach the purse net, a very large group of fish is likely to begin to swim in a circle. The large circling group can be easily pushed into the purse net once the coir nets are closed around them.

This surround method gets the larger reef fish such as sea bass, grouper, parrotfish, and surgeonfish, as well as smaller reef fish such as butterfly fish, angelfish, moorish idols, boxfish, puffer fish, toad fish, and file fish. The main difference between netting on the reef flat and netting from the lagoon is where the purse net is placed and how the rope is handled. Figures 3.5 and 3.6 show two placements of the rope and the net.

Netting

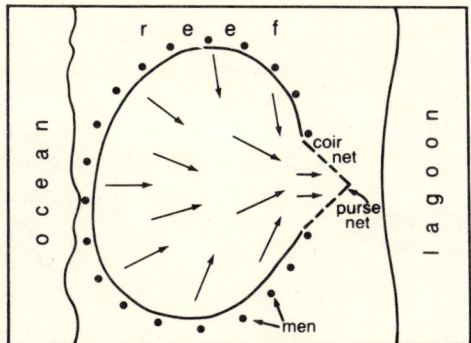

FIGURE 3.5 Di gubenge lou niu (coconut leaf netting) on the reef

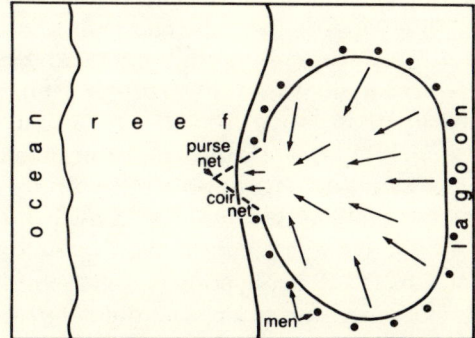

FIGURE 3.6 Di gubenge lou niu (coconut leaf netting) in the lagoon

The men I talked with stressed that this technique had to be used judiciously, since it would clear a large area of the reef of fish. That area could not be fished again for several weeks. Thus, this method put a premium on movement to various parts of the reef and on men's knowledge of the best places to do this sort of netting.

Now 'coconut leaf netting' and 'pushing up to the lagoon beach' procedures might strike you is pretty routine, but there is an intriguing aspect to it that is as political as it is technical. Purse net placement is critical to the success of a surround. It has to cover the habitual escape routes of the fish, and the wider the area covered by the surround, the more routes that have to be covered by the net. This is where knowledge, secrecy and politics come together. Fish habitually follow certain routes to the lagoon, and ambitious men are constantly on the lookout for these routes during an expedition. Once discovered, a man marks that spot (by triangulation). He keeps his discovery secret for later use in his own bid for prestige and leadership (of a men's house). Like the high priest, the men's house headman held his position as long as he demonstrated his knowledge with consistently good catches. Challengers quietly waited for him to fail.

'Coconut leaf netting' is the prototype held up by the Kapinga as the standard for communal fishing. It was a community activity in two senses. All members of the men's house were obligated to participate (unless one had a good excuse not to), and the catch was distributed to all the households on the islet, whether or not any of its members had participated. This is one of the very few traditional techniques that has survived the colonial era to the present. It's the fall back position for a hungry population--this one, along with goatfish methods will always produce fish. This is why consistent failure of a headman is intolerable.

I think of goatfish as the true hobos of the reef, which makes them dependable sources of food when nothing else is working. You've already seen how Kapinga get them in the channels. During windy season, the outer reef flat produces consistently good catches. The method, *Di gubenge gala i dua*, 'netting goatfish seaward,' can be used on any afternoon high tide when goatfish move from the lagoon to the reef flat to feed. They prefer the reef flat seaward of the southern islets, particularly at Hale islet. Using a standard surround with coir nets attached to a goatfish trap set close to the islet shore facing seaward, ten men form a wide circle on the reef flat, using a gentle sweeping motion with punting poles to herd the fish toward the coir net's V. Once the fish got close to the trap, the net was closed behind them, and they were picked up in the trap. Three or four passes could be made in a single afternoon.

Another reef hobo is the squirrelfish. Kapinga could get them all year around, but they became most important during windy season. *Di gubenge haadolo*, 'netting squirrelfish,' was designed to get them in the evenings in the interislet channels when the tide is between fifteen and eighteen inches, as illustrated in Figure 3.7.

Using a method very similar to that for catching goatfish, the men sweep the interislet channel starting from the tidal fan. There are two ways to do this--either using a rope with coconut leaves tied to it every five feet or so or using punting poles to sweep under the surface of the water. Either one will drive the fish toward the shallow water of the interislet channel, but the rope and leaf, though slower, gets more fish. Several men form a line in the interislet channel extending from one side to the opposite side. Beating the water with poles, they keep the fish from going across the channel to the outer reef. The fish circle toward the sand spit opposite to the line of men, where a goatfish trap is waiting on the sand spit. A coir net attached to one edge of the trap stretches across the interislet channel and prevents the fish from swimming back to the lagoon once they have been driven into the channel. Once the fish

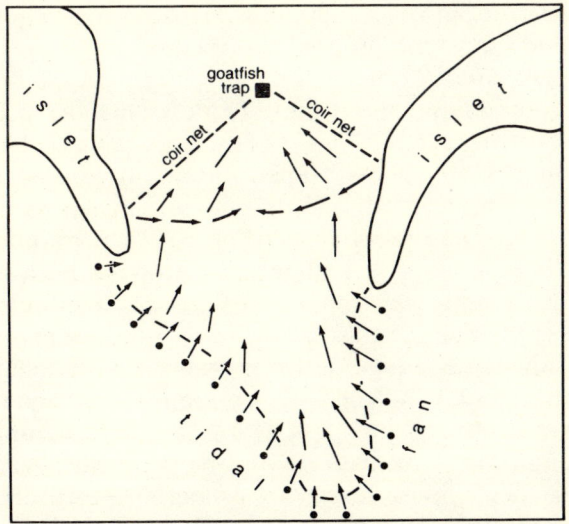

FIGURE 3.7 Di gubenge haadolo (netting squirrelfish)

have circled to the sand spit, two to four men close the two ends of the coir net behind them.

For pure finesse, nothing comes close to trying to get fish that are feeding in the waves at the outer reef margin. Three methods with different names do just this. I'll start with the most difficult, *di gubenge abi*, 'netting spotted surgeonfish.' Spotted surgeonfish are afternoon feeders on the outer reef margin in the breakers. On a day with weak wave action, up to twenty men surround the fish just beyond the breakers. They use punting poles to gently push the fish into a surge channel just lagoonward of the breakers where a *hulihuli* net is set for them. This is not as quick or easy as it might seem, as spotted surgeonfish spook very easily at the sight of anything unusual. Fishermen have to surround their prey slowly and quietly, fanning out in deep water and staying low in the water as they swim toward the fish. The poles are used in a slow sweeping motion to move the fish toward the area of the breakers where the surge channel stands. This cannot begin until all the men are in position. One clumsy move by any of the fishermen can scatter the fish.

Di gubenge manini, 'netting striped surgeonfish,' is identical to 'netting spotted surgeonfish,' but a lot easier, because striped surgeonfish don't scare as easily, making this method much faster. Maybe this is why this method ranks at the very bottom of the prestige ladder. One man called it a *balu gubenge* 'useless netting (method)'. This is a stop-gap method of getting food when nothing else works. When anglers come back empty, they can stop on the way home and net striped surgeonfish--a sign of defeat but not a total loss. Fishermen also got squirrelfish with this method, and with an ease about equal to that for striped surgeonfish, only without the onus.

Since I've been talking about prestige, now I'll show you prestige, *di gubenge manu*, 'netting birds,' finesse with a vengeance. This method is for rainbow runners, who show up periodically in large schools, usually near the end of a lunar month. 'Birds' is a euphemism for the flocks of birds that hover around the school feeding on three kinds of very small fish, called *malau woo*, that the rainbow runners are also after. Fishermen follow the birds to locate the school. This is one of two netting methods done seaward of the reef in open ocean, and it is by far the most dangerous of all fishing that Kapinga do. A measure if its prestige is the fact that 35% of all extant fishing chants are about rainbow runner expeditions. Done in relatively calm seas with weak wave action, the tide has to be high enough to permit passage of canoes over the reef. Under the direction of the men's house headman, canoes surround the school and slowly push it toward the reef. As the school nears the reef, the men drop off into deep water, and the canoes let out the coir nets behind them.

Once the school is surrounded by the men and nets, the problem becomes one of finding a suitable spot on the reef to get the school over the breakers and into either a coir net or a weir constructed on the spot. Once a spot is selected, the coir net is dropped into the water from the canoes. Each man in the water holds his section of coir net behind him to hide it from the fish lest they see it and begin to leap over it. This is the dangerous part, because these fish have hard beaks and they leap blindly and fast, striking anything in their path with considerable force. Several men have deep scars inflicted by these fish. If fishermen can avoid frightening the fish and can gently push them over the breakers and into shallow water on the reef, then they step over the coir net and hoist it up around the fish. There is a chant describing one expedition where the fish were driven onto the reef just seaward of Werua islet. While people stood on the seaward edges of the islet watching, the headman had his men slowly push the fish across the reef, through the interislet channel between Touhou and Werua, around the southern sand spit, up in the shallow water at the beach, and onto the beach at the men's house. This was done for show, according to the people who witnessed it. The fish could have been netted on the reef and picked up there. But to be able to induce the school into the lagoon and onto the men's house beach was a feat of skill and a challenge to the other men's houses to try to match it. The entire procedure is conducted silently using only hand signals and whistles and may take as much as six to seven hours to complete.

Netting

Two other surrounds require some technical trickery to do well. One that I already hinted at is *di gubenge hoologi hagabae*, 'netting (by) pushing (toward) rock piles. Kapinga fishermen maintained rock piles on the inner and outer reef flat (see Map 4). Rock piles on the inner reef flat were larger (six to eight feet in diameter and three to four feet high) than those on the outer reef (four to five feet in diameter and two to three feet high). The rock piles on the inner reef flat were frequented by larger fish that moved onto the reef from the lagoon, while the piles on the outer reef were frequented by the smaller fish, such as striped surgeonfish, that feed at and around the breakers and surge channels. The rock piles were constructed in layers with larger stones and boulders on the bottom and progressively smaller stones placed on top of the larger ones. Fish at the large rock piles included emperor fish, parrotfish, sea bass, *Caranx*, bream, toadfish, unicornfish, and spinefoot. Around smaller rock piles were surgeonfish, smaller wrasse, and small sea bass.

Up to twenty men would work as a group when fishing at the larger rock piles, while eight to ten men would be sufficient at the smaller rock piles. The same general method was used for each, but the nets used at the smaller rock piles were of a smaller mesh. Just after the full moon during late May through July, when afternoon high tides reached about 14 inches, the men would spread out on the reef in a rough circle around the rock pile, using punting poles on the water surface to frighten the fish toward the rock pile (Figure 3.8). The men would encircle the rock pile with a coir net (Figure 3.9), using one of two alternative methods to get the fish. One (Figure 3.10) was to take a length of coir net and lay it flat on the reef beside the rock pile. Then while one or two men discarded and scattered the rocks from the pile, others made a second pile on top of the coir net. The fish would escape from their rapidly disappearing hiding place into the second rock pile. When all the fish had escaped to the second, smaller pile, the coir net was pulled up around it and the rocks inside discarded, leaving only the fish remaining inside the coir net.

The alternative method was to build a second rock pile inside a *huli-huli* net, as in Figure 3.11. Usually done at the smaller rock piles on the outer reef, this net was well suited for smaller fish and had the advantage of making it easier to discard the rocks. Two or three men rebuilt the rock pile when the fishing was done, while the others could move on to another rock pile.

The other technically tricky method was *di gubenge tebu*, 'netting (by) diving,' which is exactly what the name implies. It required a twenty inch tide that stayed steady with a following slow ebb, i.e., early and late phases of calm season or a calm day during windy season. The main pass at the southeast quadrant of the reef has several large and small

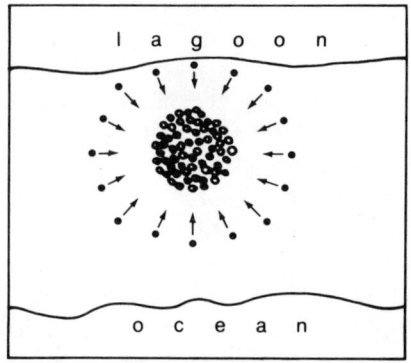

FIGURE 3.8 Surrounding fish and driving them to the rock pile

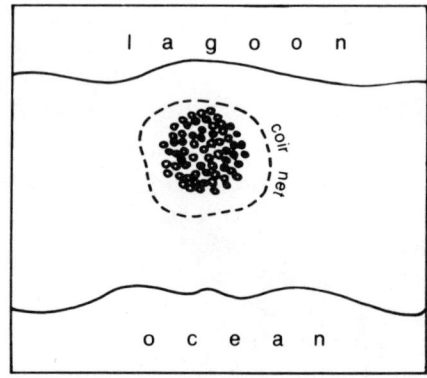

FIGURE 3.9 Coir net encircles the rock pile

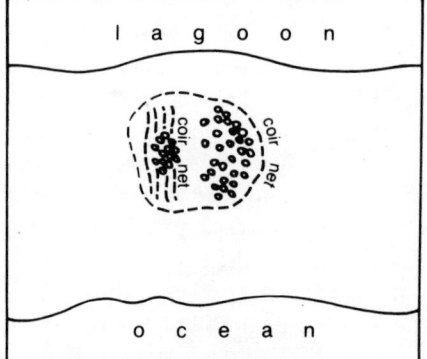

FIGURE 3.10 Building a second pile on a second coir net

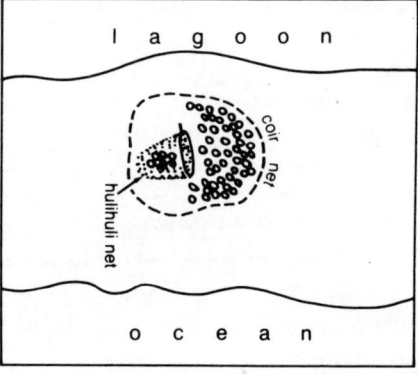

FIGURE 3.11 A second pile built inside a hand net

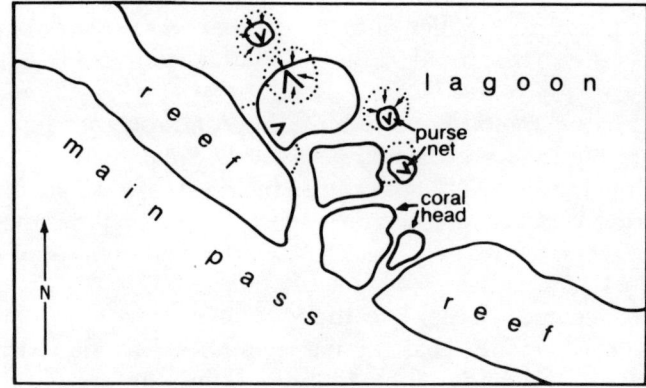

FIGURE 3.12 Di gubenge tebu (netting by diving)

73

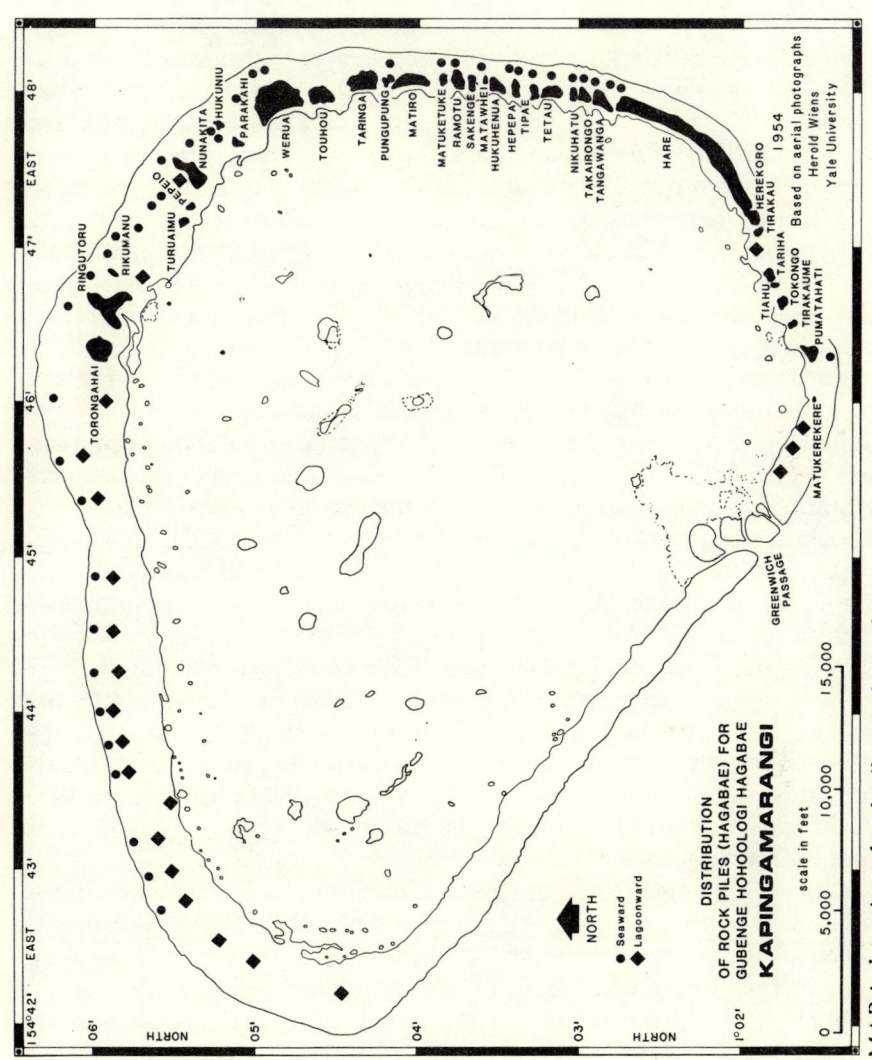

MAP 4 Location of rock piles on the reef

coral heads with intervening deep ravines. Each coral head is loaded with several varieties of surgeonfish, unicornfish, sea bass, parrotfish, emperor, and spinefoot. With a purse net set up at the top of the coral head, twenty or so men dived down to the deep water to circle the base of the coral head. Using poles, they would gently and slowly herd the fish up to higher water and eventually to the top of the coral head, where they herded the fish to the purse net. Men would take turns in the water; as one man came up for air, another would replace him. Herding slowed down as the fish got closer to the top of the coral head. The reason for this was that when nearby fish saw a large group of fish swimming in one place, they would often swim over to join it. If the tide held steady and the catch was relatively small, the group could move on to another coral head. Figure 3.12 illustrates the net positions and directions of approach at coral heads in the channel.

The last two surrounds are examples of organized opportunism that takes advantage of sudden, unpredictable windfalls. The first is practiced only when flying fish entering the lagoon in the evening remain there overnight. When spotted, the men's house mounts *di gubenge tawe*, 'netting flying fish.' A group surrounds the fish, gently beating the water with paddles to herd them toward the beach. Once in shallow water, punting poles dragged through the water herd the fish together, where the coir net surrounds them and two or three men scoop them up in *huli-huli* nets.

A frequent windfall is thousands of Waigeu drummers (or rudderfish), who come to the atoll with drift logs. Once near the reef, the fish move to the big boulders on the southern reef flat. A few men will test their numbers by fishing with pole-and-line for the men's house headman, who announces the timing of *di gubenge ngadala agau*, 'netting Waigeu drummer.' Once announced, the fish are the property of the men's house (or men's houses, if more than one cooperate).

During high tide, there are certain boulders near the seaward reef that the fish prefer. A very large group of Waigeu drummers is called an *iga duai* (literally 'coconut grater fish,' referring to the fact that these fish can be baited with grated coconut). Men surround these boulders with a heavy rope, to which coconut leaves are tied at 5 foot intervals. The fish are driven to a coir net set next to the boulder, trapped inside, and then driven to a goatfish trap set at one end, which is emptied and then reset to fill again. Some fish are left for another expedition the following day or for pole-and-line fishing. The men's house group usually seeks other *iga duai* the following days.

Kapinga used two net methods to get bait--one that's exciting and skilled and another that's dull but clever. Hand netting flying fish is called *di waga llama*, 'the torch canoe,' and both Peter Buck (1950) and

Kenneth Emory (1965) have described it in great detail. I'll only summarize its main features. Flying fish are hand netted on moonless nights (around the new moon) outside but close to the seaward reef. Fishermen use torches both for light and to attract the fish, which they catch with a long handled net used only for flying fish. While several men paddle the canoe, one of them stands on the bow with a torch in one hand and the net in the other, waiting for the fish to leap and then bringing the net down on top of the fish and twisting it to trap the fish, a maneuver called *bulou*. The skilled fisherman swings the net behind him and empties the fish into the canoe without ever looking back.

The major problem with this kind of expedition, other than skill and balance, was navigating out to the main pass on a moonless night. This was done through star navigation--the only form of star navigation that Kapinga used traditionally--by sighting one point of a particular constellation and heading directly for that point until reaching the pass. Several canoes usually went out together, and on reaching the pass, certain chants had to be sung before going through. The canoes maintained a particular order of precedence from entering the pass until their return through it.

Flying fish netting was part of a boy's initiation rites. Each boy was supposed to net 1000 flying fish (actually about 860) before being allowed to go out regularly on such expeditions (see Emory 1965: 333-335). The catch was used primarily for bait, either for tuna or for rainbow runners. Anything left over was either eaten or dried into jerky.

The other bait netting method is *di gubenge gube*, 'netting small Apogon.' These are minnow size fish that inhabit small coral heads in the outer reef lagoon north of the main pass, and they are caught with a small woven mat called a *bahi gahala*, 'half sleeping mat'. Fishermen take coconut branches with them to stuff all crevices in a coral head where the fish hide except for one. Then they simply wait until the fish come swimming out of that crevice and into the mat.

A second technique is to fill all but one crevice in the coral head where the fish are. Then the fish are chased away from the coral head. Once the fish have departed, the small mat is placed in the crevice that was left open. The fishermen then just wait for the fish to come swimming back into the mat, close it up and empty the fish into the canoe. The fish are bait for lagoon angling, particularly around large coral heads fished during calm season.

I end this section on netting with a technically clever method for getting triggerfish, who will eat just about anything you offer. *Di gubenge humu*, 'netting triggerfish,' requires bait, a minimum of two canoes, and a triggerfish net. The frame is a hibiscus sapling bent into a circular shape with a thirty inch diameter and tied shut. Two slender sticks are lashed

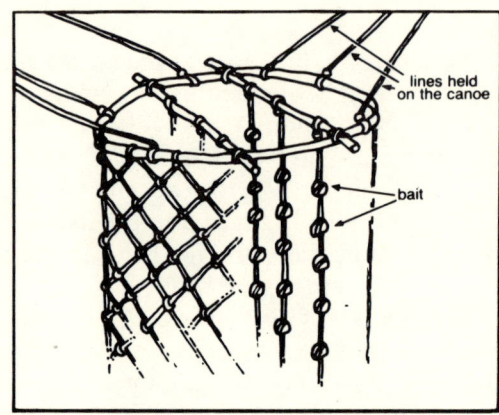

FIGURE 3.13 A triggerfish net

across the circle parallel to each other. A net woven from the fibers at the base of the coconut tree is suspended from the rim to about eight feet (Figure 3.13).

Fishermen tie bait to six lengths of sennit cord at six to eight inch intervals. Three cords are suspended from each of the sticks lashed across the frame. The bait is usually hermit crab, because fishermen don't like to waste anything better on triggerfish.

The net is weighted with stones and lowered into the water four or five fathoms. Using lines from two canoes (three lines per side of the rim), the net is slowly hauled up, its contents emptied into a canoe, and then it is baited and reset. Besides triggerfish, the method also nets unicornfish and other surface feeders, and it can be done during both the calm and windy season.

Nets required hundreds of hours of labor just in the preparation of the cordage, no less the weaving (see Buck 1950: 210-225). It is important to remember that nets, especially hand nets, also required the services of specialists, who had to be fed while they worked. Given the labor and the expense, Kapinga are very attentive to the care of their nets. A net had to be dried carefully after use, but it could not be exposed to the strong sunlight for very long. Because fresh water would quickly rot a net, men dried them in a breeze or strong wind. Once dry, a hand net was usually hung inside the house from a rafter. A coir net would be wrapped about a house beam. Some men even built special houses to keep their fishing gear (a sign of wealth and prestige).

4

Pole and Line Fishing

Nowhere is the difference between Kapinga and western fishermen more marked than in pole and line fishing, which defines sport fishing for westerners but not (with one exception) for Kapinga. For us in the "developed" world, an entire industry including manufacturers, publishers, advertizers, television programs, resort owners, guides, and professional consultants, derives hundreds of millions of dollars a year catering to the insatiable consumer demand for technology, techniques, and places to use them. But for Kapinga fishermen, who like to talk about fishing, pole and line is a workaday, serious business, devoid of fun and prestige (except for bonito fishing, their sport of kings). I've wondered about this for a long time, and collecting detailed information about pole and line fishing only made their diffidence that much more of a puzzle. Pole and line is no less tedious than netting or angling. Certainly, the technical aspects of method present a fisherman with a series of challenges, and consistently good catches require a high degree of skill.

Anyone who has done a lot of rod and reel fishing knows that no matter how good the equipment is, it can't replace or compensate for the kind of touch a skilled fisherman acquires. Knowing the direction that a fish is heading by the feel of the rod, keeping the fish's head up while fighting the drag of the water as you pull it in, keeping a steady pull after the first jerk of the line--these are the small but critical kinds of control that distinguish a fisherman from a dilettante with expensive equipment. Surely, good equipment makes a good fisherman better by making some of the work easier, but that touch has to be there, and everything a fisherman knows about particular fish and their habits and habitats has to be translatable into it. The average Kapinga fisherman is supposed to have it, and by all accounts, most did. But it was convertible only into food and not much else. WTo understand why this is so is to understand what the organization of pole and line fishing means to Kapinga fishermen.

If pole and line wasn't considered a measure of a fisherman's virtuosity, it certainly was seen as a measure of his adequacy as a provider, particularly when other methods were unproductive. The only chant that mentions pole and line (albeit obliquely) is the one used for the rite of consecration of male infants, the pre-Christian counterpart of baptism. The chant delineates the duties of a man, and the first mention of fishing is for the fire wrasse, which is caught with pole and line. The chant instructs the boy to 'chase your own fire wrasse on the reef, do not chase the fire wrasse of another.' The line has two meanings: one has to do with a man's adequacy as a fisherman, with developing the basic skills a man needs. The other has to do with fidelity, not chasing another's wife. That both ideas are joined in pole and line imagery is significant: the married man is defined as a provider of fish. Pole and line is the least ambiguous image of provisioning in this community; people have to depend on it when nothing else works.

There is a much sharper difference between calm and windy season methods with pole and line than with netting. There are two pole and line techniques (used by adults) that work all year. All but two methods are designed for particular species. While there is more choice of methods during calm season, pole and line was important mainly during tuna season, when only tuna canoes could go out. It was during windy season that pole and line was used intensively. The high winds, high tides, and choppy lagoon that make lagoon angling and most kinds of net fishing impossible serve to bring fish from the deeper waters of the lagoon to the islet shores and onto the seaward reef flat near the islets. Here they can be caught with pole-and-line. In many ways, pole-and-line fishing is to windy season what lagoon netting is to the calm season.

Other than hooks, pole and line technology was relatively simple. The poles, called *hiihii*, are made of bamboo driftwood, from hibiscus saplings, or from *Premna obtusifolia*, varied from six to eighteen feet in length. Lines were made of braided, two-ply breadfruit bast, which holds up to abrasion from coral better than sennit or hibiscus bast. Lines are the same length as the pole (see Buck 1950: 131). Hook sizes and shapes varied with the fish. They were made from shell to conform to the head and mouth of particular fish. Kapinga's hooks had no barbs, so control of the line was a finely honed skill. For most pole and line techniques, bait was hermit crab. Since this is the first mention of chum, I better tell you that chum is my translation of the Kapinga word that means 'to call together,' as when a man blows a conch shell to notify people that a meeting is about to start. Chum is fish or shellfish parts put into the water to attract fish to a single spot. Most pole and line techniques use pounded hermit crab (minus the bowel, which is bait).

Since a boy's first encounter with hooks is in pole and line fishing, where he learns the fundamentals of chum and bait, fish habitats, hand-eye coordination, the feel of different fish, etc., I'll start my description with them. I'll follow that with calm season methods and then windy season techniques. Once you get a feel for the relative complexity involved, I'll tell you why I think pole and line is so devalued.

Men make short poles with lines and hooks for their young sons to use in learning fishing skills. Even today, you can see boys at ages five and up during the day using four to six foot poles at the interislet channels and in the shallows of lagoon beaches catching minnows and small jack fish. They stand or walk slowly along the shore of the interislet channel trailing the line and hook at about four feet from the shore in shallow water. When the tide is low enough, the boys stand in the channel in the shallows. By age seven, boys prepare their own bait with hermit crab intestine and begin fishing on the seaward reef. On the inner reef flat at the deeper tide pools at low tide, boys catch damselfish and flounder with hermit crab bait, fishing in groups of three and four during afternoon ebb tides. By age nine, boys begin to fish beside the small coral heads on the beaches near the islets. They usually stand in the water next to or just behind the coral head, using hermit crab chum and bait. On occasion, they are able to get a parent or grandparent into loaning them a canoe to fish the coral heads--wealthy families even had canoes made for their young boys! This is the only time in most men's lives when pole and line fishing is play.

Men also use pole and line at the coral heads, one of the two methods that exploit an area rather than a particular species. While boys are after anything they can get, men fish the coral heads for bait when they go angling for bass at the main pass. The lagoon around the coral heads was shallow enough to stand in even at high tide, but men more often fished from canoes, so they could get their bait and head on out. The catch was small wrasse, damselfish, sergeant majors, and a variety of *Chromis*. Men and boys both used six foot poles and hermit crab bait, with hooks made of coconut shell or the bone of a small parrotfish. Men would occasionally move a bit further lagoonward of the coral head to catch scarlet-breasted Maori wrasse.

For men, *hihi nia dogo*, 'pole and line (at) coral heads,' also meant coral heads anywhere near the reef. On the far north and south ends of the reef near the lagoon shore, for example, there are numerous coral heads that can be fished throughout the year during the day or evening with a tide that is low enough and clear enough. Using a twelve foot pole and minnows or small Apogon as bait, they catch blue spotted rock cod and half-banded parrotfish, along with varieties of sea bass (in smaller numbers). They anchor the canoe and fish from it or stand next to it at the coral head.

The problems of touch here differ according to position. For these very small fish caught from a standing position and pulled up immediately maintaining a steady pressure on the line as it is swung toward the fisherman is the problem. Caught from a canoe, the problem is slightly different, since the first pull is in, then up, so the difference between drag, no drag, and swinging the line in, all with the same pressure on the fish, is one of pinpoint control. This is easier to do with heavier fish, so boys start off with the most difficult problems of control, and no barbs to secure the fish. It's all line control, all fisherman.

The other technique targeting an area is *hihi leduge,* 'pole-and-line (for) handfish,' which is a metaphor for the outer reef margin and surge channels where handfish, moon wrasse, fire wrasse, sea Bass, triple-tailed Maori wrasse, tropical bream, and snapper are caught. bass, tropical bream, and snapper are caught with a twelve foot pole and hermit crab chum and bait. This is done during the late afternoon when the waves are low and weak. The chum is thrown out on the waves to be carried inland by wave action, luring the fish into the surge channel. The hook is then baited and put into the surge channel as the waves carry the fish into it. At rising tide, tide pools immediately inland of the surge channels are also fished (both by men and adolescent boys). Men use this method as as a stopgap when other methods are unproductive.

The only pole and line fishing done consistently all year was *hihi humu* 'pole-and-line (for) triggerfish,' the pole and line equivalent of triggerfish netting done on a canoe on the outer reef slope when men didn't feel like taking a lot of equipment. Six spots on the outer reef are known to be productive. Using the direction of the surface current, a fisherman lets the canoe drift into one of these spots, scattering hermit crab chum behind the canoe to get triggerfish to come up to the surface. Then the hooks are baited with hermit crab bowels using a twelve foot pole. About 60 to 70 fish are considered a good catch.

Nothing could contrast more with a triggerfish expedition than *di waga diu* 'the dipped canoe,' the ultimate in sport fishing on this island. Done once or twice a year by a priest or a *tomono* fortunate enough to own a bonito canoe, it was the most prestigeous and economically the least important of all fishing methods. It was the pinnacle of a man's career. The canoe was specially equipped with a seat and a frame for holding the fisherman's legs steady. Few men had the clout or the resources to pay for having one built. The closest most men ever got to bonito fishing was being taken along to paddle while someone else fished.

Bonito are plentiful toward the end of tuna season, and the fisherman went out when the tide was high enough to allow the canoe to get over the reef. Fishing was done with a six foot pole and the traditional pearl shell shank and turtle shell hook, lashed with breadfruit bast and left with one shredded bast end for a lure (see Buck 1950: 238-239). The fisherman stood facing the stern of the canoe to fish, trailing the hook in the water between the wakes left by the hull and the outrigger float. Bonito fishing took great strength, as the fisherman not only had to keep a steady pressure on the line but also to hold the fish steady at the side of the canoe while a partner clubbed it before pulling it into the canoe.

On the rare occasions when bonito entered the lagoon, they could be caught with a surround technique using a coir net and purse net. But the leader of that netting expedition had to be a man who owned a bonito canoe, and the purse net had to be carried by the bonito canoe. A story is told about such a surround being organized in 1860 by Haiadu, a secular chief who was to become a high priest. His name, meaning 'does bonito,' indicates his status as a fisherman. The men's house had already surrounded the bonito in deep water off Nunagida islet. Haiadu instructed the men to wait until he came back with his bonito canoe. Instead, Haiadu's brother directed the surround in his absence, setting the nets on the beach at Nunagida. By the time Haiadu returned, all the bonito had died and were floating on the surface of the water.

The only other calm season pole and line fishing done during the day was *hihi ngadala agau*, 'pole-and-line (for) Waigeu drummers,' a windfall technique. One or two men fished for Waigeu drummers when they first migrated from the drift logs to the coral boulders at the southern quadrant of the reef. Pole and line at this time was used more for determining their numbers and locations than for food. Chumming with soft coconut meat, the fisherman begins by throwing pieces of coconut meat toward a spot near where the fish are congregating. Once he attracts a large group of them, he will bait his hook and begin catching them. With a 12 foot pole and sufficient coconut meat, a fisherman standing on the reef at high tide can get as many of these fish as he can carry home. More important than the catch was the information he conveyed to his men's house headman. If the numbers of fish justified the effort, the headman would mount a netting expedition. Once that decision was announced, the fish were the property of the men's house until the headman explicitly said otherwise. Only at that point or on a decision not to net them were fishermen allowed to use pole and line to fish on their own.

Kapinga used three pole and line methods at night during calm season, each one curious in its own way. All three depended on tide patterns much like netting, but that is not what makes them curious. *Hihi dangau*, 'pole-and-line (for) snapper,' is the only method in the repertoire that used two different hooks, one with bait and one with a lure. Snappers abound on the reef flat in the northern outer reef (away from the islets). Beginning on the evening before a half moon, the tide stays at one height with little fluctuation for three days, and this is the best time to get snappers. Standing on the reef, men used a twelve foot pole and and minnows or Apogon (gotten at nearby coral heads) as bait on a shell hook placed directly in the water. If bait was not available, fishermen used a pearl shell and turtle shell hook with a lure that is in every way a miniature version of the bonito hook. While the bonito hook was a prized possession and the subject of myths, this one was so ordinary that not one Kapinga ever mentioned its existence to Peter Buck when he was collecting his information on fishing technology in 1947. Two men told me about another one, slightly larger than the mullet hook, used for jackfish, but they were vague about it. What can I say? Looks aren't everything.

The one thing that lends symmetry to a lunar month in calm season is two three day periods, one six days after a new moon and the other six days after a full moon, when the reef crawls with wildlife. These two periods are called 'mullet days,' and they coincide with migrations of hermit crabs and sand crabs out to the reef by the hundreds as the tide rises. The crabs' eggs form a thick foam on the water, attracting hordes of mullet, who come in to feed on them. This is when fishermen do *hihi dalinga*, 'pole-and-line (for) mullet.' Done either just seaward of the islet shore or at large coral boulders like the one on the outer reef flat at Touhou, two or three men using twelve foot poles fish together, usually spaced far apart and with as little movement as possible, as these fish scare easily. Two or three men can get 100 to 150 mullet in an evening.

Just before the 'mullet days' is a three day period in the third quarter of the month when the tide is very low at night. At this time, anglers go after crimson squirrelfish to use as bait for sea bass and big groupers in the main pass. The use *hihi malau pungu*, 'pole-and-line (for) crimson squirrelfish.' These squirrelfish are plentiful along the lagoon beach slope just lagoonward of the tidal fans. When the moon rises it is bright enough to allow fishing from a canoe. Using a three fathom pole and hermit crab bait and chum, two men can catch 100 or more fish. Other varieties of squirrelfish are usually caught along with the crimson squirrelfish, but in far fewer numbers. The crimson squirrelfish are kept in a holding trap set in the lagoon until they are needed for angling .

What I find curious about this is the fact that crimson squirrelfish is ceremonially very important for birth rituals, for boys' initiation into angling, and for making new mats for the cult house (one of the five major cult house rites)--but *only when they're caught by angling*. This is when people--almost entirely women--eat them, though they are not particularly tasty or filling. Their major economic importance is as bait. It's as if the economic and ceremonial values of this fish vary in an inverse proportion. I'll try to solve this puzzle when I get to the description of angling for them.

There are two places that fishermen can use a pole and line during windy season. One is the inner reef flat just off the seaward shore of the islets. The other is at the lagoon beaches of the islets. Three kinds of fish are caught in large numbers during high tides close to the seaward sides of the islet (inner reef flat). They are the *madu*, a kind of goatfish, the *dangau kila*, a snapper, and a garfish variety called *iha gaa*. All three fish are caught in roughly the same area--just seaward of the islet edge (the fisherman standing on the islet) or in the interislet channel just beside the beach.

Hihi madu, 'pole-and-line (for) goatfish (variety),' requires four to five days of chumming with hermit crab, beginning the day after a full moon. The baited hook (on a twelve foot pole) is not offered until there are are enough fish collected to make it worth the effort. Once fishing does begin (at the afternoon high tide), a fisherman can continue fishing for two or three days.

Hihi dangau kila, 'pole-and-line (for) snapper (variety),' uses a similar procedure, but differs in that snapper is caught throughout the month during high tide. Fishermen use minnows (preferred), hermit crab, or sand crab for chum and bait. The technique is identical to that for goatfish, except that chumming and fishing are done on the same day.

Hihi iha gaa, 'pole-and-line (for) garfish,' takes advantage of a garfish variety that prefers the inner reef flat rather than the channels and coral heads. Both kinds of garfish arrive at the same time, late November or early December. Fishermen work together to take advantage of the large numbers of these fish and to compensate for the time it takes each one to get an *iha gaa* off his line once he catches it. Standing on the seaward shore with fifteen foot poles, the fishermen offer the fish not a baited hook but a lure made of shredded breadfruit bast soaked in salt water, pounded, and dried, as illustrated in Figure 4.1.

The garfish's long nose and jaws get tangled in the lure once he bites it. The fisherman jerks the lure from the water, untangles the fish, and

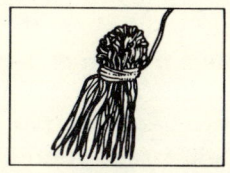

FIGURE 4.1 Garfish lure-hook

puts the lure back into the water. Fishing continues for as long as the garfish hold out.

Two species, goatfish and blue spot mullet, are caught on lagoon beaches during the day at high tides. Both require prior chumming for several days before fishing begins. *Hihi gala*, 'pole-and-line (for) goatfish (variety),' required hermit crab or sand crab chum and bait, a twelve foot pole, and lots of patience. These fish congregate at lagoon beaches or at the interislet channels near the beaches. One or two fishermen had to scatter pounded chum into the water each afternoon for three to five days, whatever it took to attract large numbers of goatfish to the area. Once collected, from four to six fishermen using twelve foot poles and crab intestine bait stand on the beach and catch the goatfish. Fishing continues for up to five days, until the fish run out.

The relationship between fishermen and blue spot mullet requires not just patience, but something between Pavlovian conditioning and foreplay. *Hihi ganae*, 'pole-and-line (for) blue spot mullet,' is possible at only two places: at the lagoon shore on Bumadahadi islet and at one spot on the southern lagoon shore of Werua islet. These fish are easily startled so that the sight of a man standing on shore feeding them is sufficient to cause them to scatter as chumming begins. Eventually the mullet become accustomed to the sight of the fisherman--only one man does this--scattering pounded hermit crab or sand crab. Chumming goes on for about four days, at which time the fisherman waves a pole slowly back and forth over the water while he chums. The fish are startled at first, but eventually they become accustomed to the sight of the pole. This is when fishing starts. A fisherman can get up to 100 or so fish per day over a five day period, using a twelve foot pole and crab intestines for bait.

There is also a good deal of skill involved in landing this fish once it bites. The *ganae* hook is designed not so much for holding the fish as for getting it off the hook quickly. The hook and shank are set at about a 120 degree angle for each other, and the part that actually hooks the fish is a very slight curvature at the very end of the hook, as in Figure 4.2. Once the fish bites, the fisherman gives the line a gentle jerk and then maintains a steady pressure as he backs up toward the beach a few steps. Then he quickly jerks the pole upwards and backwards in an arc towards his right. This motion pulls the hook (and the fish) out of the water in an arc that takes the fish over the fisherman's head. While the force of the line movement pulls the fish toward the beach, the line slack at about mid-flight is usually sufficient to cause the hook to drop out of the fish's mouth. The fish lands on the beach behind the fisherman, while he retrieves the hook, baits it, and continues fishing. This is touch!

FIGURE 4.2 Ganae (blue spot mullet) hook

Pole and line fishing lacks two things that would lend it prestige in this community. One is danger, which I'll go into later. The other, and probably more important ingredient is an appreciative audience. With a couple of partial exceptions, pole and line fishing is a lonely business, the only sort of fishing that does not involve the fellowship (or the competition) that characterizes most Kapinga activity. With the exception of pole and line fishing, all of what Kapinga think of as work or play is done in the company of others. Work, Kapinga style, produces goods and meals, but it also produces social relationships. The two are ordinarily inseparable. This might be hard for us westerners to fathom, since we scheme and save to get away from people and place such high value on what the individual is able to accomplish. I'll argue later that the individual as we understand it is meaningless in this community. That's not what a person is. The relative value placed on fishing activity varies with its context, and a person alone does not constitute a normal context, necessary as solitary fishing may be. Consequently, of all the western fishing technology that has excited Kapinga interest, the one thing that fishermen could care less about is rod and reel technology. For any kind of fishing to have high social value, it has to be more than a living.

5

Weirs

I think of weirs as designer purse nets made of rocks and tailored to the fish. Placement is everything, and it depends on an intimate knowledge of the migration habits and preferred routes of particular fish: minnows, goatfish, and garfish. Of these, only garfish weirs were private property (others built and maintained by men's house labor). Map 5 shows their locations. None of these remain today aside from one built south of Matiro islet before World War II.

The weirs getting the heaviest use were minnow weirs--and one can see in Map 5 that they far outnumber the other two. The minnows, called *daueni*, provided bait that just about any fish would take. They were taken in calm season as they crossed the reef flat to the lagoon at rising tide and again as they crossed back at ebb tide. The larger weir, illustrated in Figure 5.1, catches the minnows at rising tide. The open apex of the two converging, one foot high rock walls was usually left open until men needed minnows. At that point one man simply covered the apex with a minnow net (see Buck 1950: 214). When the net was full, one or two men would empty the minnows into a basket and either replace it to get more or head out to deep water.

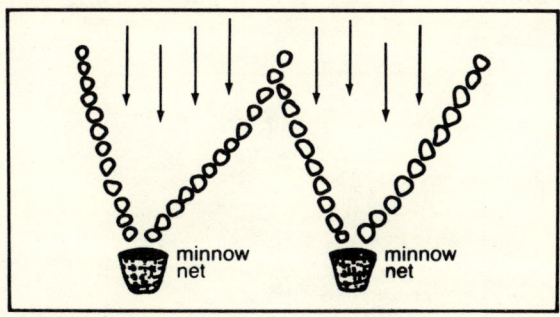

FIGURE 5.1 Large minnow weir, lagoon to reef

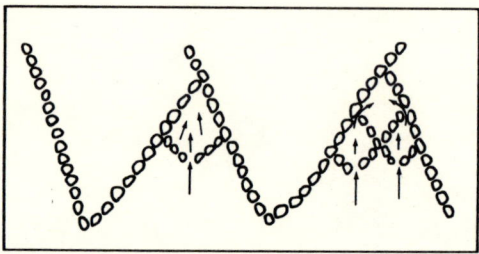

FIGURE 5.2 Single chamber and triple chamber minnow weir

Smaller minnow weirs were constructed on the sides of larger ones whenever two or more large weirs were built adjacent to one another. These small weirs (used to catch minnows at ebb tide on their return to the reef flat from the lagoon) were of two sorts: a single chamber or a three-chamber weir as shown in Figure 5.2. As the chambers filled with minnows, they were simply scooped out with minnow nets. Either the large or small weir could be used day or night depending on tide and need.

Goatfish weirs took advantage of the habits of one goatfish variety called *gala*. Beginning on the day after the new moon and continuing for three or four days, the tide begins a slow rise in the early evening. Goatfish begin crossing the reef on the way from the lagoon to the reef as the tide reaches eight inches or more. Fishermen refer to this tide pattern as a 'goatfish tide.' These goatfish have only a few habitual routes across the reef, and the locations of the weirs mark the ones that fishermen knew (or cared) about. When the tide reaches five to seven inches in height, one or two men fill in the open area of the long wall of the weir with rocks, allowing the weir to fill with goatfish. As the fish continue to trap themselves inside it, a goatfish trap is placed in the center of the round portion of the weir. Then four to eight men fan out in the lagoon surround style around the open end of the weir, using poles to beat the water

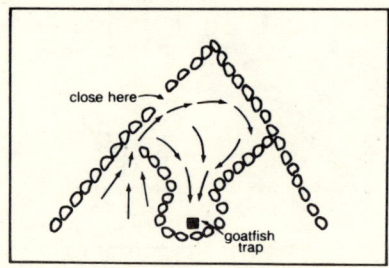

FIGURE 5.3 Goatfish weir

and scare the fish into the the apex of the weir and from there into the trap, as shown in Figure 5.3. Fishermen could also scoop the fish up with a *hulihuli* net once they reached the apex. A hundred or more fish was a good catch, and fishermen could return to the same weir as long as the goatfish tide lasted.

Goatfish and minnow weirs were community property, built and maintained by men's houses under the authority of the headmen and the *tomono*. Garfish weirs were built by what Kapinga call 'high people,' men of chiefly and priestly families and considered family property, but it was spiritual authority that protected family prerogatives. Garfish weirs were located on the northern outer reef flat (see Map 5). On days when the garfish were plentiful and the winds low, fishermen caught them in weirs rather than netting them at the interislet channels. During the latter part of the lunar month in windy season, the tide rises in the early morning to between 8" and 12" heights. The weirs are approximately 12" high.

A men's house group, using a technique similar to that for surrounding and netting flying fish, uses canoe paddles to beat the water around the small coral heads close to the lagoon beach, driving the garfish toward the reef. The men get out of their canoes and move up on the reef as the garfish approach the reef. They drive the garfish to the enclosed area of the weir (as in Figure 5.4). There, they can wither be driven into a goatfish trap or simply scooped up with minnow nets.

There are two garfish weirs shown in Map 5. The one closest to the islets was owned by the family of a high priest, who purportedly built it. Ownership rights involved a ritual presentation of garfish to the people in the chief's house on Ringutoru Islet at the conclusion of an expedition. The prescribed ritual was enforced by the spirits that inhabited the islet. Failure to perform the ritual would anger these spirits, who would retaliate by withholding fish from any subsequent expedition other than that led by a family member.

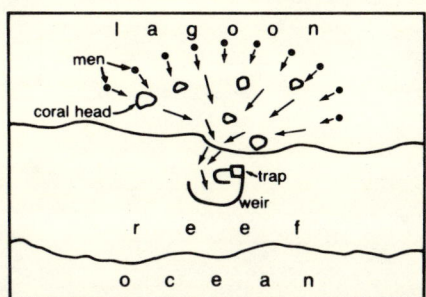

FIGURE 5.4 Di gubenge iha (garfish netting) on the reef

90

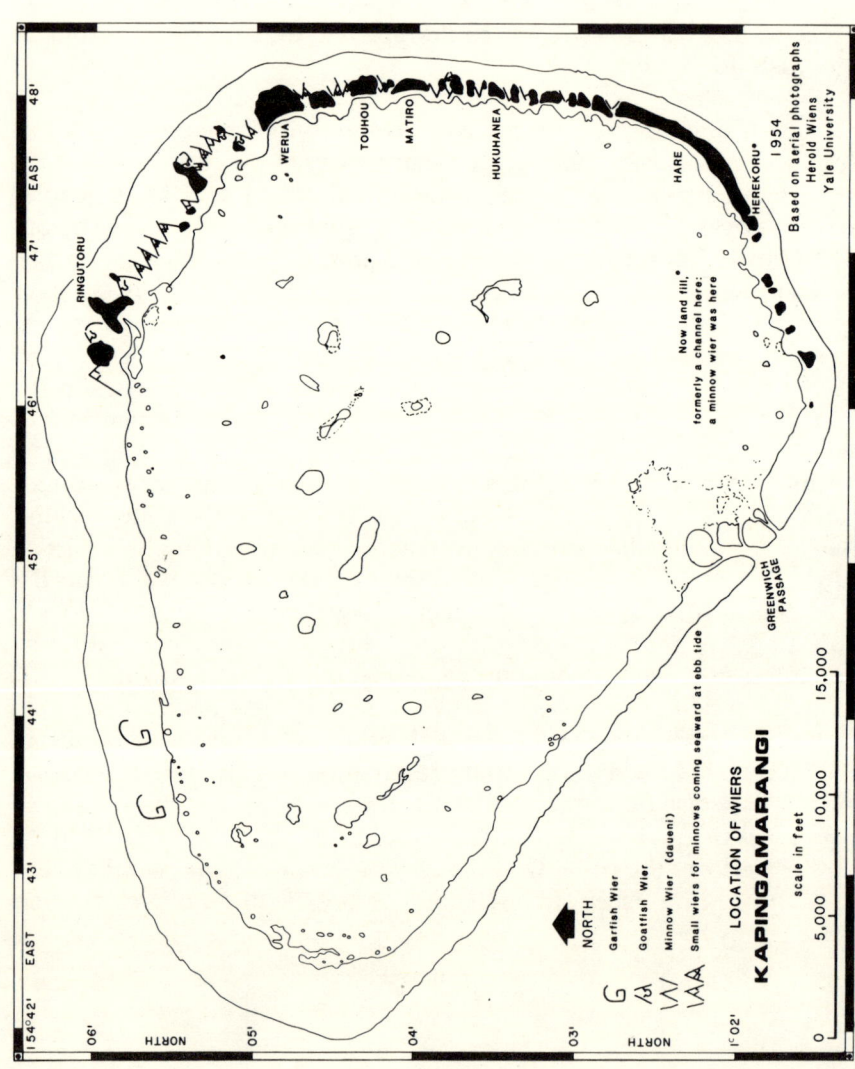

MAP 5 Location of weirs

6

Collecting

Hefty people with big appetites, under constant pressure to produce, are not above scrounging. There is enough useful stuff on an atoll reef to keep the most inveterate of reef rats happily employed. There is food: some of it delicacy, some of it just to keep your stomach from growling. There is also bait, and, most plentiful of all, shells of all kinds. There is little of it that Kapinga didn't scrounge and use before white rice and Sears catalogues became available.

My favorite scrounging is for large crayfish (Florida lobster type) and crabs that migrate across the reef from the breakers twice a month during calm season for three day periods and occasionally during windy season. For three days at the start of the second quarter and another three at the beginning of the fourth quarter, hundreds of these shellfish appear on the reef as the night tide rises. They're easy to get—just pick up the small crabs and step on the tail of the crayfish, being careful to pick them up just behind the antenna or your hand will get turned into hamburger. Coconut crabs also migrate across the reef during the fourth quarter night tide, but most people get them on the the outer islets during daytime. You grab these crabs from the back, behind their powerful claws. There are only a few migration spots on the reef and a few destinations (like Taringa islet) for these crabs, and you have to be there on time, as you only have forty five minutes before they're gone or lost in the tide. These are delicacies.

Women regularly collected sea urchins on the reef. This was the women's only involvement with fishing other than occasionally joining a *modoholo* expedition and cleaning and cooking fish. According to older women, hunting sea urchins was both food production and a welcome break from their normal routines, a chance to get out of the compound and play with their friends. Sea urchin was a very important part of the diet, however, a very dependable stop gap. In fact, when both men and women talked about a normal diet in the 'old times,' it was sea urchin and coconut.

Men and boys caught octopus on the reef flats and in the interislet channels. If they were in shallow enough water, men would dive for them, being careful to kill them quickly by biting the eye. To get a small octopus on the reef, you pick it up grabbing the inside of its belly and then getting your hand out of there fast before he digests it. Starfish were occasionally collected on the reef for use as bait.

Hermit crabs (and, less often, sand crabs) were and still are collected on the islets for use as bait for pole-and-line fishing and for catching triggerfish and small fish in the lagoon. They were buried in the sand in large baskets to keep them cool for a day or two until fishermen were ready to use them.

The giant clam is gotten in quantity during the calm season. *Tridachna*, was used both for food and for its shell. Divers would approach it from the rear and cut the valve muscle, then cutting the meat away from the muscle. If the shell was not too cumbersome, it would be brought up to the canoe and taken home for use in making adze and hand axe blades and other cutting tools. Small *Tridachna* shells were also used in shark hunting, two shells being rubbed together under water to attract sharks to the canoe.

Finally, and most importantly, calm season was when people collected the raw materials for tools. This was a continual process of being on the lookout for various kinds of small mollusks both on the reef and in various areas in the lagoon for use as scraping, grinding, and cutting tools. These include *Cardium orbita*, *Barbatia candida*, and *Asaphis violaca*. Several species of *Turbo* were collected on the reef for food. A black shelled *Avicula* species was gotten, along with pearl oyster shell, by diving in the deep water of the main pass. Kapinga men used both shells for making fish hooks.

7

Trapping

Of all fishing methods, none better illustrates the adaptation of technological ingenuity to an intimate knowledge of fish habits and the variability of the environment than trapping. Kapinga traps are basically porous boxes with one opening designed as a tunnel leading to a loosely lashed, hinged door that opens in with gentle pressure but will not open out. Once a fish gets inside the box, the only way it ever gets out is by the fisherman removing the top or part of the back of the box. Designed to mimic coral formations, all traps are baited and depend on calm waters so that fish can see them and on currents that will carry the scent of the bait. Since trap technology on this island stimulated some of the best ethnographic description in my discipline (Buck 1950: 251-256), I'll only touch on those details here. The concentration on trap use, however, will give you your first taste of the subtle, arcane world of secrecy and deception among fishermen, of how knowledge was convertible into personal power to manipulate others.

The first three traps described here are the work horses. Two are identical except for their relative sizes. They are the 'red squirrelfish trap' called the *uu daa* and the 'stinky trap' or *uu hagabilau*. The second trap, which seems to have been one of the few pieces of traditional technology that escaped Buck's notice, is about two and one-half times larger than the Red Squirrelfish trap but is otherwise identical in its construction.

The 'red squirrelfish trap' gets small fish like squirrelfish, sea perch, small parrotfish, spinefoot, red emperor, orange gilled surgeonfish, coral trout, and small sea bass that are around the lagoon shore. A man sets the trap at the base of a tidal fan, usually near a small coral head, or in some of the smaller interislet channels. He baits the trap with coconut meat tied to its sides, positions it, and covers it with stones, leaving only the entrance funnel clearly exposed. He can leave the trap for one to three days. The squirrelfish enter the trap to get at the coconut meat, while other fish may enter the trap to get the squirrelfish or other small fish that have entered. These are all fish that move from deeper water to near lagoon shores to feed during rising tides. The trap can be placed any time, but it is necessary for the water to be reasonably clear for the trap to be effective, limiting its use to calm season. Twenty to thirty fish are a good catch with this method.

The 'stinky trap' gets its name from its bait, a kind of starfish that is cut up and roasted before being put into the trap. Measuring six by four feet and standing about six feet high, the trap is for the larger fish that feed in the main passes at the western reef--giant Jewfish, larger sea bass, blunt headed parrotfish, and red bass. The trap is set at the base of a coral head in the main pass and covered with rocks, exposing only its funnel opening. It is left for four or five days before being retrieved. If productive, it is emptied and replaced. If it is not productive and the fisherman has brought along more bait, it will be replaced, moved, or taken home.

In constant use during the calm season is the *uu baabaa*, 'flat trap' for catching small, white reef eels that inhabit the reef flat and interislet channels. The trap (Buck 1950: 253) is placed on the inner reef flat in the interislet channel. The positioning of the trap depends on the particular channel. Men learn the areas that white eels are most likely to search for food, but positioning of the trap also depends on the current patterns in the channel. Fishermen need a place that has a reasonably steady current that will carry the scent of the bait (octopus or clam). The trap is set on the reef, covered with small rocks, and left for a few hours.

With the *uu dagabe*, 'sea perch trap,' we encounter the analog of what would be magic elsewhere in the Pacific. Sea perch are very tasty fish that congregate near coral heads, but only in certain spots. A fisherman finds these spots, called *daula*, meaning 'to anchor, anchorage,' by trial and error. There is no way of predicting when the fish will be there, so a fisherman normally tests his anchorage on the way to or from angling at coral heads. Using minnows or small Apogon, he tries angling at about thirty to forty fathoms. If he gets sea perch, then he will go home, get his trap, and return to the anchorage. This trap is baited like a triggerfish net, by tying bait at short intervals to strings that hang down from the top of the trap. Weighted with rocks placed inside the trap, it is taken down to about forty fathoms and left for about an hour. The fisherman either goes off to fish a coral head or he stays put and angles for a while, pulling up the trap to check it. If there are fish there (usually several varieties of sea perch and emperor), he will replace the trap up to three or four times. A good catch of 100 or more fish is enough to convince him to try again the next day. Once these fish run out, they're gone for the season. Another anchorage might produce sea perch, but only once a year, which is why these spots are such closely guarded secrets.

Like magic in many Melanesian societies, everyone assumes that everybody else knows at least one anchorage. The trick is to discover the other guy's spot and hide your own. So when fishermen are out on the lagoon, they're not only scanning the environment, but also each other. When a man is fishing his anchorage, he's also scanning for others who may be scanning him. As soon as he sees another canoe, he moves off to another spot. The problem comes if he decides to leave his trap for a while, because he has to tie a wood float to his line to locate it and pull up the trap later. Crafty fishermen know to look for those little pieces of wood that seem to be drifting but aren't moving anywhere. Then the potential thief has to test the float without the trapper knowing that his spot has been discovered. This is only part of the cat and mouse game, however.

A man's patrimony consisted of land, taro patches, and whatever arcane knowledge his father chose to reveal to him. This sort of lore included chants, land history, myths, family lore, and fishing spots. There was nothing automatic about the inheritance of any of this stuff. A man could reveal or withhold this knowledge just as he could will land to or disinherit his children. From a father's point of view, this knowledge was his social security. He could use it to compel obedience and reasonable care from his children in his old age. He could also use his knowledge to manipulate his children, who knew they had to compete with one another for these things. Men tended to wait until very near death before choosing which child would get what, often engendering bitterness and mistrust among surviving siblings thereafter.

Even more restricted than sea perch anchorages was the arcane lore that made it possible to catch moray eels. It was not the fishing technique that was secret. The technique is common knowledge. Anyone with an *uu haganiga*, 'rounded trap,' could catch them. This is the most technically elaborate of the traps Kapinga men make. About two or so feet long, a foot deep, and oblong, this trap has a sloping corridor that forces the entering eel to move upward into the trap, over a rise and then downward. Helped by gravity, the eel's own weight and momentum carry it through the trap door toward the bait it seeks. This trap is the only one still in regular use on the atoll, as the moray eel is a delicacy in great demand for special occasions, such as the feast for a child's first steps (or the first birthday feast at present). Fishing begins about two weeks before the fete, using any number of traps, each of which is checked every two days. The traps can be baited with clam or *Acanthurus*, cut up and tied to the inside walls. Traps are set on ledges of the reef slope known to harbor the eels. High tide, light wave action, and a gentle current are necessary to carry the scent of the bait to the crevices in the slope where the eels hide. The trap is weighted with giant clam shell with an abalone shell lashed to the top, allowing the fisherman to see the trap from the surface. Although sighting the trap required clear waters, even in more turbulent water, fishermen used the trick of chewing up coconut meat and spitting in the water, creating a clear area to look down. The trap could hold up to five eels before it had to be emptied. Eels are transferred to the canoe by gently lifting them with two hands. They are taken to the lagoon and transferred to a holding trap weighted with rocks and placed at the base of a tidal fan. The holding trap with a capacity for about twenty eels, is called an *uu hagadali*, 'waiting trap.' This is a generic name referring to both the trap to hold eels until a feast and the one holding crimson squirrelfish until they are needed for bait.

Anyone with a bit of experience and a trap can catch eels. But what enabled a man to use the traps was a set of chants to the spirit that guarded the outer reef slope, and very few people knew these chants. The adept had to recite them in the water and out of earshot of other men in the canoe before letting a trap touch the water. Very few men knew the chants, and they willed them to only one of their children. There is a story about a man who had caught eels and neglected to give one to his son, who was furious about it. In his remorse, the fisherman wanted to go out for eels, but was taken ill. He called his son-in-law, taught him the chant, and sent him out for eels for the son. People tell the story as an example of wasting a family's wealth.

I've already mentioned one other trap without specifically describing it. This is the one used as a receptacle for small fish to replace a purse net. it is called the *uu hagabagibagi*, 'beating (the waters) trap,' referring to the technique for driving fish by beating the water with poles or paddles. Though physically a trap (see Buck 1950: 257-259) with small coir nets attached to each front corner, it is not used to attract fish, but rather as a container for fish driven into them. It is constructed so that only the smallest fish can swim out of its sides. It is designed to hold small fish, such as goatfish, some of which can escape through the mesh of the purse net. It does not require the same care as a purse net, and it is easier to construct, requiring much less cordage to complete. The one part of its construction that is at all complex is the recessed funnel that takes up all of the front of the trap.

Finally, one for the kiddies. This is the *ulu dahi*, 'enter once,' a coconut shell trap used throughout Oceania. It is made of a half coconut shell with holes bored around the rim for attaching a square mesh net of coconut fiber. The small net has a square opening at its center that could be closed with a draw string. It was baited with chopped hermit crab and left in the interislet channel close to shore, where small fish would enter it. The trap was used by small boys and formed their introduction to catching their own fish. The small fish were usually used to feed pet birds (the noddy tern and the sooty tern). Older people stressed that this sort of trapping was important for two reasons. One was to involve young boys (as young as four and five years old) in the excitement of catching fish. Though it was play, this sort of fishing had its own associated ritual, a chant sequnce that sounds a lot like "counting out" rhymes that western children use for games. As a fish enters that trap, the child sings *ulu dahi*, 'enter one' for the first fish, 'enter two' for the second, and so on. Thus, *ulu dahi* was not just play, but a rehearsal of both the technical and the ritual aspects of fishing. The second purpose that it served was early training for taking responsibility for the care of something other than oneself. In this case, it was the feeding of a pet bird. Little girls at the same age were already involved in the care of their younger siblings. This was a little boy's first taste of what would become adult responsibilities.

The construction of traps was usually done in the men's house so that anyone who wanted to learn and practice their construction had ample opportunity. Older men said that the actual construction of the traps was not all that arduous, although it required careful attention to the details of cutting, shaping, and lashing the wood fittings. The fabrication of most traps could be completed by an experienced craftsman within two or three days of part time work. The most time consuming part of trap construction was the making of cordage for the lashings. For the larger traps, this meant hundreds of feet of cordage. Making cordage is something that only the older, partly disabled men can do on a full time basis. Preparation of the cordage for a trap could take months to complete. Therefore, there was a premium placed on proper care of traps, which included careful drying after use and hanging the traps in the house, usually from a ridge pole. A trap could last for a dozen or more years with proper care. Repair of traps usually involved having to use new cordage to redo lashings that had rotted. All of these traps were individually owned, although each men's house usually had at least an eel trap, holding traps, and, possibly, a large 'stinky trap.'

8

Angling

Angling, called *aangoli*, is what a Kapinga fisherman lives for, the big career step of a man who is making it. But that step brought new problems with it.

Calm season was busy for anglers, as for all other fishermen, what with the lagoon and deep sea open to them. Getting to the deep sea required more work, however, since high tides were still too low for a man to float his canoe across the seaward reef from his islet. He had to sail out either to the main pass in the southeast quadrant or to one of the smaller passes in the northern part of the reef. Windy season cut off the lagoon, of course, but the high tides did permit an angler easy access across the reef. Nor was rain a particular impediment, unless it was a real downpour. A fisherman could always paddle the canoe, especially if he and his partners were fishing close to the seaward reef. The windy season problem was bait, much of which came from the lagoon. Apogon, for example, are available throughout the year. The problem is getting to them.

Lagoon angling and deep sea angling share many features, but they are different operations in many respects. The fish caught, the kinds of areas fished, the equipment, and some of the methods are different. Most lagoon fishing, for example, is done near coral heads or at tidal fans. Deep sea fishing concentrates on the outer reef margin, terraces, and slopes, and the same spot, say at the outer reef slope at thirty fathoms, yields different fish depending on whether the angler works during daylight or at night. Lunar phases are important for both lagoon and deep sea angling, but its importance has more to do with tides in the lagoon and light and wave action in the deep sea. For lagoon angling, fishermen use a two-ply line with a single hook, while a deep sea angler usually uses a heavier line with a hook at each end. Anglers use two different chumming techniques. One is what I'll call scatter and sink--the fisherman breaks up, cuts up, or chews up the crab or small fish into small pieces and scatters it in the water over an area, letting it sink to attract fish to the area. The second method is for chumming at depths greater than fifteen fathoms. The cut up or chewed up chum is put (or spit) into a breadfruit leaf with a heavy rock sinker. The fishermen closes the leaf over the rock and chum and winds the end of a fishing line around to make a package. He lets the line down to the desired depth and then jerks it upward, causing the line to unwind and release the package. As the leaf opens in the current, the rock falls out and the chum is released into the water. Four or five repetitions are usually enough to gather any fish that are around. Lagoon angling uses more scatter and sink, while deep sea angling depends more on the leaf package technique.

It should be pretty obvious by now that I'm going to divide up my presentation by lagoon and deep sea angling. I'll continue to order the presentation by categories of technique, since I'm trying to show you how fishermen used variations on a technical theme to fit varying environmental conditions. You'll see, however, that I won't be able to do this consistently, since there is more to the environment than fish and coral, particularly once you get outside the reef.

Lagoon Angling

The first angling that a boy does is with older boys in the evening around the small coral heads in the northern reef. With *aangoli daa*, 'angling for red squirrelfish,' he gets his first experience collecting minnows, preparing chum and bait, and angling. He learns how to use minnow weirs and nets, and, more importantly, how to make himself a desireable member of a crew. Chumming is not so different from what he has already done with hermit crabs and sand crabs at the coral heads at Touhou, scattering pieces of minnow lagoonward of the coral head to draw fish away where he has less chance of snagging his line. Using two to four fathom lines, he and his friends can catch twenty to thirty squirrelfish (along with a few sea bass) in a good evening.

A variation of this technique used during the day is *aangoli muu*, 'angling for large eyed sea bream.' These fish gather at smaller coral heads near the lagoon shore. Young men gather sand crabs for chum and bait, pounding and scattering the chum about thirty yards lagoonward of the coral head and letting it sink to lure the fish away from the coral head. Using a ten fathom line, fishermen catch several varieties of bream, spinefoot, red emperor, and long nosed parrotfish that feed with the bream. As they fish, they try to shorten the line, drawing the fish up to shallower water. Hermit crabs can substitute for sand crabs, but the catch will be mostly parrotfish.

There are two other contexts for scatter and sink chumming: lagoon beaches and the large coral heads at the main pass. Both areas can be fished both day and night, and both yield the same fish and require the same bait. Scatter and sink chumming at the main pass takes advantage of the current to carry the chum while using a rising tide to carry chum at lagoon beaches. The idea is to attract fish to an area clear of coral that would snag or cut a fisherman's line.

The lagoon beach technique for daytime angling is *di uga danudanu i dai*, 'the buried line lagoonward.' This technique is exactly what the name implies. It involves setting a baited hook so that it sticks up from the sand at the base of a tidal fan where it slopes into deep water. A fisherman buries three feet or so of the line (up to the hook) under the sand so the fish cannot see it. He holds another five feet of line in shallow water, waiting out of sight of the fish for a bite. This is best done at a late morning or early afternoon low tide just as it begins to rise. The fisherman heaves chum into deep water lagoonward of the tidal fan where the rising tide can carry it toward the beach. When a fish takes the bait, the fisherman just pulls it in and replaces the baited hook in the sand. The fish most often caught with this method are trevally, jack, green jobfish, short nosed emperor, threadfish, napoleonfish, large eyed sea bream, queen triggerfish, and flounder. Fishermen prefer octopus as bait and chum, because all these fish will eat it. Octopus also has the advantage of being very chewy and thus difficult to dislodge from the hook. If octopus is not available, then other small fish or hermit crab will do, but each is rejected by some of the fish.

Aangoli i di awa, 'angling in the pass,' gets the same fish as 'burying the line' just described, but it was a gentle current rather than a rising tide that fishermen needed to carry the chum. You usually get a current like this five or six days after a new moon. The idea is to scatter chum--minnows, small Apogon, octopus, or any small fish or hermit crab in a wide arc lagoonward of the pass and let the current carry it and the fish into the pass where a fisherman caught them with a ten fathom line from a canoe or standing on one of the coral heads in the pass at low tide. Like its lagoon beach equivalent, the chum and bait used determined which fish would bite. All of them take minnows, Apogon, and octopus. Only some take hermit crab or small fish like cardinalfish or squirrelfish.

There are two techniques very similar to 'burying the line' used at night: *dabu ae dono di ae hanga*, 'fishing at the base of the tidal fan' and *dili duu langa*, 'creating steps (on a) coconut tree.' Both require sandy beaches with a gentle slope that are clear of coral heads or rocky outcrops that can snag a line. Both are done during the last week of the month with its very low tides and dark nights. Without a rising tide to carry chum, what fishermen do is to imitate the action of a tide. One man paddles toward the tidal fan from deep water, making a wide arc, while his partner scatters chum into the water on both sides of the canoe as they go. This is the same sort of arc a surround would form, and it makes a trail of chum from deep water, attracting fish to the tidal fan.

'Fishing at the base of the tidal fan' is done nearer the central islets like Touhou, using minnows, small Apogon, or hermit crab as chum and bait. When the chum is scattered, the fishermen anchor their canoe at the tidal fan and bait their hooks on a ten fathom, two-ply breadfruit bast line. The catch is several varieties of sea perch, red emperor, short nosed emperor, great trevally, and several varieties of tang.

Dili duu langa uses the same chumming technique on the same nights, but the similarity ends there. Done at the clear beaches in the southern quadrant (like Pumatahati islet), this technique is what separates the men from the boys. The reason Kapinga use the coconut tree metaphor for this method is that, just as a man climbing a coconut tree uses steps cut into the trunk to hold his position, the fisherman using this method has all he can handle to hold his position (on the canoe or on the beach) when the fish bites. These fish are the big ones--red bass, great trevally, giant sea bass, big grouper, large, big headed jack, and larger sea perch, tang, and jobfish. This method is most often used just after a flying fish expedition for chum and bait. After anchoring the canoe at the beach, one man begins the fishing, putting the hook in the sand in shallow water. Using fifteen fathoms of three-ply tuna line, the angler stands either in the canoe or on the beach. The battle begins when one of these fish bites and tries to run with the line. The angler tries to hold his position while the fish tires itself out, pulling it in when it weakens. His partner baits and resets the hook for the next bout. This goes on until the interval between setting the hook and a fish biting it is only a few seconds. At this point there are so many fish at the beach that anglers dispense with the bait and just toss the hook into the shallows. Two or three partners usually take turns, one angling while the other(s) rest and reset hooks. As you can imagine, fishing becomes a two-way contest--one between fish and fisherman and one between fishermen.

Anglers can choose the pass to get the same fish with the same bait at the same time. The advantage that the pass offers is a current to carry the chum, but because the current in the pass is faster than that near a beach, fishermen have to chum a much wider arc starting further lagoonward. The major disadvantage of the pass is that there is a lot better chance of snagging a line with all the large coral heads that make up the pass. Finding a clear place for the line means anchoring the canoe in the pass and having to fight the current and the fish. Alternatively, an angler can stand on a coral head, but keeping a foothold can be hard on the feet and legs. Fishermen have to compensate with a shorter line (ten fathoms), making for a tougher battle with the fish.

The two other scatter and sink methods are for gold banded fusilier and for Waigeu drummers, both in the southern quadrant around the small coral heads there. *Aangoli uli,* 'angling for gold banded fusilier,' is done any time during the lunar month in daylight. These fish require three or four days of chumming with minnows or Apogon before baiting a hook on a six fathom line from a canoe. Whenever a fisherman chums for this long a period, he tries to do it at the same time of day each day, getting the fish used to the food and the timing. When he baits his hook, he does it at the same time he'd be chumming. One man put it this way, "The fish get used to being fed at a certain time, so by the time you give them the hook, they're already there waiting for dinner." After three or four days of chumming, one or two men can fish for three or four days before the the spot is exhausted, catching scad and mackerel with the fusilier just lagoonward of the coral head.

Men go angling for Waigeu drummers during the later phases of their migration cycle, after they have left the reef flat for the lagoon. Netting will have finished by this time, so those left on the reef are caught with pole and line, while those in the lagoon are caught with hand lines around the coral heads. Unlike pole and line on the reef flat, where chumming is immediatly followed by line and hook, Waigeu drummers at the coral head have to be chummed with coconut meat for three days during a high or rising tide. Once they have been chummed, fishermen angle for them just off the lagoonward side of the coral head with a six fathom line. As fishing proceeds, the fisherman shortens the line, but in this case as a response to the fish, who seem to come up to the surface to feed on their own. Once they get close to the surface, however, they move toward the reef, forcing the fisherman to follow them and switch to pole and line on the reef. The fisherman can come back to the same coral head for three or four days before the fish run out.

Lagoon anglers use leaf package chumming for fish in deeper water, usually at the larger coral heads off shore. Two methods target specific fish--Vlaming's unicornfish and the black jack--while one targets an area.

Aangoli gelu, 'angling for Vlaming's unicornfish,' requires four to five days of chumming at a spot just a few yards off a coral head in the deep lagoon. Using minnows or small Apogon in the leaf packages, fishermen take the chum down at increasingly shallower depths each day until they are ready to fish. Then one or two canoes will fish the spot for three to five days until the fish are exhausted. Using six to ten fathom lines, black barred surgeonfish and other varieties of surgeonfish are usually caught with the unicornfish.

Unlike other lagoon angling, *aangoli kau*, 'angling for black jack,' is a windfall technique. Black jack are deep sea fish that occasionally come into the lagoon to feed around the larger coral heads. Fishermen sometimes notice them on their way to or from the deep sea and go after them. Using minnows, octopus, or flying fish, they take down four or five packages of chum and then fish with ten to fifteen fathom lines. Twenty to thirty jack are a good day's catch.

Using *aangoli ni daula*, 'angling (at) the anchorages,' fishermen target an area rather than a specific fish. You've already encountered 'anchorages' in pole and line for sea perch, and you know that a fisherman sometimes angles for the sea perch, *aangoli dagabe*, while waiting for his trap to fill up. Sea perch spots are one sort of anchorage. Another is in deep water near the larger coral heads in the western half of the lagoon. What fishermen are after here is *di iga daudahi*, 'the fish (that) counts as one.' This name refers to the fact that long nosed emperor, green jobfish, blue finned trevally, and a small jack fish called *di iga mahi* always travel together, whether in the lagoon, on the reef, or in the deep sea. For example, fishermen occasionally encounter them on the inner reef flat when they go netting at the rock piles. When they do, the netting group will divide, one group concentrating on herding *di iga daudahi* to the outer reef flat for a separate surround while the other concentrates on the rock piles.

Those fortunate fishermen with anchorages--and every angler is certain that every other angler has an anchorage stashed away somewhere--go about testing them regularly during calm season on their way to or from some other expedition. A man tests his spot by chumming with leaf packages of minnows or octopus at thirty fathoms. After four or five passes, a baited hook goes down. If no fish bite, the angler can try another anchorage or another method. If fish do bite, they will be trevally, small jack, and scad initially. Catching a few of these is enough to convince an angler to return the next day with more chum and bait. The second day produces more trevally, jack, and scad, along with a few jobfish, tang, and golden jack. By the third day, all the fish, along with emperor, are biting at six to twelve fathoms as the jack and trevally come up to get minnows, salmon jack, and other smaller fish taking the chum. The anchorage is usually exhausted after about four days of fishing, which will be interrupted by the sight of other anglers in the vicinity. Once the anchorage is exhausted, it will be months before it can be fished again.

I'll complete the description of lagoon angling with my favorite method, *aangoli dalinga*, 'angling for mullet,' familiar to some of you as a technique practiced throughout the Pacific. The fisherman takes a short (one or two fathom) line with a small hook baited with hermit crab and tied onto a float, which can be made of any stick of light wood, breadfruit being common. The line and float are then simply thrown out into the lagoon from the beach. Once the mullet takes the hook, he will run with it until he gets tired. At that point, the fisherman simply goes out on a canoe and collects the float. A number of these floats and lines were thrown out and then collected together and the process repeated. The mullet hook is a wide V-shape with a small but sharp inward curve at one end, much as in the rest of Oceania. Its shape is the same in its metal form today as it was in the precolonial shell version.

Deep Sea Angling

Of sixteen deep sea angling methods, five or six of them could be used throughout the year, the rest depending on chum and bait available only during the calm season. Unlike lagoon angling, all deep sea methods save one use chum and baited hook on the same day. Scatter and sink chumming is used close to the reef, while leaf packages are used in deeper water. Every one of these techniques required ritual appeasement of the appropriate god before fishing began. The deeper the water fished, the older the man performing the ritual. Although I'm describing the skeleton of a "typical" expedition in each case, keep in mind a few things that apply to any of them. Any expedition would have to be aborted if a crewmen sited a shark, a ray, or a whale, porpoise, or dolphin where it is not ordinarily expected. If the siting were confirmed by another crewman, the crew could assume that it was a god in fish form. The problem became that of fending off the anger of the god, the responsibility of the elder of the crew, while the rest concentrated on getting back to the islet as quickly as possible to notify the high priest of the siting. This was a dangerous time, since one or more of the high gods was known to be restless and agitated. Until the priest found out why, the lagoon and deep sea were taboo to everyone until the priest lifted the taboo.

Talk on a canoe, particularly in the deep sea, was very circumspect. Fishermen were, after all, on the gods' turf, and they could assume that the gods could hear them. No large fish was ever referred to by its proper name but always by the name of a much smaller fish of the same variety. There was even a special vocabulary for counting fish that proposed much smaller numbers of fish than were actually caught. Metaphor and euphemism were the jargon of the deep sea canoe, all purposes of self-deprecation to present a pitiable image of people to the gods. Crew solidarity was essential on deep sea expeditions, so men were careful even about the way they joked with one another. This made for reasonably stable crews over time.

Let me begin with the quintessential deep water angling technique with the perfect name--the *uga hagalala*, 'deepened (fishing) line.' This technique employs a single line with a hook at both ends. Fishing begins with a chum package of flying fish taken down to sixty fathoms. Once the chum is released, another package is placed at the free end of the line and sent down as the other end is pulled up. After several passes at chumming, the hook is baited and carried down on a sixty to ninety fathom, three ply breadfruit bast line. When the line is pulled up to get the fish, the hook at the other end of the line is let down.

For fishing at these depths, certain spots are known to be more productive than others. These favored fishing spots, some of which are secret knowledge, are called *malua*. When more than two men and/or more than two canoes are fishing at the same spot at the same time, all use a uniform line length. If an older man decides to change the length of line he is using, all the men change to that length. This was typical of all angling done by several people in the same area before colonial contact.

Fishing usually begins at sixty fathoms, testing the waters at that depth and moving down until the fish bite or the fishermen quit. Fish ordinarily caught with this method are black jack, small toothed jobfish, dolphinfish, barracuda, emperor, rainbow runner, tang, red bass, giant Jewfish, dog toothed tuna, green jobfish, and sailfish. If one spot is not productive, then the fishermen move on to try another. While fishing, one man controls the canoe's position, using a paddle to keep it from turning and tangling the fishing lines, as there are usually at least two lines in the water at a given time. Once fish are biting, fishermen will try to get them to move up to shallower waters by gradually shortening the line. The large fish are always clubbed senseless before being taken into the canoe. If a spot has been particularly productive, the fishermen would return the next day or two, usually with success.

Four other methods are variations on the 'deepened fishing line.' *Aangoli kau*, 'angling for black jack,' identical to the 'deepened fishing line,' differing only in the forty fathom line length and size (two instead of three-ply) and the hook size. Chum (minnows or flying fish) is taken down to forty fathoms on a line with a hook at each end. When the black jack are plentiful, they exclude other fish, but when they are few, the catch includes sea bass, jobfish, long nosed emperor, and tang with them. If the fish bite at forty fathoms, then the fishermen gradually move the line up to draw the fish into shallower water, eventually to ten fathoms. Then the canoe is moved slowly toward the outer reef margin and anchored, leaving all the men free to take lines. Thirty to forty fish per canoe is a common catch size with ample bait and three men with hand lines.

Very similar to angling for black jack is *aangoli gelu*, 'angling for Vlaming's unicornfish.' These fish are found in shallow waters, usually at twenty fathoms. Fishermen use minnows, small Apogon, or hermit crab chum and bait on a two-ply breadfruit bast line. If the fish are in deeper water, then fishermen extend the line length to begin, but try to coax the fish back up to shallower water. These unicornfish usually feed with an *Acanthurus* variety called *huubaga*. Fishermen usually catch them while angling for fusilier, thereafter abandoning the fusilier to go after the unicornfish. Once the unicornfish and *Acanthurus* begin to bite, the fishing expedition continues for several days. The first day's catch is usually small, five or so fish. But the following days are much more productive--twenty or so per day. As the catch size increases, several other canoes may join in angling at that spot. By the third day, black jack, jobfish, other unicornfish, and surgeonfish are also caught with the unicornfish. Since this method could use hermit crab, it could be employed throughout the year.

Another variation of the 'deepened line' technique, used at night, is called *lullulu nia hadu*, 'jerking the stones.' The name refers to jerking the fishing line upward to release the stone and chum in the leaf package. Done on bright nights following the full moon, fishermen use minnows or Apogon as chum and bait on a two-ply breadfruit bast line at thirty fathoms, paddling from spot to spot along the seaward reef testing for fish. Once fish bite at that depth, they include a wide variety of night feeders--groupers, bass, several varieties of emperor and jack fish, wahoo, leatherskin, cardinalfish, and unicornfish. Fishermen usually return to the same spot over the next several nights, gradually shortening the line to move toward the outer reef margin. By the second or third night, larger jack fish begin to move up after the smaller fish. Fishing at that spot usually continues until the nights are too dark for fishermen to see well.

Finally, we have the *waga madaligi*, 'canoe of the Pleides.' The Pleides, remember, is the constellation that is the metaphor for calm season. It is also the metaphor for the tuna canoes. Tuna, like rainbow runners, come to the atoll seasonally following other fish. They move in a line at about thirty to forty fathoms, and the canoes initially try to locate them by chumming with minnows or flying fish at that depth on a three-ply line. The canoes spread out 200 to 300 yards apart, each getting one or two tuna as the line passes. What the canoes try to do subsequently is to take the chum down to fifty or sixty fathoms, spreading the canoes in a rough circle. They try to keep the tuna circling at that depth to get the chum and bait. This is when they get fifteen to thirty tuna per canoe (and why a uniform line length was so important). Tuna will return to the same spot daily until they leave the atoll.

Ritually and economically, tuna fishing was the single most important fishing activity there was in this community. Once the tuna fishing canoes went out, no other fishing using a canoe was permitted. The number of canoes going out depended on the number of old men who 'knew' the proper chants to the gods. Crew members were established at the beginning of the season and remained intact through the season. Crewmen were under strict taboos on food and on sexual activity.

The tuna canoes remained on the beaches protected from the sun with leaves on their return rather than being stored in canoe houses. Canoes were kept inside small wooden fences, and only the members of the canoe crew could enter the enclosure. As the yellow fin tuna were brought back to shore, most of them were taken to six high ranking compounds, cut into long strips, dried and smoked into jerky, which was stored until the completion of the expeditions, when it was divided among the crew. The jerky was a hedge against poor fishing during the windy season. This gave the crew members a good deal of prestige, as well as economic power.

By the end of July, the *waga madaligi* was retired by the high priest, and other fishermen could go out for tuna, but they were restricted to only two tuna per canoe. (This restriction was expanded to four fish per canoe during a famine in the mid-nineteenth century).

While Kapinga were adopting and adapting to western technology, including western style lines and hooks when they were available, tuna fishing retained its technology until 1917. By then Kapinga were using and coveting European fishing gear, but they rejected metal hooks for tuna and bonito fishing for fear of angering the gods. Not until conversion to Christianity did the 'canoe of the Pleides' lose its integrity as a sacred endeavor. Kapinga were convinced of the superiority of metal hooks by 1910, but there was more at stake in tuna fishing than mere technical efficiency. Kapinga did not maintain the integrity of tuna canoes and their technology out of a sense of nostalgia or sentimentality or inertia, but rather for purely pragmatic reasons--its sanctity was part of what ensured its success. Once they were convinced that this was not true, they abandoned the ritual constraints on tuna fishing without regret.

The high priest usually retired the 'canoe of the Pleides' near the end of a lunar month to coincide with the arrival of rainbow runners to the atoll. This was also the period when men netted flying fish, so there was plenty of chum and bait, and they could be supplemented with minnows if need be. During the day, men would look for rainbow runners around the southern quadrant outside the reef. Once found, they chummed with leaf packages using a two-ply line with double hook at about twenty fathoms. Rainbow runners tend to stay at the same place, so the canoes would go back to the same spot each day until the fish left the atoll. Night angling for rainbow runners immediately follows flying fish netting, using a single hook on a line at eight to ten fathoms. Chumming at night is a scatter and sink technique, with the canoes making a trail of chum as they paddle from the flying fish area to the area for angling. Other small fish can be substituted for flying fish, allowing angling for rainbow runners in windy season.

Another method alternating scatter and sink with leaf package chumming is *dabu ae tagihagi*, 'fishing by picking.' The word *hagi*, 'to twist off (as breadfruit from the branch), to pick off,' refers to the idea of taking whatever is there to be taken. This is an appropriate referent for this kind of angling, done throughout the year. It will usually produce fish when other techniques will not, because the method concentrates on day feeders close to the outer reef slope who take almost any kind of bait. These include flagtail (cod), several sea bass varieties, red flushed rock cod, several varieties of emperor, and black jack. The method will also pick up other varieties, such as jacks and groupers, particularly when men use longer lines. Bait includes octopus, white reef eels, small surgeonfish, or almost any small fish. The striped surgeonfish, for example, can be caught with pole-and-line or by a surround to provide bait for up to six canoes. Angling begins anywhere outside the reef that is convenient.

Fishing usually starts at ten fathoms, the canoe drifting with the current as chum are spit into the water. When the canoes reach an area where the fish are biting, they remain there. If only a few are biting, they may move to deeper water, say at forty fathoms, where they use leaf package chumming. Fishermen come back to a productive area for several days.

The five deep sea techniques using a strictly scatter and sink method to chum form a mixed bag, each of which is different from the others. There is, for example, a seaward counterpart for the 'buried line lagoonward.' It is, appropriately enough, *danudanu i dua*, 'buried seaward.' On a day with small waves at low tide, this can be an effective method for catching red bass, coral trout, green jobfish, large *Epinephelus*, and long nosed emperor. A canoe paddles northward, following the outer reef margin from Touhou toward Nunagida islet, scattering flying fish chum aft. Just south of Nunagida, there is a spot that is sandy and very smooth in about three feet of water. A hook is placed above the sand and three feet of a ten fathom line is buried under the sand or small rocks, the rest held by a fisherman in the canoe anchored just north of the fishing spot. Ten to twenty fish is a good catch.

Another method used at shallow terraces of the outer reef margin is *hagalulu bongoo*, 'chumming the hole.' This refers to dropping chum, minnows or small Apogon, into the shallow water at the outer edge of the reef slope where soldierfish, squirrelfish, rock cod, and sea bass are known to hide in crevices on the slope. A man can stand on the reef with a short line and drop the baited hook into the crevice or he can dive down to the crevice and place the hook in it. This requires a two ply, 6 fathom line. I tried this method myself at small coral heads while vacationing in the Virgin Islands. I collected hermit crabs, pounded up chum, and used proper procedure. After thirty five minutes of concentrated labor, I managed to catch a single, scrawny, red squirrelfish. As I held my prize aloft, an observer (who will go unnamed) managed to blurt out (between cackles), "Bring home the bacon, honey!"

A night fishing equivalent of 'jerking the stones' takes advantage of what fishermen know about patterns of movement of particular sorts of fish over a month. The same emperor, grouper, bass, wahoo, leatherskin, and cardinalfish that feed at thirty fathoms at mid-month come up to much shallower waters by the end of the month. Fishermen use *dabu ae hagalewelewe*, 'fishing (that) causes (something) to fall freely.' The name refers to chum spit into the water to sink. This scatter and sink method does two jobs. It gets fish at particular known spots immediately following a flying fish expedition. The procedure is identical to the one for rainbow runners, except that the line is twenty fathoms rather than ten, at least to start. If the fish bite at twenty fathoms, then the men shorten the lines to about ten fathoms. They come back to the same spot for three nights or so. The second function of this method is to test the waters to locate rainbow runners. If fishermen catch one or two with the other fish, then they break off the *dabu ae hagalewelewe* to go after rainbow runners.

There was only one deep sea method that required several days of chumming: *aangoli malianga*, 'angling for fusilier.' These fish feed in the shallows oceanward of the outer reef margin. Fishermen usually notice them on the way to another expedition and return the next day for them. These fish require three days of chumming with minnows or small Apogon using scatter and sink. One or two canoes with five or six fathom lines get sixty or seventy fish per canoe (often with a few unicornfish mixed in). After a good catch, the canoes will return to fish the same spot over the next four or five days.

The last chumming method here is the most recent. Called *gadigadi laa nua*, 'biting in the shallows,' it is a form of trolling introduced by Tuu, a Nukuoro man that lived on the atoll in the late 1870s. His sister introduced dry taro, *Cyrtosperma*, and he attempted to introduce a form of bottom fishing, catching at least one fish that Kapinga fishermen had

Angling

never seen before. The method never caught on, but the fish still bears his name, 'Tuu's fish.' His trolling method used a scatter and sink chumming with the chum being tossed aft as the canoe was slowly paddled close to the seaward reef margin. Done during the third quarter of the month during high tide in the early morning using flying fish or minnows, a four fathom line trails behind the canoe. Twenty to thirty fish, mainly red bass, was a good catch.

If none of these angling methods worked, and if no other techniques produced fish, then anglers would go out after sharks. Things had to be pretty desperate, though, because Kapinga don't like shark meat. It smells awful when cooked, and people usually used it for fertilizing taro patches. There were two occasions for shark expeditions. One is what I think of as "You gotta do what you gotta do" fishing. This is *di waga hogoulu*, 'the shark canoe,' also called *di waga olo gima*, 'the grinding clam shells canoe,' referring to the giant clam shells rubbed together in the water to make a sound that attracts the sharks (mainly Oceanic white tipped and grey sharks). This is usually a men's house expedition using the men's house canoes. The canoes go out over the reef when the tide permits to areas of the outer reef known to produce sharks. Men noosed the sharks as they surfaced (see Buck 1950: 249-250). If they do not surface they are given a baited hook, using any conceivable kind of bait, including a slice of shark that has been cut from one that has been noosed. The shark hook was a large, wooden hook (Buck 1950: 235).

Di waga hoologi 'the pushing canoe,' took advantage of drift logs off the seaward reef that bring with them hundreds of sharks. Given the hundreds of tons of fish under these logs (albeit only in the early morning and again in the early evening), both Kapinga men and I were puzzled that sharks were all that fishermen caught at drift logs. Getting them was very easy. They were noosed at the surface next to the log. While four or five sharks are a good catch for the 'shark canoe,' twenty per canoe were typical for the 'pushing canoe.'

Finally, I conclude this description with a catch technique whose method is transparent but whose meaning is not. *Dabu ae hetau*, 'fishing to fit (one another)' refers to angling for crimson squirrelfish in order to bring together a boy and a fish in a continuing relationship, at least at one level of interpretation. This introduced boys to the deep sea and initiated men to fatherhood. The birth of a man's first child entailed his obligation to catch a crimson squirrelfish for his wife before he could cut his hair and shave (from which he has abstained during his wife's pregnancy).

Bait was hermit crab, and these fish were not chummed. The canoes would fish just off the northernmost islets, the known spots for crimson squirrelfish. Using a ten to twelve fathom line with rock sinkers, fishing was done on bright nights as the moon appeared on the eastern horizon. About 200 or more fish was considered a good night's catch.

Boys are taken out for their first angling when they are still very young, between three and six years of age. The expedition is mounted during the ceremony for making of new mats for the gods in the cult house. Boys go out with their fathers or other sponsoring relatives who fish for them. Each man must catch his charge's quota of squirrelfish (200 or so). If the quota are not caught on the first try, the sponsor must go out again the next day. Fishermen returning with their catches cooked the fish and gave them to the women to eat. Although not terribly difficult to catch, men competed over the size of the catch much as they did over flying fish, which were also part of boys' initiation rites. When I asked why these fish should have been so important, older men and women were vague, saying only that this fish represented blood because of its color, and a child gets its blood only from its father.

Crimson squirrelfish is not considered a particularly tasty morsel, nor does it require special technique or virtuosity to catch. Because this is so, it is perfectly suited as a metaphor for blood and the relationships with which blood is associated. It has only two notable properties--its color and its location in the northeastern quadrant, a sector associated with women (the area of a female spirit who would attack men unaccompanied by a woman but to whom women were immune). As a symbol, in other words, the crimson squirrelfish has the advantage of being relatively unambiguous in the messages it communicates. You wouldn't confuse it with something that tastes good or something that is dangerous or something that requires skill, strength, courage, or special knowledge to acquire. What this fish represents is a conjugal relationship and all the reciprocity that relationship implies. Men know where to find it, and they have to go to its habitat, just as a man does when he courts. When these fish wander, they are caught with pole and line near the islets and are of no ritual consequence. Only when men angle for them are they ritually important. This is significant, because a man's access to a canoe is provided by his father-in-law. This would make the competition over numbers a representation of fecundity, which is particularly salient in a community where two thirds of the female population were infertile or nearly so, only one third of the women providing children for the rest of the population (see Lieber 1970). Finally, the larger context of angling for crimson squirrelfish, renewal of the gods' sleeping mats in the cult house, concluded with a feast and ritual orgy in the men's house on Touhou. This was the only time that women could enter the men's house, reversing the men-going-to-women symbolism of *dabu ae hetau* in a kind of ceremonial play.

9

The Ordering of Constraints on Fishing Activity

In Part Two, I have described a set of fishing practices and their environmental contexts as they existed around the turn of the 20th century. By that time, however, Kapinga people had been in contact with Europeans and other islanders visiting the atoll, including Nukuoro, Samoans, and Melanesians, for about 25 years. A few Kapinga had been to Port Moresby and Rabaul, some learning to speak Melanesian pidgin. European dress and furniture, steel tools, glass, pigs, chickens, dogs, jewelry, sugar, tea, and tobacco were familiar to them by that time. Kapinga traded copra for these imported goods, and that in turn was changing the vegetation patterns on the islets, coconut trees replacing many pandanus plantations. Imported foods, such as tinned meat and rice, were familiar but not highly valued. Except for tea, sugar, and *Cyrtosperma* or dry taro, the Kapinga diet remained unchanged during that period. The introduction of dry taro probably made imported foods less attractive than they might have been. Dry taro grows larger, faster, and with less effort than the *Colocasia* (or sweet taro) that it largely replaced. Sweet taro had been a feast food; dry taro quickly became a staple. Fish remained the major protein, and fishing methods changed little during this period of rapid introduction of western goods.

Part of the reason for the stability of traditional fishing technique was the lack of a dependable alternative. The only western fishing technology that had excited Kapinga interest was metal fish hooks and canvas canoe sails. But the most powerful factor contributing to the stability of the traditional system was Kapinga religion. The subject of that religion was food and the gods that controlled its productivity. The high priest was the critical link between the community and the gods, the liaison who represented each to the other. As long as the high priest did his job effectively, his power was unquestioned. An extended period of poor fishing and poor land productivity was a sure indication of the gods' disfavor, and he would be replaced (see, for example, Emory 1965: 41-43). High gods each had his or her territory on the sacred islets and in the ocean. Each had to be notified of the presence of people, and each had to be soothed and reassured of the fishermen's good intentions. Depending on the particular god, certain people could address him and certain people could not. This, as we have seen, depended on relative age. Kapinga's understanding of their universe, although expanded, continued to maintain the power and privilege of priests and of the age stratified social order among men.

The power of the priest, the secular chief, and age stratification was most importantly expressed in the limitation on the number of available canoes. Use of canoes was further constrained by the ritual requirements of tuna fishing, obviating canoe use for other purposes. Given these constraints and those of season, tide, etc., on collecting and pole-and-line fishing, the majority of fish that people ate over a year came from netting expeditions done by groups of men. This lent particular salience to men's houses that organized and controlled these expeditions. The salience of men's houses and the individual efforts of pole-and-line fishing, however, had important ecological implications.

Given that the majority of the men likely to be fishing on a particular day were more often than not fishing in groups--mainly netting groups--that activity was then subject to the constraints that made some sorts of fishing more productive than others on that day. In other words, if netting is what is being done on a particular day, then the group is going to concentrate on the most predictably productive kind of fishing. But this depends on which fish are likely to be available that day, and that in turn depends on constraints represented by tides, wave action, and resulting concentrations of particular species in particular places. The changes in tide patterns over a lunar month determine what fishing methods are chosen for particular tide patterns. During calm season, we see that the pressure on different sorts of fish are distributed in such a way that no species becomes a target of exclusive concentration.

The ecological outcome of Kapinga organization of their fishing activities is a wide range of relations between people and over two hundred varieties of fish. None of these relationships are exclusive of the others. Even during the calm season, when reef and lagoon fish are exploited most intensively, particular varieties were rarely ever sought for more than six days out of a month, and then only for relatively brief periods as the tide permitted. The variety of areas exploited and species sought also characterized windy season fishing, despite fewer alternative catch methods available. The few species singled out for sustained effort--yellow fin tuna, Waigeu drummers, and rainbow runners--are migrant species that are not native to the atoll.

We see in these data an ecological balance between human and fish populations, sustaining people without threatening fish species with extinction. This was an ecosystem in homeostasis, and that steady state held well into the 20th century.

Now, the reader will inevitably make what he or she will of the stability of this marine ecosystem according to personal preferences of ideology, theoretical commitment, or political position. One could argue that primitive people are closer to and more in tune with nature, or at least more constrained by it. One could single out the limitations of Kapinga hardware and technique as making overexploitation of fish species virtually impossible. One could point to the pragmatism of Kapinga fishermen, whose calculations of cost (in time, effort, and materials) against returns in catch size should be sufficient to regulate catch pressure. One could view religion (or the political order) regulating the distribution of catch methods (perhaps as a by-product of maintaining the unequal distribution of privilege). There is ample evidence above to substantiate each of these positions, as each one addresses a major category of variables constraining fishing activity. This still leaves open the question of how these constraints are organized and, thus, how these explanations fit together. Figure 9.1 illustrates one possible way of integrating this explanations.

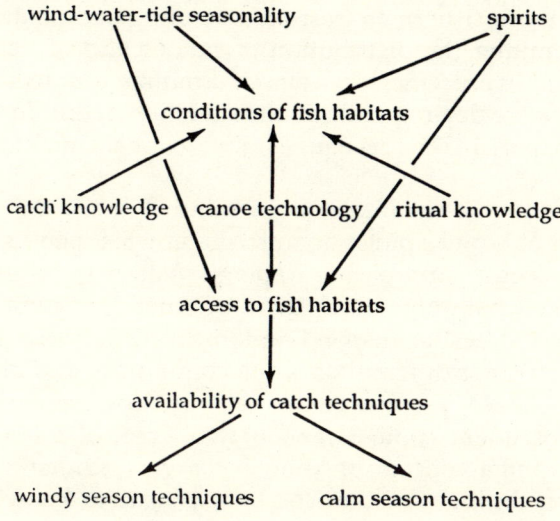

FIGURE 9.1 Constraints on catch techniques

From both a Kapinga and an observer's point of view, wind seasonality with its associated patterns of variation in water surface, tides, and the consequent availability of fish species, is an all encompassing variable shaping the deployment of catch techniques. Fishermen take account of wind-water surface-tide patterns, i.e., they *perceive, interpret, talk about,* and *respond to* seasonal patterns and their daily variations. The kinds of differences these variations make are shaped at least in part by their equipment, catch techniques, and water craft. Similarly, the importance of rain is determined by the form of the canoe, e.g., the unwieldiness of pandanus mat sails when wet. Access to possible fishing areas and, thus, to possible varieties of fish are constrained by wind, water surface, and seasonal tide patterns in the ways that they are only because the Kapinga fishing technology is what it is.

It is equally clear that the gods, those of the deep sea and those of the cult house, are every bit as encompassing a category of environmental variables as wind-water surface-tide patterns. Both sorts of gods were whimsical, sensitive to intrusion and insults from people, and quick to vengeance. Cult house gods in particular could endanger fishermen on the water by altering their daily routes and coming back early to the island. As a category of environmental variables, they contextualize every catch method in the Kapinga repertoire in terms of dangerous and safe areas to fish--the areas where fishermen are most and least likely to encounter them. The minimization of danger lay in limiting contacts with them to those fishermen best able to recognize them and to deal with them. Limiting the distribution of canoes and of fishermen over dangerous areas were efficient ways of limiting contacts. While it is obvious that we are dealing with ritual regulation of environmental relations (cf. Rappaport 1971), it is equally obvious that ritual is not the only regulator.

With these two generalizations in mind, I think that the clearest approximation of how Kapinga organized constraints on fishing activity is a common sense approach. Kapinga fishermen organized their responses to their environment in terms of what they *knew* about it and about their capabilities for responding to it. This is true of any community, of course. What differentiates one community from another is its particular epistemology--what counts as knowledge and how one gets it--and the consequent contents and organization of the known. Very briefly, the Kapinga concept of knowing is very similar to the French *savoir*, knowing through experience. In Kapinga, 'to know,' *iloo*, means 'awareness of differences or distinctions.' One comes to know something through a sequence that begins with 'learning,' *kabe*, which means to 'dislodge something from its matrix,' followed by repeated experience, *agoago*, 'practice,' which results in becoming familiar with and comfortable with, *woowoo*, 'accustomed to' what one learned. Usually used as a verb, when 'know' is a noun, it follows a personal pronoun, denoting a set of facts that someone has about a particular subject. 'To know' is distinguished from hearsay and memorized material, although one can 'know' a story, a chant, or historical lore (if one has the right to tell or sing it). What for us would be "common knowledge" is, for Kapinga, common experience. Even the most private of experiences, like dreams and visions, do not count as known experiences until a child learns to distinguish them from each other and from waking experience and thought.

The apprenticeship of a fisherman, starting at six or seven years of age, brings him successively into repetitive contact with different parts of his environment. Beginning at the interislet channels, where he learns the difference between the swift currents of the deep channel and the slower currents of the the shallows, he moves on to the tide pools of the inner reef flat. Here he learns the difference between a gradual ebbing of the tide that empties the tide pool of fish and a rapid ebb, leaving flounder taking refuge only to be caught with a pole and line. By age nine or ten, the boy and his friends are learning to fish off the small coral heads near the Touhou beach, using a small paddling canoe for their first taste of angling. Variations in wind, tide, and water surface leave clear water for fishing or turbulence that makes the water murky and fishing impossible. Boys come to know these areas and the variable conditions that characterize them through repeated experience. In practical terms, these experiences are mediated by the hardware and catch techniques they bring to the activity. In epistemological terms, what the boy learns about fishing technology determines what he knows about his environment. Knowing the technology and its deployment is *how* a fisherman comes to know the marine environment. What an angler knows about the fish at a coral head is different from what a spear fisherman knows. The angler sees the fish from the water surface one at a time, while the spear fisherman sees them in their habitats together with other fish. It is also true that the apprentice fisherman learns about the technology and the environment simultaneously in relation to each other.[1] The same holds true for ritual as the way in which a fisherman comes to know about the gods: ritual formulae and the times and places of their deployment are as much a part of fishing technology as lines, hooks, and canoes. What distinguishes hardware and catch methods from ritual as a way of experiencing one's environment was the differing organizations of wind-water surface-tide patterns and of the gods and how these differences were communicated to fishermen.

Seasonal winds, their associated water surface and tide patterns, and their consequent effects on the availability of particular fish varieties vary on a daily basis within a known range. This allows for rapid adjustments of catch technique. Apprentice fishermen come to know the range and alternative responses to it through a variety of ways--being told and shown by others, by being directed by others, through trial-and-error, through criticism by elders and peers, and through listening to conversations about expeditions just concluded. If conditions at a tidal fan do not allow a surround, the group can move to another. If a thirty fathom line is unproductive, then try a different line. If the current is too strong in one part of the channel, the eel trap can be moved to an area with a slower current. The sort of response demanded to an environment with a known range of variation is one of *accuracy*. This is possible because one can always try again.

Spirits are far less predictable as environmental variables. Jealous of their prerogatives, e.g., the taking of their fish from their turf, suspicious of the intention of intruders--the first line of the chant of placation is "Nothing is hidden from (lost to) You"--and whimsical, the six gods of the deep were easily insulted. The cult house gods were even more whimsical, demanding, and ornery. They demanded to be fed, housed in clean, quiet surroundings, and attended to even when their desires were not clearly communicated. One or more of them might suddenly decide to break off their daily journey to the horizon and return to the island, expecting their usual but unscheduled pampering. Refusing to be seen, they disguised themselves at these times in the forms of sharks or rays or porpoises. When angered, they could bring sudden disasters, or they might send omens of impending disaster, leaving a confused populace to figure out why they were angry and what they wanted.

Given the many uncertainties in the relationship between the gods and the community, boys were trained by their fathers from an early age to know the regularities in the habits and habitats of sharks, rays, and dolphins (the guises of spirits) so that they could recognize omens encoded on any radical departures from their usual behavior. They were taught the chants to mollify these spirits (as a temporary palliative) while they hastened to notify the chief priest. Boys memorized the chants to the gods of the deep along with the named sites along the oceanward reef by which they could pinpoint the area of each of the six gods by triangulation. Kapinga today refer to these evening training sessions as the 'school of the old days.' Elder kin taught not only recognition of omens and ritual formulae, but protocol on a canoe and between canoes in a group, including division of labor and deference patterns associated with them (particularly younger to elder), the euphemisms that one used for particular fish, for the numbers of fish caught, and for particular kinds of expeditions, and order of precedence in a line of canoes entering and leaving the main channel. All of these procedural details were signs of deference to the gods and to those who communicated with them. These details were critical not only to a particular fishing expedition, but also to any that might follow. Even an unintended slight to the gods could result in their withholding fish from all canoes that went out. Kapinga coped with unpredictable gods--and, in essence, an unpredictable environment--by making their own actions as predictable as possible. The more routine the appearances and conduct of fishermen, the less likely that spirits would notice them. While the predictable range of environmental variation demanded an accurate response (a second try almost always being possible), knowing the least predictable part of the environment required a *precision* of response (cf. Bateson and Bateson 1987: 42-43). The fisherman had to get it right the first time or else.

What Figure 9.1 shows is how two differently ordered sets of known experiences intersect in constraining access to and deployment of canoes, which in turn constrains access to fish habitats, which access constrains the selection of catch techniques. While Figure 9.1 gives a clear picture of a general hierarchy of constraints on fishing activity, it does not display the constraints that distribute people over space, which accounts for catch pressures on fish species. Figure 9.2 opens up the category of ritual knowledge to display its hierarchy of constraining variables, which delineate different categories of fishermen in a ritual context. These differences are integrated in the men's house, which constrains individual decisions, thus regulating the distribution of fishing activity over space and time.

Figure 9.2 shows the relations whereby the organization of ritual knowledge limited the number of canoes and their distribution by ritual fiat, discriminating between anglers and non-anglers and, in turn, between available habitats, species, and techniques. But while ritual constraints determine categories of possible activities available to categories of fishermen, they do not specify the organizational requirements for these activities, which are determined by species or area exploited and the technique used for them. While angling is most efficiently done by two to four men--one preparing bait, one keeping the canoe steady, and one or two manning the lines--netting usually requires many more men with a single leader, two men on the nets, and the rest surrounding or driving the fish, while a single man can use pole and line, walk the reef, or collect garfish at a weir. Unlike other methods, angling and pole and line use a two step procedure, requiring bait collection (and its equipment) followed by angling (with its equipment). Although these different methods could be used simultaneously because of their differing requirements, ritual exigencies could act to eliminate many or all possi-

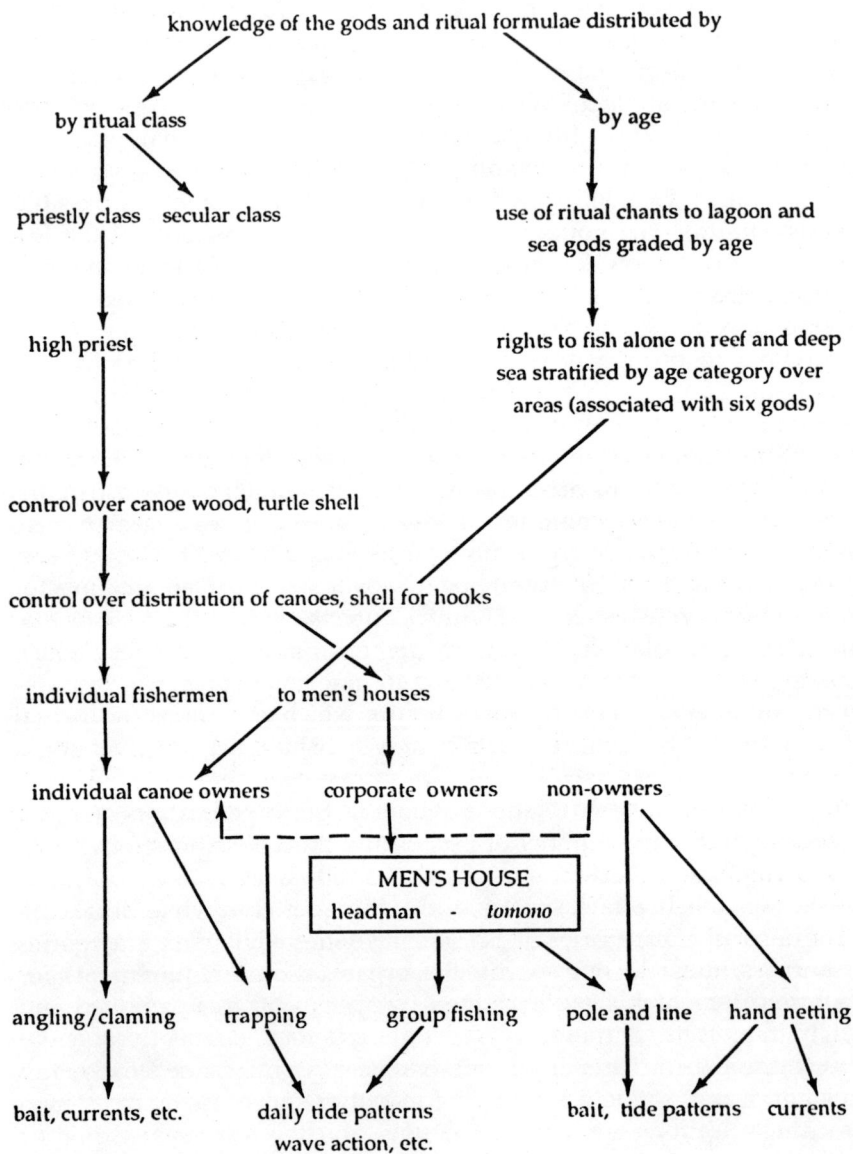

FIGURE 9.2 Ritual knowledge: its distribution and integration in organizing fishing activity

ble methods but one, e.g., tuna fishing, which excluded all other fishing requiring canoe travel, or angling for crimson squirrelfish, obligatory during the ceremony for renewing the bleached mats in the cult house (Emory 1965: 236). The complementarity of these various categories of method, however apparent, is only the most skeletal of pictures.

Netting methods shared enough features with one another *and with* angling, claming, and trapping to create potential conflicts over equipment, personnel, and locations of fishing activity. All but six netting methods require coir and purse nets. Of these twenty one methods, seven can substitute a goatfish trap for a purse net. This same trap is used at goatfish and garfish weirs. These shared features can present problems during calm season when more than one kind of expedition is mounted during a single day. Take the new moon in June, for example. Plugging the channel, followed by spinefoot netting, followed by netting at the rock piles all require a small mesh coir net, kept in the men's house. While there is ample time to return it after plugging the channel, finishing spinefoot netting may overlap with beginning rock pile netting, particularly if the two are done in distant locations. The problem of coordinating the transfer of equipment and personnel between the two is compounded by two other sorts of overlap. Both netting methods require more than twenty men--they are two of nine netting expeditions with big manpower requirements. Spinefoot netting is also one of eight of the large scale methods that shares a crucial feature with angling--a requirement of more than the two men's house canoes. The twelve netting expeditions requiring less than twenty men can usually be mounted with one or two men's house canoes for transporting the nets, the expedition organizers, and the fish. The eight large scale expeditions done on the outer reef, of which spinefoot netting is one, depend on several privately owned canoes being conscripted to transport men, equipment, and fish.

These sorts of equipment and personnel problems were dealt with by the men's house in two ways. One was maintaining an equipment inventory sufficient for multiple uses, e.g., two or three canoes, two goatfish traps, and enough lengths of small mesh coir net for two medium size expeditions. Wide mesh nets did not require that many extra lengths, but both sizes required constant attention for tears and rotted sections. Splitting equipment between expeditions or transferring it from one to another became more difficult when some of it was out of service. Coordinating personnel and canoes became a problem when two or more expeditions were mounted either simultaneously or in succession at different locations. So, for example, the transfer of coir nets from spinefoot netting to rock pile netting groups was less of a problem than transferring personnel, since both require a sizeable group. One option was to move all or part of the spinefoot group to rock piles at the southern quadrant of the outer reef flat. Another was to split the rock pile groups in two, with one manned from spinefoot netting near the southern islets and the other originating from the men's house, netting at rock piles near the central islets. This would mean leaving one of the men's house canoes behind for the central group and and substituting a privately owned canoe for it in spinefoot netting, a preferable strategy when the size of the spinefoot catch was uncertain, e.g., on the first and third days. Men's houses could also alternate days, each doing rock piles on one day and spinefoot netting on another.

All of this coordination took place at evening meetings in the men's house, attended by all members, anglers and those not in angling crews. Anglers are an important source of information for men doing netting, since they commonly see variations in fish concentrations on the outer reef. Their reports are important in the same way that reports of men using pole and line for Waigeu drummers are. Anglers' reports are also important to one another, e.g., whether it would be adviseable to take along a pole and line for triggerfish the next day because of marginal catches today, etc.. Men doing netting commonly reported tide conditions, whose range of variation can be considerable. Planning the next day's activities is conducted (by the men's house headman) on the basis of these reports and the sorts of prognostications that they enable. Private canoe owners were not free agents in these planning sessions. Their membership in the men's house required their participation in large expeditions like spinefoot netting when their canoes and/or labor were needed. Those not committed to particular group expeditions were free to pursue their own plans. The *tomono* had the power to enforce this requirement, e.g., punishing a recalcitrant member by sending men to his land to gather food for the men's house or to chop down his trees. This was rarely necessary, since there was a reciprocal advantage to the men's house lien on an angler's time and canoe(s). Given the severe limitations on bait collection during the windy season, one possibility was coordinating coconut leaf netting with angling, giving all the small fish caught to anglers for bait and taking the larger fish home for food. This practice was also used during tuna season when other netting methods were unproductive. Coconut leaf netting was justified as providing bait for tuna fishermen, while it actually provided food for a hungry population.

Clearly, the men's house was not simply a standing group composed of losers in the competition for canoes and places in angling crews. It was a multi-purpose organization whose activities included such periodic ones as providing labor for work on the cult house and the election of a new high priest and, more importantly, the day to day coordination of fishing activities both between its own members and in concert with those of other men's houses. The men's house was *enabled* to coordinate fishing activity by using ritually determined differences between fishermen as sources of information about conditions of fish habitats and by its control over members' choices of activities and over equipment for group netting. It was *empowered* to coordinate fishing activities of all its members through the ability of its *tomono* to punish non-compliance with the group's decisions. These decisions could override categorical differences between fishermen, e.g., by forcing anglers to be members of group netting expeditions when necessary. From the point of view of organizing activity, the men's house is an *institution* as Goodenough uses that term (in the Foreword). Its critical property as an institution is its control over sources of information about fishing conditions and over the processing of that information, differences that make a difference in how men and equipment are allocated over specific habitats. It is in the men's house that information about performance of groups and of individual fishermen is communicated and performances judged. Negative feedback--information that allows for correction of errors of prognostication, planning, staffing, equipping, and performance of expeditions is--thus, *institutionalized* in the men's house context. From a cybernetic point of view, the men's house--and any other standing group--is an institution if and only if it serves to regulate activity, and it does so only to the extent that it controls (has access to and processes) all information about its environment and its members necessary to allocate people and equipment to planned activities and to correct errors in planning and/or the conduct of the activity.[2] Clearly, the men's house did all these things both internally and in concert (and competition) with other men's houses. These institutions, however, were in turn regulated by another one: the cult house.

The organization of the cult house was both hierarchical and ranked in terms of the distribution of particular ritual tasks (Emory 1965: 223-236). Like the men's house, the cult house organization was responsible for monitoring environmental conditions with information provided by fishermen (anglers and netting groups, particularly at the outer reef slope). It was the presence or absence of gods and their disposition and the distribution of canoes, turtle shell, standing breadfruit trees, and drift logs that had to be kept current. While the purpose of men's house monitoring was the maximization of fish catches, that of the cult house was the safety of the island and its population. This difference accounts for the difference in how each institution regulated fishing activity. The men's house regulated activity by allocating men and equipment in amounts varying with environmental conditions over specific places on an as-needed basis. This is similar to the distribution of pigments into cans in a paint factory (on the basis of current orders) or the speedometer, odometer, and fuel guage in the driver's panel of a car--these are all examples of continuous variables. Thus, the organization of men's house regulation resembles that of an analog computer, i.e., in terms of how much of what goes where. The high priest regulated fishing activity not only by controlling canoe production (by permitting or prohibiting construction) but also by prohibiting access to the lagoon and/or deep sea and/or the outer reef, by limiting access to any of these areas to certain people, and by limiting personnel on canoes to, say, sacred class men, all by the use of taboo. The priest, in other words, controls a set of fishing areas, means of access to areas, and categories of personnel on canoes, each of which has two possible states--permitted or prohibited. This is similar to mechanical devices, like pianos or multi-toned accordions, and electronic devices like light panels or computers that operate with a set of on-off switches. Cult house regulation of fishing was organized digitally with "off" as a default setting, i.e., the men's house headman could assume that any and all areas were open to fishing unless notified otherwise.[3] Indeed, the men's house headmen were the first to be notified of the placing or lifting of a taboo, and they notified their members at the evening meetings. These institutional relations are summarized in Figure 9.3.

The hierarchy of constraints on fishing activity in Figures 9.1, 9.2, and 9.3 show a peculiar property: what we westerners think of as "natural" or "ecological" variables are distributed at the very top and at the very bottom of the hierarchy. Currents, daily tides, fish schooling, bait, etc., are contextualized by ritual knowledge and its distribution through the population; they only kick in once the ritual conditions have been satisfied, first as information used in men's house decision making and then during the actual expedition. Since this is one of the most significant findings of this part of the research, I want to be very clear about what its significance is.

I am *not* arguing that cultural variables are more important than natural variables in organizing traditional fishing activities. All of the variables that constrain fishing activity are cultural variables. What I am arguing is that the Kapinga's knowledge of their ecosystem render wind-water surface-tide patterns and spirits as sets of differently ordered ecological variables, the former being more predictable than the latter. Requirements of precision in the use of ritual techniques for interacting with gods engendered a set of social discriminations between categories of fishermen considered best and least able to deal with gods. Cross-cutting categories of ritual class and relative age were the bases for delegating responsibility for interacting with gods and its associated privileges of canoe ownership, men's house leadership, and membership angling

Ordering of Constraints

crews. This differential distribution of privilege distinguished fishermen with access to the deep lagoon, outer reef, and deep sea from those with access to near shore lagoon, inner reef, tidal fans, and outer reef flats within walking distance or on men's house canoes. These distinctions generated differentiated sources of information about environmental conditions enabling the high priest to regulate fishing for the safety of the the island and the men's house to regulate it to maximize fish catches. This hierarchy of constraints had the effect of distributing the attention of fishermen over a wide variety of species.

The ecological outcomes of a hierarchical organization of fishing activity certainly give the appearance of a system designed with conservation in mind, reminiscent of the situation on Palau and Tobi Atoll

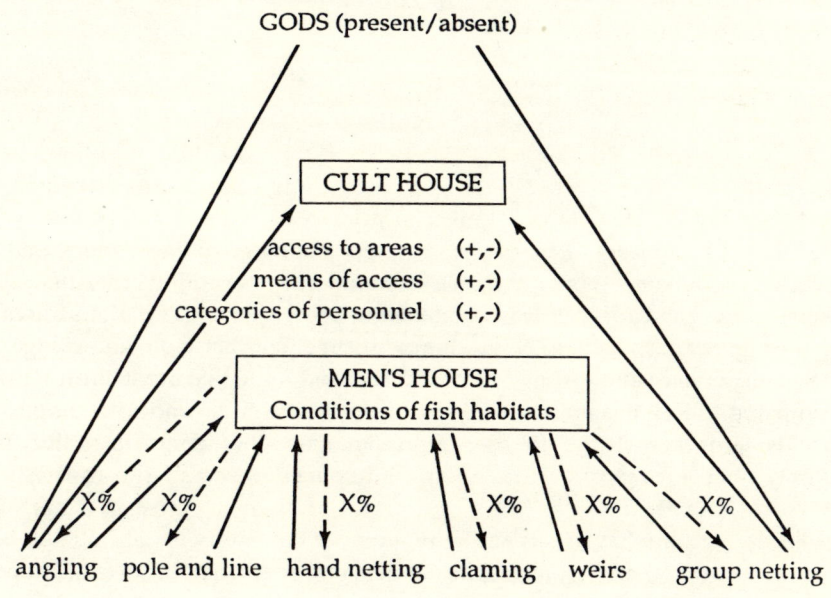

FIGURE 9.3 The organization of regulatory activity in the institutional hierarchy.

described by Johannes (1981). Johannes notes that the organization of fishing activity on these islands seems to presuppose principles of conservation (though not necessarily consciously so). This is a reasonable hypothesis, particularly given a Kapinga epistemology that takes relationships as what one knows about--and difference is a relationship--seeing learning as a process of distinguishing things from their contexts. It is a short logical step to infer that Kapinga fishermen would regulate their own activities according to their observations of their effects on the fish, limiting their concentration on particular species accordingly. I tested this hypothesis repeatedly in 1977, 1980, and 1982, by which time the constraints on both fishing activity and the social order had changed dramatically. That test simultaneously involved testing the accuracy of the model of constraints on fishing activity. I turn to these matters in Part Three, the account of change in Kapinga fishing activity and in the social order that is its context.

Notes

1. This is not a statement of a universal principle. In a society like ours where people hold a concept of *knowledge*, an impersonal body of facts, ideas, and lore available to anyone, there are many ways to know something other than direct experience. The variety of ways of knowing and of personal relations to what is known generates, among other things, distinctions between knowledge and belief, experience and revelation, verification and faith, that are interesting when compared to Kapinga epistemology but inapplicable to its understanding. I will use the term "knowledge" for ease of presentation with the understanding that it is only a tag, not a gloss or translation of a Kapinga construct.

2. Focussing on what fishermen know appears commonsensical initially, but it makes theoretical and ethnographic sense, since regulation of any sort depends on the control of information. The source of information by which both the men's house and cult house regulate fishing activity is fishermen's knowledge of the current state of the environment. This is the reason for not distinguishing between knowledge and belief, which would add to this account only invidious distinction between what the fishermen and the observer count as knowledge. But that distinction is already disallowed for discriptive purposes by the definition of constraint presented in the introductory chapter. What anthropologists call cultural relativism is, in other words, built into the very definition of a system *in relation to the observer*. One analytical advantage of that strategy is the observation, in this case, that the sociology of knowledge and the sociology of religion are folded into the sociology of work (cf. Lansing 1991).

Ordering of Constraints   127

3. This regulatory pattern of a digitally organized component controlling a component whose processing is analogically organized is rather common in biological organization, e.g., gene systems and nervous systems. What distinguishes human social systems (and man made machines) from biological systems in this regard is the human tendency to organize digital regulation with the default setting at off. One metamessage of the gods' daily round is something like "Unless you hear from us otherwise, you are free to do what you planned." Gene systems and nervous systems normally operate with sequential switching on and off of polygenes and nerve nets to regulate cell and nervous activity. In social systems, this sort of regulation would be thought of as micromanagement, although some of the more complicated, robotically controlled industrial processes appear to be regulated more on the gene model than the social system model.

PART THREE

Changing Contexts and the Contexts of Change

130

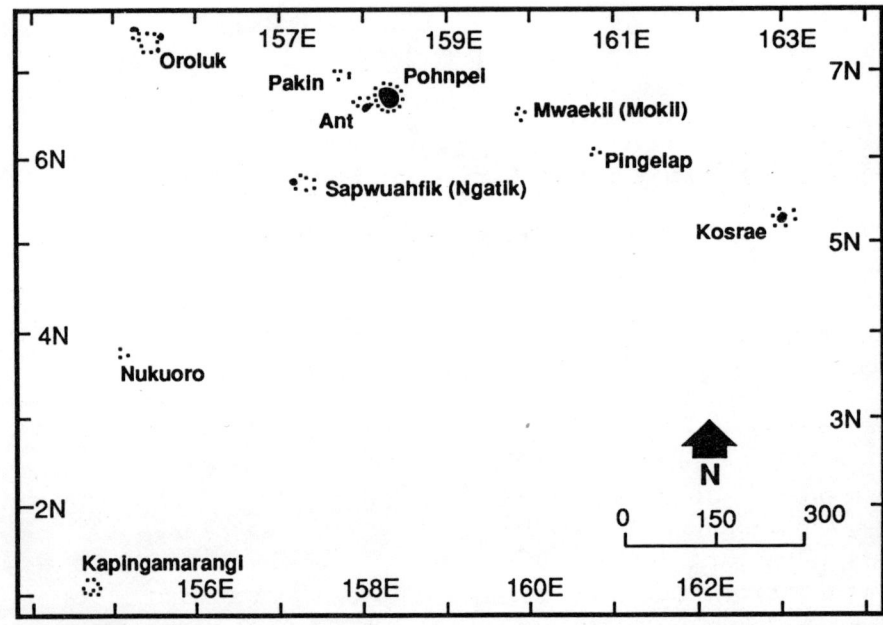

Source: Bryan, 1971

MAP 6. Pohnpei State, Federated States of Micronesia (after Vern Carroll, *Pacific Atoll Populations*, [Honolulu: University Press of Hawaii, 1975], p.345)

10

Coping with a Changing Environment

Despite over 50 years of rapid technological and social change, the homeostasis of the Kapinga marine ecosystem held well into the 1950's (see Wiens 1956, Niering 1956). But by 1980, there were signs that this ecological balance was being upset. At least two species--both of the spinefoot varieties--appeared to be endangered. Not only were there fewer of them to be caught, but those that appeared were much smaller than normal adults, evidence that the fish are being taken faster than they can reproduce. With fewer spinefoot, attention was turning to sea bass at the same fishing site (the channel), and at least one variety appeared to be headed the way of the spinefoot. Octopus and turtles are now rarely seen on the atoll, and those that make an occasional appearance are very small. Several other species that used to appear on the reef in large numbers are also rarely seen. At the same time, there are changes in coral form at two small channels resulting from changes in angling procedures.

These ecological changes correlate with changes in fishing activity and the technology that implemented them. The spear gun in particular has brought about dramatic changes in the productivity of individual fishermen since its introduction in 1963. The endangered spinefoot and sea bass varieties have been caught almost exclusively with the spear gun. As early as 1965, older Kapinga fishermen were blaming the spear gun for decreasing productivity of netting and angling in lagoon fishing. But their complaints had no effect on the popularity of spear fishing, which has increased with the easy availability of a cheap, light, aluminum variety that can be operated with one hand.

These changes were apparent before I began my research, and like older fishermen, I assumed that they were the result of a new technology whose implications fishermen had yet to understand. I also assumed without much question that pre-colonial technology did not permit over-exploitation of any species. Given the relational, contextualizing character of Kapinga epistemology, I hypothesized that Kapinga would perceive variations in abundance of fish native to the atoll in terms of their relations with them and regulate their activity accordingly. Kapinga, hypothetically, should be optimizers, regulating their activities to take what they needed and not much more. After repeated testing, it is clear that this hypothesis is false.

Kapinga fishermen are maximizers, not optimizers of fish catches. They will, according to what they say and what they do, take every available fish on an expedition whether or not they will eat them and regardless of whether they have the canoe space to transport them all back to the islet. Fish can always be given away, and someone can always be dispatched to the islet to summon other canoes to transport the fish. The idea is to get them all. So, if traditional fishing activity appeared to achieve an ecological homeostasis of human and fish populations, it wasn't because Kapinga fishermen were conscious or unconscious conservationists.

The assumption that Kapinga fishermen did not have the technology that could threaten the breeding stock of local fish populations is also false. Curiously enough, the netting technique used for the endangered spinefoot and bass populations was capable of overfishing these species. What made the technique potentially devastating to these populations was (a) that it got them before they reached the channel to breed and (b) that it could get every last one of them over the nine days of schooling each month. Monthly use of this technique over all nine days of the May through August season would have reduced each population to the point that natural predation would finish off whatever fishermen did not take. With the technological potential and a maximizing ideology, what kept fishermen from overexploiting these fish?

Three sorts of constraints prevented traditional fishing activity from exterminating these fish. Because tuna fishing, which precluded any other fishing using canoes, occurred in mid-calm season, bass and spinefoot populations proceeded unmolested to the channel for at least one and usually two months out of the four month breeding season.

Another constraint on spinefoot netting was collecting the requisite manpower and canoes, which depended in turn on alternative activities and how fishermen scheduled them. Sea bass and spinefoot netting began at the end of a lunar month, when fishermen were also engaged in netting flying fish, several kinds of night angling, blocking the channel, netting rainbow runners, netting at rock piles, and day angling. All but one of these required private canoes for transport. Getting enough fishermen and canoes for sea bass-spinefoot netting might be possible for one or at most two days of each three day period, but rarely all three. No men's house headman would opt for spinefoot over rainbow runners, and none would try to force the men into an expedition they did not want--not if he wanted to keep his job.

Rain could be a constraint on netting. Once pandanus leaf mat sails get soaked, they become heavy and unwieldy. To tack a canoe, a man has to pick up the yard and the boom, folding the sail between them, and carry the entire assembly from fore to aft, placing the forked end of the yard on the gunwale rail, converting stern to bow and *vice versa* (Buck 1950: 206). This procedure is difficult when the assembly triples its weight, so fishermen would rarely attempt sailing in the rain.

None of these constraints are applicable at present. Tuna fishing is no longer sanctified, and anyone who can get the tree can have a canoe. Manpower is not an issue when a fisherman with a spear gun can get over 100 fish in an hour. The use of outboard engines (or synthetic sail cloth) precludes problems with heavy sails. As many as eight or ten spear fishermen can fish the channel in less time and with less work (no bait) and gear than it takes for tuna fishing. If spearing spinefoot had the same constraints as netting them did, or even one or two of them, these populations could never have been overfished. Clearly, it is not the technology that threatens these species, but how the activity that deploys the technology is organized. It is organizational change, not technological change, that accounts for overfishing these two species.

The virtual disappearance of hawksbill turtles from the atoll is a more obvious instance of change resulting from the lifting of traditional ritual constraints. Turtles were taboo before 1917, being taken in secret and left for the high priest's disposal. Conversion to Christianity obviated these restrictions, and turtles have been taken enthusiastically for food and shell for handicrafts (Lieber 1984a).

Octopus, like turtles, have been harvested with increasing intensity since 1917, because more fishermen are angling and because octopus is the universal bait. To understand what increasing intensity means, consider this--angling techniques constituted a third of the total inventory of discrete fishing activities before Christianity; they now constitute two-thirds. The only netting techniques still consistently practiced in the 1970s and 1980s were coconut leaf netting, used occasionally on Saturdays and for feasts and flying fish netting. The only trapping still practiced regularly is for moray eels and that only for important feasts. Adding to the pressure on the octopus population has been the disappearance of the other universal bait--minnows (called *saipi*) from the atoll in the early 1960s.[1]

Six-horsepower engines mounted on the canoe's outrigger boom make the main channel easily accessible, so that two smaller channels in the northeast quadrant are no longer used to get over the reef during calm season. Before outboard engines, anglers used to police these channels, removing coral growth, but unimpeded growth had blocked the channels by 1982. Using public works funds (granted by the Pohnpei State legislature) to pay workers, the Kapingamarangi council organized crews to remove new coral outcrops and smooth down the reef in the two channels in August, 1982. Older men and women were disgusted at the need to pay people to do what fishermen had always considered part of their routine.

Compared to the oil spill off Prince Rupert Island or the disaster of Czernobel, the ecological changes I'm describing here are small potatoes. The Kapingamarangi ecosystem is not nearing a state of collapse, nor do Kapinga sense a dire emergency. But Kapinga men and women saw these changes as symptoms of a malaise that encompassed the entire community, and they were very uneasy about them. Over the years between 1978 and 1982, I could feel a growing, pervasive *angst*, a vague sense of uncertainty and impending chaos--and helplessness to avert it-- that people expressed when talking with me and with one another. The nature of this generalized anxiety began to become clear in a very curious way when I began work on 20th century changes in fishing activities. This was by far the most frustrating part of my research.

Getting people to list and describe traditional techniques had been easy. Getting a list of new methods, no less descriptions of each one, was impossible. People would answer my initial questions, giving me details about one or two new techniques, and then change the subject, always in the direction of politics--the state of the community in general or specific issues like maintaining two small channels in the reef, squabbles over the construction of the large pier in the Souhou lagoon, council issues, and the like. Their transitions between fishing techniques and the state of the community all followed a single pattern. Listen to what people had to say:

> Before, when fishermen came back from netting, every household got a share of the catch. Now, only those who went out get to take fish home.

> Not so long ago, when a fisherman came back to the islet and neared another canoe that had no fish, the fisherman always gave some to the man with none. If the fisherman saw anyone standing on the beach when he came in with fish, even a small child, he would have to give some to that person. Now, a returning fisherman looks at no one and gives fish to no one. He just takes them all home.

> Fishermen need to obey the orders of the men's house headman when netting. People had to be particularly careful when closing the coir net behind the circling fish to push them into the purse net. Today, instead of holding

up the net around the circling school, the young men abandon the coir net to shoot the fish with spear guns. So most of the fish escape through the openings in the coir net that these younger men left. That's why the headmen don't like to take groups out netting anymore.

Before, we fished together with the men's house; we went out together to get flying fish with each canoe in its assigned place. Each father taught his son how to act on the water. Now every man has his own canoe and his own gear and does what he wants. Just like the community. It's just like what I'm talking about with fishing. No one listens to the men's house headman, no one listens to the chief magistrate or the council. We just do whatever we want and then gossip about each other.

Fishermen would go out to one of the small channels on the reef and wait until high tide to get their canoes through. They would always get there early to spend time stamping on and clearing out any new corals that grew in the channel. You have to keep the channel clear and smooth or the coral will just grow up and clog up the channel so it can't be used. Now no one will go and clear out the channel. We have to pay people to do it.

Before, the community was sacred. Now each person has his own knowledge and his own truth, and the community is nothing.

I might have dismissed these statements as the sour grapes of older people over their loss of influence in the community if younger people had not been saying the same things. They were explicit about problems with fishing and with one another resulting from people's failure to subordinate their personal interests to community interests and a failure of the community to exert authority to compel such subordination. Although fishing still symbolized the social order, it had clearly become the most bitter of ironies: a metaphor for *disorder*.

To understand the nature of this irony is to comprehend ninety years of profound social transformation under the hegemony of three different colonial masters. From the first colonial contacts in 1877 until 1914, Kapinga experience a new source of and a new kind of power impinging on them from outside their community, and their responses to colonial agents involve changes in their technology and in their activities. With the arrival of the Japanese as colonial masters, followed quickly by conversion of the population to Christianity, Kapinga reorganize their social order by recombining parts of the old one with novel institutions. Under the United States administration from 1947 to 1979, Kapinga again reorganize their social order on a Western model of democratic (and bureaucratic) institutions. Throughout this period, fishing activity changes in three ways: (a) fishermen adopt new technology and new catch methods; (b) angling increases in frequency at the expense of group organized netting; and (c) there is a profound change in the connection between fishing activity and the larger social order.

All of these changes are parts of, or aspects of a single process of transformation whereby the *environment* of fishing activity--in the widest sense of that term--changes. So, for example, we know that the gods are part of a fisherman's environment. Their presence impinges on fishermen and on fishing activities in a way that demands a response. We see that response in the ways that fishermen conduct their fishing activities and their relationships with one another. When the gods cease to be part of the fishermen's environment, the organizations and techniques designed to respond to them cease to have any salience, resulting in a reorganization of fishing activity. As contacts with colonial regimes and their agents become more frequent and predictable, their presence becomes part of fishermen's environment, impinging on them and on their activities directly (in the form of the availability of manufactured gear, for example) and indirectly through the reshaping of the atoll social order.

Generally speaking, as the environment of fishing activity changes, the constraints on that activity change, so one could reasonably expect that the activity should change accordingly, and indeed it does. But generally speaking is also loosely speaking. Environment is a very slippery term, more evocative than it is descriptive. I do not mean to say that environmental change causes change in fishing activity. An environment doesn't *cause* anything; it is a set of conditions that a system must take account of (or not take account of, depending on the particular system). How a system takes account of the condition and how it responds to it depend on the system--how it transforms inputs, how it processes them, etc.. Applying these general considerations to the Kapinga case, what they amount to is this: you won't be seeing anything in this account about the "impact" of colonial regimes and policies or about economic and political "forces" on Kapinga social order and fishing practices. Impacts and forces and the like are what explains why a billiard ball moves in the direction and velocity it does when struck by the cue ball. People are not billiard balls, and the communities they form are not mechanical devices (or dynamic systems) that can be impacted, impressed, or driven. If they were, then we should expect that all of the islands under the same colonial administration on Pohnpei should have developed the same sort of relationship with and the same sort of responses to that administration. So Nukuoro, Ngatik, Pingelap, Mokil, Pohnpei, and Kosrae islands should all have the same relationship with the administration and should have changed in the same ways as Kapingamarangi. This is clearly false (see Carroll 1977 and Lieber 1990 for specific examples).

What you will see in the account that follows is how the relationship between the colonial administration and the atoll forms the *context* of change in the atoll social order, which in turn forms the context for change in the organization of fishing activity. The form of the relationship between colonials and atoll people, that is, the *pattern* of messages exchanged between them (Bateson 1972: 257-258), depends on how the parties perceive one another. Thus, how Kapinga people respond to colonial demands and policies depends as much on Kapinga premises about the nature of relationships between themselves and outsiders as on what colonial authorities may have had in mind. These premises, because they are largely unconscious, abstract models of relational form, are not subject to conscious reflection and are, therefore, resistant to change. For these reasons, there is nothing linear about the history of change in this community. That is, there is nothing domino-like in the progression of events that produce change in how activities are organized: A happened, which caused B to happen, which caused C to happen, etc.. Change is of a part-to-whole character such that (a) fishing activity changes as it is recontextualized, remaining part of the atoll social order, but a differently organized part of a differently organized whole, and (b) understanding what has changed and how it has changed depends on understanding what has not changed (cf. Carroll 1977). Specifically, I'll be focussing on how a changing social order is shaped by unchanging premises about what it means to be a person, what it means for people to live together, what authority is and what its sources are, and what change and innovation mean to a Kapinga person.

Persons, Groups, and the Location of Authority

Kapinga people define "the person" in a way that makes what it means to be a person identical with what it means to live together. Unlike our western understanding of the person as an "individual," a self-contained, self-motivated, self-reliant being describable in terms of his or her attributes, Kapinga see the person as a *relatum*, as one end of a social relationship. The person is a locus of shared biographies, a node where social relationships intersect and where things and messages are given and received.

It is the relationship that defines the person, not *vice versa*. For example, Kapinga distinguish people from animals in terms of the ability to establish and maintain differentiated categories of relationship. Kapinga observe dogs and cats mating with their siblings and their offspring, saying that "Animals do not know who their relatives are; people do." In another example, a woman is considered promiscuous not for having sexual relations with more than one man at a given time, but for maintaining several sexual liaisons without establishing the formal relationship of 'lovers' with any of them.

People are distinguishable from one another by the styles with which they conduct their relationships with others and with non-human things around them. Speech styles, types of humor, special interest in particular crafts or with special aspects of craft production, etc., all become foci of personal differences that people actively cultivate. The way that Kapinga label differing personal styles illustrates how the idea of the relationship defining the person is embedded within the language. What we would call a carpenter is, literally in Kapinga, a 'person who fabricates things.' A fisherman is, literally, a 'person who works (with) fish.' A comedian is a 'person who causes other people to laugh.' In each case, what we think of as individuals' special skills and talents (properties of a person) are, for Kapinga, properties of a relationship between people or between persons and things.

Now, this way of defining the person, that is, as a part of a larger whole (the relationship) has a crucial implication that contrasts sharply with our western conceptions of the individual and the social order. We see persons as individuals, complete in him- or herself, such that individuals are somehow naturally self-contained. To generate a social hierarchy requires people to do something, to consciously create an otherwise artificial social asymmetry through negotiation: the social contract of Hobbes, Locke, and Jefferson (Becker 1958). Indeed, we continue to couch the community-person relation in terms of the collectivity versus the individual, both in popular and academic parlance. But from a Kapinga point of view, hierarchy is the natural state of human existence. Just as the person is part of a relationship, those relationships coalesce in a number of ways to form larger sets, like cliques and gossip networks, or groups like families, men's house groups, work groups, the priesthood, and the like. These groups are part of the larger 'community,' which is part of the island. Each level of the hierarchy constrains the one below it, as is evident in Figures 9.2 and 9.3 in Part Two. At the top of the traditional hierarchy were the gods, who were not constrained by anything, but who could be importuned--by the right people--if addressed properly. The Kapinga conception of a universal order is that of a hierarchy wherein constraint is applied in a top-down direction: the gods constrain the island; the high priest, through communication with the gods, constrains his assistants, men's house headmen and their *tomono*, and heads of families, all of whom, in turn exercise control over their members; social relations between people serve to constrain the parties to that relationship, who in turn constrain their own inner selves--the lowest level of the hierarchy and the domain of true chaos. While personal style channels a person's ways of dealing with others and makes him or her predictable to others, it also masks the inner self, which Kapinga call a person's 'insides' (cf. Mageu 1989, 1990).

A person's inner self consists of desire, emotion, will and thought. Each of these parts of the self develop at different times during infancy and are thought to act independently of one another (in contrast to the integration expected of the Western individual). Without constant vigilance, unconstrained will or desire, etc., may surface unbidden, dominating the person's actions with disastrous results. Unconstrained thought, for example, causes insanity. Unconstrained desire leads to one's being constantly duped or to sexual involvements that rupture important relationships. Unconstrained emotion can be an omen of someone's impending death or can attract the attention of spirits. Most dangerous of all is unconstrained will, which always involves disaster to others. A fisherman thoughtlessly announcing what fish he is after risks insulting the gods, who will withhold those fish from him and from other fishermen. One high priest defied the rule that priests must be buried in the sacred area on Souhou, demanding instead to be interred oceanward on his own compound. High waves hit that islet, disinterring his bones and causing damage to his and other families' land. These examples illustrate the necessity to control the self, and that control is embedded in the hierarchy of constraint that begins with the gods.

The sort of hierarchy described here is a conceptual hierarchy, a principle by which Kapinga people appear to organize their experiences, acts, and utterances. They talk and act in a way that is consistent with the principle that people do what they do either because they are constrained to do so by others or by their own habits of style (or because expected constraints have somehow failed to operate properly). Ask any Kapinga why he or she is doing something, and the answer is always that some other person or group of people told him or her to do it. Even when the task is done gladly, it is never because one wants to do it. To admit that is to admit to willfulness. One's intentions, in other words, are carefully managed.[2]

While the Kapinga conception of hierarchy may give the appearance of people and groups as automatons awaiting the next instruction from above, this is an appearance based on western premises of individualism and personal autonomy. Kapinga people certainly don't think or act like automatons. The relevant considerations for deciding and acting for Kapinga are one's own needs, the nature of the current situation, the people present in the situation, and what likely effects on one's relationships might follow from a particular course of action. Rather than an inherent right to do what one wants and to be what one chooses to be (or any obligation to be self-reliant), Kapinga think of a person as responsible to others--minimally for being attentive to who they are, what they need, want, and deserve, and for responding accordingly. Personal initiative is not expected; adaptability to situations and to people is. The western notion of autonomous action has as its Kapinga counterpart the value placed on flexible response. Flexible response presupposes some latitude for people to choose how they will respond to others, but wrong or inappropriate choices are not overlooked. There is a thin line between being accommodating and being patronizing, between being knowledgeable and being boastful, or being helpful and being willful. People cross that line with some regularity.

The Kapinga conception of hierarchy shows one other peculiarity, a very important one, that differentiates it from western thinking. We think of a hierarchy as almost always involving a potentially infinite regress of levels, e.g., from gene to chromosome to nucleus to cell to tissue and so on up to the biosphere and beyond. Any whole can be seen as part of some yet larger whole that contextualizes and constrains it (Berrien 1968, Whyte, Wilson, and Whyte 1969, Simon 1968, Pattee 1973). Not so the Kapinga hierarchy. The gods that constitute the top level of the hierarchy constrain the community, but neither the island nor the community is considered to be part of the gods. Nor are the gods part of the community, even though they sleep there. The gods are beings apart from and outside the social order, who control the environmental conditions on which human survival depend. It was this knowledge that formed the basis of the Kapinga conception of power, authority, and their sources.

Since power originates with the gods, community authority is based on the differential distribution of the capability for communicating with them, then power and authority ultimately comes from outside the community and remains there.[3] So when someone tells you that he or she is doing something for X or because X needs it done, what you are hearing is a justification for a personal decision based on a relationship between that person and X. The higher the hierarchical level that relationship is (family, men's house, etc.), the more legitimate and compelling that decision is. Thus, personal decisions are empowered by their contexts, and the higher the level of context, the more authoritative the decision is.

The Kapinga conceptions of the person, the social hierarchy, and authority not only shape the ways Kapinga understand and conduct social relationships and social activities in their many contexts, but also the ways in which these are most likely to change over time. Change of any sort begins with innovation that is subject to public scrutiny, implying a personal decision and its public enactment. How Kapinga people regard an innovation is determined by the same premises of personhood, relationship, and hierarchy that shape people's perceptions of any other personal decision and its enactment.

Kapinga regard innovation in their community with a great deal of ambivalence, because creating something new is an act of sheer will. The innovator is greeted with ridicule until his or her creation proves to be useful or aesthetically pleasing (until it is clear that the innovator had others' interests at heart all along). For example, the young man who undertook to build the first Nukuoro style canoe on the atoll was taunted unmercifully over the months it took to complete construction. When he demonstrated the canoe's superiority over the Kapinga model, he was celebrated.

There are two sorts of exceptions to Kapinga's mistrust of innovators. One is the person who is known from childhood to be creative, the composer of songs and chants and the habitual innovator whose creativity is regarded as part of his or her personal style. A habitual innovator is called *dangada dili mee*, 'person who creates things,' puzzle solvers, as Kapinga describe them. One man, referred to above, figured out how to make the triggerfish retract its fins using "goosing" someone as an analogue. Similarly, others described were people who Westerners would call clever, solving difficult problems by identifying some aspect of the situation that can be manipulated.

The second exception to the Kapinga response to innovation is the class of novelties introduced from the outside. New food preparations, plants, tools, techniques, goods, and ideas are viewed with skeptical reserve until people are satisfied with their utility. The source of the novelty has a lot to do with people's readiness to give it a fair test. The higher the level of the hierarchy the source of the novelty, the more worthy it is of consideration. The new, the unprecedented, and the exotic is more or less empowered by its source. The person who first adopts a novelty is at less risk when he or she can say "X told me (showed me how to, suggested that I) to do this, so I'm trying it." The more powerful, prestigious, and further removed from the atoll X is, the less likely people are to denigrate the innovator.

The description of social change that follows will provide ample illustrations of how the Kapinga hierarchical empowerment of decisions and their implementation have shaped the changing organization of the social order and of the fishing activity that is part of that order.

Recreating the Social Order

At the outset, colonial interest in Kapingamarangi was mainly commercial. Ships from Rabaul and Port Moresby came occasionally after 1877 to trade manufactured goods for copra and beche-de-mer. Trade was organized by resident Europeans or Americans, mainly beachcombers and two Europeans married to Kapinga women. They negotiated exchanges with ships' supercargo for imported goods, which they doled out to their client producers. If marine ecology was not affected by colonial contact, land ecology certainly was as pandanus trees were replaced by coconut stands and taro pits increased by 40% to accommodate the role of *Cyrtosperma* (introduced by a Nukuoro in 1879) in the diet. Commercial interests were supplemented by occasional visits of tourists from Rabaul, and anthropologists of the Thilenius Expedition spent eight days on the atoll in 1910 (Eilers 1934). Other than the anthropologists, colonial agents were not very interested in internal community affairs, nor did they need to be. The *tomono* who was their liaison with the community catered to their every want. Assuming that he was the authority in the community, they referred to him as king, a title that Kapinga eventually adopted. For most Kapinga, whatever their reservations--and there were some--the high priest retained the authority on which the community's welfare depended.

The traditional task of the *tomono* was that of enforcing men's house decisions, provisioning feasts and organizing labor for men's house and cult house work projects, and assisting in the ritual initiating canoe construction. When the first Europeans came ashore and/or settled on the atoll, the task of dealing with them fell to him. Kapinga people were terrified of these early outsiders, and for good reason. In their experience, these *baalangi*, as they came to be called, were whimsically violent and benevolent, administering beatings, committing murder, demanding food, service, and copra, and bestowing western goods. By dealing with the ships' captains, the traders, and the beachcombers, the *tomono* took on the dangers but also reaped the benefits of his role, accumulating tools, utensils, clothing, and other goods, including firearms.

The *tomono* used his wealth and firepower to coerce relatives into ceding land rights to him. While the high priest maintained his position in the cult house and continued to exercise ritual restraints over fishing, the gods he represented were no longer the only powerful outsiders with whom Kapinga had to contend. One measure of power obvious to any Kapinga was that Europeans could disparage the gods and violate ritual taboos without any apparent ill effects.

Kapinga quickly learned the advantages of maintaining good relations with visiting or resident Europeans. Access to such things as sailcloth made fishermen's lives a lot easier. Even if metal fish hooks were available, they were not very useful without a dependable supply of files and pliers, for example, since barbs made fish difficult to get off a line once caught. Kapinga filed the barbs off and modified the tips of the hooks with pliers to match the head shapes of the fish for which the hooks were used. Gaining access to such goods without being dependent on the whims of the *tomono* had clearly become an issue by the late 1880's. A group of ten men formed a copra producers' association and approached a Danish sea captain married to a Kapinga woman and residing on Touhou, asking him to act as their trading representative with visiting ships. By the 1890's this group competed with the *tomono* and his partner, a resident Englishman also married to Kapinga woman. If fishing activity did not change dramatically following colonial contact, issues of access to resources for it had begun to change the shape of other economic activities and their political ramifications.

When the Japanese colonial government acquired hegemony over Micronesia from the Germans in 1914, administrative control of Kapingamarangi shifted from Rabaul to Kolonia Town on Pohnpei. The atoll became one leg of a regular shipping route from Pohnpei, going to Ngatik, Nukuoro, and Kapingamarangi, collecting copra and passengers and unloading goods to be exchanged for copra. The Kapinga's first experience with the Japanese was a detachment of soldiers that landed, marching double time with fixed bayonets to the central square on Souhou. No one remembers exactly what the commanding officer said, but what Kapinga heard was something like, "Do what we tell you or you will have to deal with these people (soldiers)." A volley of rifle shots and the presentation of the Japanese flag underlined the point. The administration sent a Japanese employee of the Nanyo Boeki Kaisha trading company to the atoll in 1915 to organize copra production, market retail goods, and to represent the administration as its local affairs officer. When this man, Furia, took up residence on the atoll, it was that detachment of soldiers that he was thought to represent.

Furia ran a retail store on the atoll, trading goods for copra. He organized a school where he taught Japanese language, writing, and arithmetic. He sent promising students to Pohnpei for schooling or for apprenticeships in the trades. He found himself in a political situation that had already undergone change from that encountered by Europeans thirty-seven years earlier. By 1914, the high priest's power had been diluted from that of his predecessors, while the power of his erstwhile underling, the *tomono*, had grown.[4] Although Furia was approached by the competing copra producers' group to act as their agent soon after taking up residence, he preferred to deal with and act through the king until he had become familiar with the populace. By 1917, he faced his first two major crises. One was a drought that began in 1916 and was to last for two years. The other was the incapacitation of the king by a stroke.

Furia continued copra production until the drought threatened the supply of drinking nuts. By early 1917, starvation and dehydration were the major problems and the king was clearly ill. Furia appointed one of his cronies to replace the ailing king and instituted a number of measures designed to conserve coconuts and stave off starvation. Furia employed the group of ten copra producers as police to enforce his conservation measures as the drought became a famine. Called "masters," they conducted surveillance of coconut use, organized netting expeditions, and administered punishments for theft, including public flogging, being staked out on the beach in the sun, and being forced to stand naked before the assembled community. But the rationing of drinking nuts and severe punishments for coconut theft were acts of desperation. By mid-year, people had begun to die.

The Nukuoro had heard about the Kapinga's plight via ship passengers. Their chief, Lekka, an ordained Protestant minister, had his people collect a ship's hold full of drinking coconuts. He sent them, along with a group of church elders, whose task was to convey the gift and convert the population to Christianity.

By the time this group of missionaries arrived on the atoll in late 1917, the cult house lay abandoned. The high priest reigning in 1916 had abdicated in favor of a younger man, who later abandoned the cult house when it became clear that nothing he could do was helping. The missionaries' task of conversion was easy. The demoralized Kapinga were perfectly prepared to believe that their false beliefs were the cause of the drought. After all, the food that the gods did not send were brought to them by people representing this new deity, and the arrival of food is, traditionally, evidence of efficacy. Conversion of the populace was accomplished rapidly. When the missionaries boarded the ship for Nukuoro, they left behind one of their number, a younger man who, with the help of two men who would both become ministers and kings, set about organizing a congregation, destroying the cult house, and building a church in its place.

The outcomes of this radical organizational change did not become immediately apparent. The atoll was still in the midst of the drought, and netting expeditions were being organized on a daily basis, employing both men and women at Furia's insistence. The expeditions were aimed at giving people some fresh water from the fish themselves, at maintaining a steady source of food, and at preventing the theft of coconuts by keeping the able bodied population off the islets. This strategy ameliorated the effects of the drought somewhat during the calm season, but with fewer netting options available during the windy season, the death toll began to mount rapidly. When the rains began again in 1918, sixty people had died (Emory 1965: 20).

An already chaotic situation was exacerbated by several events by the end of 1918. Open defiance of the masters destroyed their credibility; Furia's appointed king was forced to abdicate by public outcry over his breaking his own rules against adultery, and Furia was recalled to Pohnpei when word got back to the administration (through ship passengers) about the famine and the cruelty of punishments being administered by the masters. The son of the former *tomono* and king was elected king in a community meeting, but he resigned after six months out of fear of having to deal with the Japanese. The administration sent a man to the atoll to investigate the allegations of cruel and unusual punishment by Furia and the masters. The people interviewed all protected the masters by blaming their depredations on Furia, who eventually faced charges in an administrative hearing on Pohnpei.

The Japanese administration was not pleased with Furia's handling of atoll problems. Its interest in the atoll was that of a steady supply of copra and laborers and a dependable market, not in managing atoll crises. Kapinga were free to regulate their own internal affairs as they would with the tacit assurance that the administration would back the island chief if need be (which they did on at least one occasion). The death of the old king and the abdication of two successors set the stage for a new political era by 1919. The king was, for the first time, appointed by consensus of the adult population. Following traditional rules of succession, however, the consensus choice was in the line of patrilineal succession of the *tomono* of the central Souhou men's house. This man, King David, was also a leader of the fledgling church and its strongest local advocate. He would become its first native pastor. For the first time, ritual and political authority became fused in a single, secular position. The power of that position derived, as it always had, from powerful agents outside the community: the Japanese colonial administration and the little known Jehovah.

David could and did employ the threat of sending those who violated his edicts to Pohnpei for corporal punishment by the Japanese. This threat was made credible by reports of public flogging of Micronesians and at least one Kapinga on Pohnpei, and it lent the image of autocratic power. His power was both constrained and made legitimate by his position in the church. One of the great appeals of the new church was its ideology of social equality of its congregants. Calling the pre-Christian era a 'time of darkness,' church leaders used the social and ritual inequalities of the sacred-secular class distinction as examples of the unenlightened wickedness of 'the time of darkness.' High priests and their functionaries could coerce land owners to cede plots to them, using these ill-gotten gains to purchase sexual favors, according to church members. This ideological contrast served to constrain the king to be even-handed in his dealings with his subjects. Indeed, King David is remembered with reverence and admiration for his scrupulous fairness and devotion to meeting the needs of the island and its people as he perceived them.

One of the needs people considered to be urgent was a dependable supply of cash. For those without access to work or close relatives on Pohnpei, the only source of cash was copra. This depended on access to land resources, which, by the turn of the century, had become a constant source of inter- and intrafamily land disputes. Following a precedent set by Furia, David handled land disputes by calling community meetings and taking testimony from all adults with relevant knowledge of the history of the land in question. Based on this testimony, David would render a decision, either awarding the land to one claimant (and his or her family) or dividing the land and awarding portions to both claimants. These hearings were precedents for what became a new embodiment of the community, a kind of monthly town meeting with a majority rule-consensus mix for ratifying community policy. The meetings would begin with a prayer, followed by the king's sermon on proper behavior (especially that of young people, the categorical culprits) and the king's announcements of new policies on such subjects as organization of house roofing, assessments for feasts, or major construction projects. In the discussion that followed, the king might (but did not have to) modify details of his announcement. While this has the image of autocratic decision, the realities were far more complex than that.

The king already knew what the responses to his announcements would be before the meeting began, since he and his assistant and secretary (his half-brother, Duiai) had already floated the issue in informal discussions months before the meeting. These discussions typically took place in the men's houses on Souhou and Weelua during those days and evenings when men gathered to work on gear, plan expeditions, and converse. While the king and his assistant were subtle in floating trial balloons or simply raising issues with a question, their fellows soon came to understand the significance of these conversations. The men's houses became the major centers of political activity where, the details of public policy were aired, directions of opinion determined, and nascent consensus built. What appeared publicly as authoritative pronouncements of orders of the king were actually the representations of public consensus emanating from the men's houses.

By combining the moral authority of the church and consensus developed in the men's houses (and ratified in community meetings) with the political authority of the colonial government, David managed to reorganize the Kapinga polity by late 1919. To appreciate the magnitude of this accomplishment, you need to consider that, in going from chaos to reorganization within five months' time, David began with the stigma of membership in the masters (albeit the most moderate of them), with no guidelines from the colonial administration, and with at least three possible modes of leadership that he might have adopted. These included the high priest model of unilateral authority backed by outside agents, the *tomono* model of the enforcer backed by henchmen, and the men's house headman model of the consensus builder recontextualized in the monthly community meeting. Each of these posed its own problems and uncertainties, but the constraints on his authority were clear enough at the outset.

Commanding older people would be difficult. Any arbitrary punishment for violating rules would not be tolerated by the populace or by the administration on Pohnpei--David had barely dodged a bullet as one of the masters, and he knew it all too well. The new church was aggressively formulating rules for personal conduct and demanding cooperative labor for church projects. Every one of David's decisions would be subject to to review in the men's houses, at church elders' meetings, and gossip networks. While the community meeting had been useful as a formal instrument for announcing decisions and hearing land disputes, it had its own pitfalls, particularly if community opinion was opposed to a chief or a chiefly decree. Consensus building was the most viable operating strategy for a young leader who was certain only of the constraints on his authority and uncertain of the extent of his responsibilities and the power he could command to implement his decisions. The men's houses were the natural loci of consensus building. All of these issues crystallized into matters of operational convenience and efficiency in the first test of David's leadership in late 1919.

Before he left the atoll in early 1919, Furia arranged for ninety adults to be transported to Pohnpei to reduce the population pressure on the slowly recovering food resources. Hired as laborers for the Nanyo Boeki Kaisha plantations and shipping facilities, half of these people died in a dysentery epidemic by mid-year. The colonial administration, at Furia's urging, offered the bedraggled survivors a leasehold for Kapinga to live on while on Pohnpei. Kapinga chose a site allowing easy access to the lagoon, twenty-one acres just north of the administrative center overlooking an inlet between Kolonia Town and Sokes Island. The area is called Porakied, and the Kapinga village established there bears that name. The administration considered the village a colony, and its development was the new king's problem. The land, half of which is steep cliff, was undeveloped, dense underbrush that would take a major clearing and planting operation before it could be habitable. David quickly found men's house discussions useful both for gathering information about Pohnpei from men who had been there as sailors and for developing a long term plan for rotating groups of settlers with each ship visit. Community meetings were important for gathering support and for recruiting settlers. Using a men's house model, he appointed a headman from among the first group of settlers as his representative in the village.

Porakied village, one of several ethnic enclaves in the area, provided a home base for Kapinga coming to Pohnpei as government laborers, to seek economic opportunities, medical care, schooling, church work, and adventure. Once Kapinga were able to transport canoes to Pohnpei, they quickly established a virtual monopoly over the supply of yellow fin tuna on the island, selling tuna and reef fish to Japanese and Micronesians. Kapinga were firmly established on Pohnpei by the mid-1920s. Regular shipping between Pohnpei, Ngatik, Nukuoro, and Kapingamarangi facilitated contacts, including intermarriage, among these populations.

The many discussions that went into the decisions on who and how many people would go to work on clearing, planting, and construction in Porakied, how they would be provisioned, how long they would be required to stay, what equipment (e.g., canoes, tools, cuttings, etc.) they would take, how much of their time would have to be put into village labor (versus fishing for cash), how often a group of settlers would rotate, and the like served as operational precedents for organizing the activity of political decision making. I suspect that without the exigency of organizing the settlement of Porakied, the reorganization of the atoll social order would have taken much longer to accomplish. I doubt that the results would have been much different, however, given the administration's preference for dealing with a single representative of the community, the community's preference for being represented by a single office, and the obvious constraints on anyone who occupied the liaison's position. This is not to minimize David's importance in the reorganization process, but I think that what is most significant about his personal role in the transformation other than his astuteness is the fact that because of his relative youth, because he had narrowly avoided facing criminal charges, and because of his leadership position in the church, he was probably more acutely aware of the constraints on his position than another person might have been.[5]

Thus, in the two year period between 1917 and 1919, the context of fishing activity had altered radically. The entire hierarchy of constraints emanating from the presence of the gods, along with the gods themselves, had been eliminated in one fell swoop. The men's houses no longer had the ritual sanctions nor the *tomono* positions that had buttressed their operation. Access to non-native fishing technology had become regularized, along with new avenues for acquiring it. Fishermen no longer had to depend on copra alone to buy goods. With the establishment of Porakied, they could acquire a great deal more cash by commercial fishing on Pohnpei, being assured of a place to live and wage work when fishing was unproductive. Fishing activity on the atoll, in the meantime, began to change rapidly once the drought was over and people's lives began to settle back into some semblance of normality.

The most dramatic change was in canoe ownership and canoe technology. The demise of the priesthood left landowners free to control their trees as they would. As the atoll was recovering from the effects of the drought, people without canoes began to construct them. The numbers of new canoes increased dramatically with the introduction of the Nukuoro style canoe in 1922. The Kapinga canoe, with its washstrakes, gunwale rails, three outrigger booms and hundreds of yards of sennit cord for the complex lashings (Buck 1950: 180-192) required a heavy expenditure in materials, time, and food to feed the workers. The Nukuoro canoe, a single hull craft without washstrakes or gunwales, and with two outrigger booms, was more simply and rapidly constructed, required far less materials, and was faster and more maneuverable under sail. By 1947, Kenneth Emory and Peter Buck found not one traditional canoe still in use on the atoll.[6] With the rapid increase in canoes, the numbers of men angling rather than netting began to increase.

Nukuoro fishing methods were introduced along the the canoe. Trolling under sail, enthusiastically adopted by Kapinga fishermen, replaced bonito fishing and *gadigadi laa nua*. Using lures made bait less of an issue in trolling, while current was no longer an impediment unless it was running fast at a shallow depth. Nukuoro also introduced spear fishing in the 1920s, using a long wooden spear and diving goggles acquired from the Japanese. Popular with young men, who usually go out spear fishing in groups, it brings them under water with the fish. Consequently, a new generation of men learned new things about fish, such as feeding patterns, escape strategies and routes, etc.. They found where large crayfish hide and how to entice them out of their reef rock caves. Young men were becoming the first generation to know things about fish not learned from or known to their elders (cf. Mead 1970).

The make up of the angling population changed along with its numbers. With gods no longer a constraint on the personnel of a canoe, relative age no longer determined the composition of the crew as it had previously. Age was a factor in that older men were more likely to have the canoe and the gear for angling. But even this began to change by the late 1920s.

Japanese trading companies on Pohnpei had, with government help, established a number of agricultural experiment stations and plantations producing copra, rice, tobacco, and cacao. These ventures required both labor and roads for transporting products. The colonial administration responded to these needs by conscripting laborers from all the outer islands of the Pohnpei district (including Mokil, Pingelap, and Kosrae along with the southern atolls). Each ship took a group of young men to Pohnpei for a four to six month labor contract period, paying the men when the contract ended. Some of these laborers remained on Pohnpei to acquire cash and goods through commercial fishing and wage labor. Following a familiar Pacific pattern, these men purchased goods not available on the atoll, such as lines, hooks, leaders, lures, sinkers, nets, goggles, canvas for sails, and the like to send or to take back to Kapingamarangi. They also did a good deal of scavenging at the numerous major construction sites around Kolonia Town, particularly for heavy cable for making fish hooks. Just as sail cloth had replaced mat sails by the turn of the century, purchased cord and nets had begun to replace all but flying fish nets and coir and purse nets by the late 1920s. It was younger, not older men who were the major source of supply of these items.

The introduction of the throwing net in the 1920s by young men who had learned its use on Pohnpei rendered most pole-and-line techniques and some of the netting techniques obsolete. After chumming on the seaward shore of the islets, for example, the throwing net could get most of the collected fish in a single throw. The fisherman could maximize the catch by throwing a rock seaward of the fish, frightening them into running toward the islet shore where they could be covered by the net. Surrounding fish outside the breakers and driving them toward a waiting net was replaced by a single man stalking the fish from inland. Moving slowly to observe where trevally and other surface feeders congregate and crouching to hide his presence, the fisherman picks his spot and stands up only to release the throwing net. Using this sort of technique, the throwing net replaced *gubenge taile laa dua, gubenge manini, gubenge buu awa,* and *gubenge tawe*. While the *gubenge tawe*, 'netting flying fish,' was practiced only rarely, use of a throwing net made it possible to catch flying fish as they entered the lagoon in the evening just before a new moon.

Kapinga continued to practice other sorts of netting methods in the traditional repertoire, but on a much more occasional basis than in pre-Christian days. Without the priestly controls over the canoe supply, the headman no longer had the dependable labor force guaranteed by the old ritual sanctions. The men's house canoes were no longer as important for making fishing possible, given the rapid equality of access to canoes. The men's house, however, still owned the coir and purse nets for surrounds, and the headman continued to control their use. As cheap, manufactured nets became available on the atoll, expeditions such as netting goatfish, sweeping the channel, and surrounds at in-shore coral heads could be organized by small groups of men on the spot or by prior agreement. Clearly, the headman no longer had his pre-Christian control over netting activities. During the transitional period of the 1920s, his role became that of a consensus builder. That is, he listened to discussions among the fishermen, finding out who would be angling the next day, who was available to go netting, what these men wanted to do, and summarizing the emerging consensus by announcing what expedition he (and/or the nets) would be available for the next day. The headman, too, had the option of going out angling.

The new Protestant church was not entirely passive in the gradual transformation of fishing activity and the role of the men's houses. Its most important contribution to the reorganization of fishing activity was the introduction of Western calendrical reckoning, particularly the seven day week. Sunday was the sabbath, during which no work could be performed. This interdiction required that fish caught on Saturdays be sufficient for meals on both days. Given that canoes would be out on Saturdays, Fridays would have to be used for collecting sufficient vegetable food for the entire weekend. Because Souhou has few food resources and Weelua cannot be counted on to provide sufficient coconuts, taro and breadfruit (in season) on a weekly basis, Friday food collecting almost always involves going to an outer islet with enough male labor to get and transport the food. A household with two or more canoes and two or more adult males could deploy one canoe for food collecting and another for fishing on a Friday, but only if all the necessary food could be collected from a single islet or islets in the same quadrant of the reef. In general, very little fishing is done on Fridays unless tuna and rainbow runners are in season.

The task of provisioning weekend meals (and holiday feasts) fell to the men's houses. The headman was responsible for deciding the particular netting technique employed, but the usual ones have been variations of 'coconut leaf netting,' which is now called, simply, *di gubenge*, 'the net.' The headman had other options, of course. If Saturday happened to fall on one of the first three days of spinefoot season, he could choose to do that with certain knowledge of a large catch. He might choose rainbow runners in season (coordinating with anglers to make sure they stayed clear of the nets). If tuna were in season and plentiful, the headman might eschew netting altogether (unless some families demanded an expedition). The headman could also be importuned to organize a netting expedition in special circumstances, such as funerals and first birthday feasts, especially during windy season when there were fewer productive options.

Since the 1920s, then, fishermen's work schedules have changed from a work month to a work week during which fishing is possible for five of every seven days. The men's house became central to only one of the five fishing days. The other four days might involve fishing organized through the men's house or it might not, depending on the availability of fish and of fishermen. This in turn depended on the current productivity of angling and the availability of bait.

As men's houses became increasingly marginal to the organization of fishing activity, their numbers decreased. There were five men's house groups in the 1850s, located on Souhou, Weelua, Hale, and Torongahai. By 1930 there were two, one on Souhou and the other on Weelua. This was partly the result of population shifts. During the drought, Furia and his puppet chief had the population settled on Souhou and Weelua in order to control coconut theft. The introduction of the new school and church kept people on the central islets.

Along with their numbers, the solidarity of men's houses as social groups declined. Men's houses had traditionally competed with one another for prestige as successful fishing groups. This spirit of competition extended to which group went out first after the high priest lifted a taboo on the lagoon, for example. If the high priest showed favoritism by notifying one men's house well before the others, a brawl could result. In one instance, a men's house on the ocean side of Souhou went out netting after being notified of the lifting of a taboo. The men's house on the ocean side, seeing its rival making a surround, rushed out to the lagoon and surrounded their net with its own while its men surrounded their rivals, instigating a rumble.

Men's houses commonly commemorated particularly successful expeditions by composing chants recounting their details. On occasion, two men's houses would hold a chant competition, one group hosting its rival. The guests would perform their most recent compositions first, followed by the hosts. Elders of both groups would confer to decide the winner, while the hosts provided food for the gathering. When church leaders declared traditional chanting to be 'uncouth' and 'the work of Satan,' these competitions ceased.

The men's house organization did not disappear with Christianity, nor did it cease to be a viable institution for organizing fishing activity. Men of all ages continued to gather there during the day and in the evening to work on gear, to converse, and to plan group expeditions. Age stratification continued to structure communication among the men. But the frequency of group expeditions declined with the obsolescence of several netting methods, with increasing numbers of men angling, and with the continual absence of so many younger men (through labor conscription) most likely to participate in group expeditions.

The elaborate network of weirs fell into disrepair through gradual disuse, leaving only one intact by 1947. As the use of weirs diminished, traps used at weirs also ceased being made. The use of the white eel trap declined while moray eel trapping expanded once the closely guarded knowledge of its ritual and chants became obsolete.

Fishing activity after 1917 had become recontextualized in two important ways. One was the expansion of the environment of fishermen and fishing activity afforded by travel to other islands. Pohnpei and Nukuoro became avenues for importing new gear and new techniques to the atoll, particularly by younger men who, perforce, became the middlemen in the traffic of goods and ideas, a very new position for this category of person in the social order. The second level of recontextualization was the reorganization of the atoll social order. The effects of this reorganization are palpable, but far more subtle.

Without the collapse of the cult house and its hierarchical order of constraints on fishing activity, new techniques such as trolling and spear fishing in the deep lagoon and outer reef slope would have been, like bonito fishing, the prerogatives of select elders with canoes. This would have left only the throwing net as the new technique available to the ordinary fisherman. It was the collapse of the traditional system of hierarchical constraints, made permanent by conversion to Christianity, that irreversibly changed the lives of fishermen and the organization of fishing activity. With a more or less equitable distribution of canoes over the population, canoe ownership had already tripled by the late 1920s. All of the new techniques (except, possibly, trolling) could be employed by individual fishermen, whose range (given canoe ownership) included anywhere that a technique could be used. None of these changes involved new modes of organization, however.

Fishermen in the 1930s were organizing fishing activity in the same ways their fathers and grandfathers had. Angling still required one to four men per canoe, netting still required a group with a leader, adequate manpower, and appropriate equipment, and the like. What had changed was the frequency with which each organizational mode was deployed. Angling crews and individual fishermen with spears or with throwing nets were being deployed more frequently than netting groups organized through the men's house. Men's house groups went out when there were enough men who agreed to participate in an expedition. The only ritual constraints on fishing activity were those of provisioning church sponsored feasts (e.g., at Christmas) and the seven day work week. Men's house organizing of fishing activity depended on fishermen's choices, not *vice versa*. It is precisely this *choice* that embodies change in the organization of fishing activity. This is clear even at the level of how micro-ecological variables constrain fishing activity.

The availability of bait traditionally contrasted with daily tide patterns as constraints that were salient to different categories of fishermen. By the late 1920s, their salience had become that of constraints on the choices that any fisherman could make. If bait was unavailable, angling was impossible, so netting became the next best option. At that point, the next set of choices was where, when, with whom, and with what equipment. The repertoire of fishing techniques had been transformed from that of categories of techniques available to categories of fishermen to a menu of options available to most, if not all fishermen. Fishermen were opting for the most prestigious techniques and/or the newest techniques unless otherwise constrained by microecological variables or by periodic ritual occasions (including such things as weddings, funerals, and first birthday feasts).

No one saw a problem with any of this. Fishermen appreciated and enjoyed their new-found access to the sorts of activity that every fisherman lives for. Older men got the canoes that they had been previously denied. Younger men, with their access to cash and goods, could help to finance their fathers' and elder brothers' new canoes and could look forward to getting their own canoes eventually. If enfranchisement of fishermen as canoe owners drew them away from men's house activity, their enfranchisement in the process of political decision making drew them to the men's houses, where political consensus on major decisions and personal influence were established.

This pattern of change bears some remarkable similarities to the one Ward Goodenough found on Onotoa atoll in Kiribati during approximately the same time period. I turn now to a comparison of his findings with my own.

Onotoa, Kapingamarangi, and the Organization of Change

Ward Goodenough originally developed his method of using activity as an analytical unit for the same reason I developed mine--as an efficient way of collecting lots of useful information very quickly under considerable time constraints. Using the method first on Onotoa Atoll in Kiribati and later on New Britain, he realized that an understanding of how a community organizes its activities permits an observer to assess the most probable directions social change may take when a community is confronted by unprecedented events (and/or development programs). In *Cooperation and Change* (1963: 337-347), he demonstrated the utility of activity analysis for forecasting change, focussing on fishing activity and its ramifications for the Onotoan social order.

Traditionally, most fishing on Onotoa was in-shore fishing using nets and surround techniques. A very few men practiced deep sea angling, which was prestigeous but contributed far less to the diet than group netting. The reason for the predominance of group fishing was the paucity of canoes, Onotoa producing even less suitable construction materials than Kapingamarangi. The organization of group fishing, therefore, was even more critical to Onotoans' survival than to Kapinga.

On Onotoa, fishing groups were organized by the extended family, a group of kin residing together. A married woman usually lived with her husband's family, so that the typical residential group was composed of a core of related males and their spouses and children. Extended families were parts of larger groups called *kaainga*, each of which consisted of the descendants (counted through males or females) of its founding ancestor. The *kaainga* was associated with a tract of land that belonged to its founder and was managed by its senior male headman. Extended families, thus, lived on *kaainga* land. A *kaainga* was responsible for protection of and for maintaining order among its members. It exacted revenge and restitution for damage suffered by its members at the hands of members of another group. It was from *kaainga* members that fishing groups larger than a single extended family were recruited.

The prohibition of warfare and private retribution by the British colonial government in the 19th century obviated some of the major functions of the *kaainga*, but internal order and fishing group organization remained its prerogatives. This began to change in the early 20th century, however, as British colonials began phosphate mining operations on Ocean Island. The necessity for a large labor force led to intensive recruiting throughout the Gilbert Islands, and young Onotoan males signed on as wage laborers, spending two or more years working on Ocean Island. They used their wages to buy and send back to their relatives such goods as cloth, cooking utensils, bicycles, tobacco, and steel cutting tools (Goodenough 1963: 338). But more importantly, wage workers spent a good deal of money to buy North American redwood, canvas, and paint for canoes. By 1951 over 15% of the island's population was on Ocean Island and there were two sailing canoes for every three adult men on Onotoa.

The results of these changes parallel those on Kapingamarangi. As more men acquired canoes and spent their time deep sea fishing, they spent correspondingly less time at group-organized in-shore fishing. Owning a canoe or having a partnership as a crew member on someone else's canoe (with an even split of the catch and of canoe maintenance) enabled young men to establish their own independent households at marriage rather than having to live in their father's households. With less time spent at in-shore fishing in any case, the extended family lost its major *raison d'etre* and its personnel. With the declining frequency of group fishing, group owned fish weirs fell into disrepair. Group ownership rights to fishing sites around the coral heads were allowed to lapse to the extent the lagoon had been declared public domain by 1951 (Goodenough 1963: 339). What group fishing was still done could be organized on the spot by *ad hoc* parties of kin.

As changing residence patterns weakened the organization of the extended family and the authority of its head, the larger *kaainga* that sustained and organized the extended family was similarly denuded of its personnel, its authority, and its major contributions to the maintenance of personal welfare. By 1951, problems of personal security and social order rendered

> neighbor more dependent on the good will of neighbor and increased the need for cooperation at the community level.
>
> The community meeting house, *mwaneaba*, was the remaining institution capable of meeting these residual needs. Popular acceptance of Christianity deprived it of some of its traditional functions and meaning, transferring them to the Church, but the *mwaneaba* continues to be of tremendous importance to Onotoan life. In former times, the *kaainga* stood between the individual and the community in several important matters, but it does so no longer. The *mwaneaba* is itself organized into a series of seats, *bwoti*, with which community offices are associated. All persons with the right to the same seat are direct descendants of the founding ancestor and together constitute an organized kin group in *mwaneaba* affairs. Principles of *bwoti* membership differ from those of *kaainga* membership, and their operation has not been affected by the changes we have recounted. Nevertheless, they were such as to produce a group whose local membership overlapped considerably with that of the *kaainga*, bringing together much the same kinds of kinsmen. Thus the meetinghouse was able to provide an organization of personnel ready-made to function as a substitute for the *kaainga* and to do so in the context of increased individual dependence on the community as a whole. In this way, the *mwaneaba* has, if anything, gained in functional importance as the *kaainga* has disappeared. (Goodenough 1963: 341-342)

The similarity of our approaches can account for our attention being focussed on the same sorts of constraints on fishing activity, but not for the similarities in our results. Onotoa and Kapingamarangi are, after all, atolls, both subject to periodic droughts (Alkire 1981: 27), and both supporting a limited variety of plant growth and food crops. Onotoa supports even fewer food plants than Kapingamarangi, lacking breadfruit trees, for example. Wood suitable for canoe construction was, thus, scarce on Onotoa. According to Goodenough (1963: 338), "...much labor was required piecing together small irregular planks adzed out with shell tools."

The only protein source in plentiful supply on either atoll is fish, although shellfish seem to have been more plentiful and more regularly captured on Onotoa than Kapingamarangi. Given their relative sizes, numbers, and habitats, as well as constraints of available technology, deep sea and lagoon fish are captured most efficiently with line and hook from a canoe. Reef and lagoon shallows fish are captured most efficiently by the coordinated effort of a number of people using a surround technique. Either alternative for capture is capable of satisfying subsistence needs, but each has different technological and organizational requirements. Two or three persons form the most efficient angling group, while many more people are required for surround fishing with nets and traps. Any constraint that limits the number of available canoes limits the capacity of fishermen to satisfy food requirements with off-shore fishing techniques. This leaves group organized expeditions to take up the slack. In order to be dependable, however, surround techniques demand a dependable supply of manpower whose size must at least equal that required by those techniques in the repertoire deploying the largest number of people to be effective. A standing group of some sort, however recruited and organized, is a minimal requirement for group fishing on a regular basis. Conversely, any change that obviates constraints on the number of available canoes, enabling off-shore fishing dependably to satisfy food requirements will (a) make group fishing less imperative, (b) draw off the standing group's manpower, and (c) threaten the integrity of the group that organizes surround fishing. From this point of view, the processes of change on these two islands would appear to be identical.

The organization of fishing activity does not change qualitatively on either island. While there are new items of hardware, e.g., metal fish hooks, manufactured nets and lines, canvas sails, etc., and some new methods there are no new ways of organizing fishing activity invented or borrowed from elsewhere. Organizational change on both islands is a change in the *relative frequencies* with which particular organizational modes are deployed. In this regard, direction of change on both islands was identical. It is evolutionary rather than revolutionary change. The causes of change are also identical--new access to wood for canoe construction facilitated by a change in the environmental context that shaped such access. The particular historical events that reshaped the context of access to wood on each island were different but still analogous. Scarcity of wood on Onotoa is a result of island soils and rainfall. What wood was available was parceled out to to prestigeous men who control kin groups and land use. It is the relationship of the island to its larger environment, changed forever by colonial control and intense labor recruiting in the 19th century and thereafter that recontextualizes Onotoans' access to wood. On Kapingamarangi, it is the collapse of the cult house and conversion to Christianity that facilitates access to wood. This would seem to be more an internal social change, but the presence of colonialists, their imperviousness to attack by gods and spirits, and several other events had already sewn the seeds of skepticism among Kapinga regarding the efficacy of their ritual. The failure of two high priests to bring rain was simply evidence that the Europeans and skeptics were correct. That this was the case is exemplified by the fact that the cult house stood abandoned for months prior to the arrival of the Nukuoro missionaries. The point is that on Kapingamarangi, too, new access to wood is the result of people's redefinition of what constituted the environment and the ways in which the island and its environment were related. In the sense of redefining environmental context of access to canoes, Onotoa and Kapingamarangi are identical cases.

Now, this concentration on the process level might seem to gloss over some important differences in (a) the historical events that precipitated change, (b) how these two social orders were organized, and (c) the social structural outcomes of change. After all, the cult house disappeared while the *mwaneaba* did not. The *kaainga* disappeared, while the men's house did not. Historically, it is a change in Kapinga social organization that leads to the redistribution of canoes and access to deep sea fishing, while it is a redistribution of canoes and access to deep sea fishing that leads to social structural change on Onotoa. Without question, these are real differences, particularly when viewed at the level of social structures. But when these same institutions are viewed as standing groups for the organization of activities, their differences are not quite so sharp.

The *mwaneaba* clearly constitutes a standing group that, prior to Christianity, organized ritual activity and such political activities as regulating relations among the *kaainga*, receiving and feting visitors, and arranging island celebrations. It was a multi-purpose group that operated by consensus organized through internally ranked "seats." The

Kapinga cult house constituted an internally ranked standing group that organized a single category of activity--ritual. It stands to reason that the loss of ritual activity should threaten the existence of the cult house but not necessarily that of the *mwaneaba*. But even so, there is no reason to assume that abandoning cult house ritual should render its organization of ranked priests useless if that group were adaptable for other activities. It is here that we see the most profound difference between the meeting house and the cult house as institutions--in what Goodenough calls the "instrumental linkage" of activities, the extent to which activities derive their value from providing conditions necessary for the performance of some other activity or activities. Goodenough refers to this more instrumental importance of an activity as having *extrinsic* value as opposed to activities from whose performance people derive personal satisfaction--those activities which have *intrinsic* value (Goodenough 1963: 333-334).

It is clear that cult house ritual was essentially instrumental for controlling the conditions for subsistence activities. Ritual had extrinsic value to Kapinga as a means to an end. Positions in the cult house, each of which carried specific ritual duties, brought prestige to the few people eligible to occupy them, none of whom represented anyone in particular. Onotoan meeting house activity, by contrast, had instrinsic value to its members. Not only were its decisions a means of maintaining order and carrying out community activities, but public debate and oratory and the prestige derived from the considerable skills of public persuasion had value in and of themselves. The member who held a seat in the meeting house represented a group of kinsmen and spoke for that group. Because any male member of the group might succeed him to that seat, group members all had a personal stake in that position. Save for the small minority of Kapinga eligible for priestly roles, most Kapinga had no personal stake in the maintenance of these positions when their irrelevance to the activities they were supposed to promote became obvious.

The Onotoan meeting house, as a multi-purpose standing group whose activities--creating enforceable consensus on public policy--had instrinsic value to it members, is far more comparable to the Kapinga men's house than to the cult house. Men's house activities, remember, included not only group fishing, but ritual activities, work parties for construction and maintenance of the men's house and its equipment, nomination of the high priest, and competitive activities with other men's houses, such as fishing exploits and song composition. The formal positions of headman and *tomono* and the less formal ranking by relative age ordered its deliberations, which, among other things, constituted a context for subtle competition among its members for influence and prestige. Even after the men's house had lost its ritual functions and its *tomono* position (to the kingship), it continued to organize group fishing (given its ownership of netting equipment) and to nominate each new king. Indeed, in 1919, with the cult house gone, the new church just organizing, Furia having left, and two kings having abdicated, the men's house was the only remaining institution capable of exercising the authority necessary to begin the reconstruction of the social order. Like the *mwaneaba*, the men's house was the traditional locus of consensus on community issues, and, for that reason, an indispensable component of any new social order.

The *kaainga*, like the cult house, organized but one major activity by the turn of the 20th century--group fishing. That this activity had only extrinsic value to its participants is evident not only in the rapid decrease in the frequency of group fishing through the century, but also in the willingness of people to renounce all former (jealously guarded) claims to property rights in fishing sites in the lagoon, declaring the lagoon to be public domain in 1951 (Goodenough 1963: 339). Analogously, Kapinga declared their two former sacred islets as public property in 1920. More telling, however, is the fact that within a week after the initial conversions to Christianity, Kapinga people began to carry away the large, sacred stones from the *malae* (sacred plaza) for use in building their sea walls.

On both atolls, single-purpose institutions whose activities have only extrinsic value to their members collapse when the activities they organize lose their salience. Multi-purpose institutions some or all of whose activities had intrinsic value to their members not only survive the loss of ritual activities to new churches, but also take on responsibilities they had not previously handled. The *mwaneaba*, for example, finds itself dealing with disputes between neighbors, a result of changing demography, with the demise of the *kaainga*. The Kapinga king, formerly empowered to mediate between colonial agents and the community, was forced to deal with matters internal to the community during the drought and famine, e.g., promulgating rules to control the use of coconuts, prohibiting certain forms of marriage as part of an effort to control birth rate, etc.. The community meeting, created by Furia to hear land disputes, became useful during the famine for announcing new conservation rules and for trying and punishing coconut theft. After the famine, David continued to use the community meeting to try land disputes and to announce and discuss community policy. The meeting was also an ideal context for working out the organizational details for public projects, e.g., what sorts of and how many groups were necessary, who would lead each, how group members would be recruited, when work would begin, etc.. Cases of theft, assault, drunken comportment, adultery, and civil marriages were handled by the king in private hearings, either by request or on his own initiative.

When you look at these sets of activities and how they were distributed over standing groups--the Kapinga king, with his secretary and one policeman constituting a group--you see that the combination of the kingship, the men's house, and the community meeting is functionally equivalent to the *mwaneaba*, which, except for group fishing, combines the same activities in one standing group. Now, take into consideration the church and its role in formulating and legitimizing public policy emanating from these secular institutions--and on Onotoa as on other nearby atolls in the southern Gilberts, the role of the church in decision making has been considerable (Macdonald 1982: 31-53, 130) and comparable to that on Kapingamarangi. What you see on both atolls is the same process of change: single purpose institutions disappear when their activities are either obviated or more efficiently organized by *ad hoc* groups; traditionally multi-purpose institutions take on new responsibilities, and newly imported institutions organize newly introduced practices, some of which (like ritual) replace traditional practices. In the Onotoa case, the social order is reorganized as a working partnership of church and meeting house. What had been a single institution that included ritual activity became two institutions whose relationship constituted the social order above the neighborhood level. In the Kapinga case, the remodeled kingship combined with the men's house, the community meeting, and the church, all of whose leaders overlapped with church leaders. The men's houses eventually established much the same relationship with the church that they had with the cult house.

Clearly, the same transformation process, which Homer Barnett (1953, 1983) described as "recombination," served to reshape both atoll social orders at the levels both of institutions and of the relations between institutions. This is the case because, regardless of the particular structural properties of the standing groups that survived and those that did not, their constituent activities and interrelations between activities were so similar. The comparison of transformation processes, therefore, does not ignore or minimize their organizational differences. Nor does the identity of transformation processes ignore the differences in the historical sequences of events on the two atolls.

I'll stick my neck out and put the matter of historical contingency of events briefly and bluntly. The cult house organization collapsed because Kapinga people had reason to believe that it was ineffective in bringing about conditions that facilitated everyday activities. The presence of colonial agents on the atoll, which the high priest was supposed to prevent, the tangible goods and harm they brought (indices of their power) were evidence of the priests' impotence. Other incidents prior to 1916, including a failed attempt at executing a man for violating a taboo, reinforced people's growing skepticism about their commitment to the priesthood. That the famine and drought simply accelerated a process already well underway is indicated by the fact that Kapinga who went to Pohnpei before the drought had begun to convert to Catholicism a year before the arrival of the Nukuoro missionaries. They continued to do so well into the 1920s. Given that conversion to Christianity had already begun in 1916, the significance of the Nukuoro missionaries lay in ensuring that it was the Protestant rather than the Catholic church that predominated numerically and politically on the atoll.

Similarly, the power of the king had begun to erode by 1900, both because of competition from the copra producers' group and of his own miscalculation of the extent to which he could intimidate his rivals. For example, when one intended victim of a land grab attempt routed the men's house group the king had sent to frighten him, the king retreated, rifle in hand, without firing a shot, ending his land acquisition program. In another instance, the king slapped an old woman known to have inherited sorcery power from her Woleiaian grandfather. His subsequent stroke was attributed to her vengeance. Thus, when the drought began, his position had weakened to the extent that Furia appointed the masters to enforce conservation measures, and they, too, were discredited by an intended victim of punishment. Because the kingship was the only remaining leadership position in 1919, and the authority of that position was already limited before the drought, some form of consensus involving at least the king and men's house was inevitable.

Just as the days of the Kapinga cult house were numbered as soon as the first European ship entered the lagoon in 1877, the days of the *kaainga* were numbered when the British committed themselves to a colonial presence in the Gilbert Islands. Colonial systems require a dependable, mobile labor supply for their commercial operations, and pacification is always a necessary first step to ensure the safety of the operations and the mobility of laboreres. On Onotoa as elsewhere, prohibition of feuding obviated a major activity of the *kaainga*. Given the ubiquity of labor recruiting, the variety of plantations and mines as sources of work and cash and Onotoans' interest in deep sea fishing, it was only a matter of time and opportunity before wages were converted into wood. Ocean Island provided a convenient source of cash and goods, but certainly not the only one. Nauru was also an accessible and dependable source (Macdonald 1982: 55, 58; Viviani 1970). Similarly, Kapinga men began buying breadfruit logs for canoes from Pohnpeians within five years of resettlement on Pohnpei.

I am not arguing that the particular historical events triggering systemic change are unimportant. What I am arguing is that the change processes in these two communities are systemic ones: given the states of these social systems, any number of events of the same order--real events that really happened--would have produced much the same outcomes. And it doesn't seem to matter that the colonials are Germans or British or Japanese. The reason it doesn't matter is that the recombination of activities with institutions and of institutions with one another on Onotoa and on Kapingamarangi (after Furia's recall to Pohnpei) were local affairs, i.e., internally managed solutions to local organizational problems. This is not to say that the recombination process itself was inevitable, however. It is in fact one of a number of probable change processes that might have occurred. The recombination process is, therefore, historically contingent, but contingent on a non-event: the non-intervention of the colonial administration in the reshaping of each social order. Given that the British colonial administration had actively promoted programs of political change on other atolls in the southern Gilberts (Macdonald 1982: 75-93) and that the Japanese instituted schools, administrative training programs, and elective political offices on Pohnpei, the probability of colonial intervention in the reorganization of both atolls was clearly greater than zero. It was the limitation of resources and personnel that prevented active intervention of both colonial regimes in the reorganization of both atolls. Just how important this non-event is will become evident as I describe what happened to fishing activity when it was again recontextualized by a social order reshaped under a colonial regime whose *raison d'etre* was precisely that of intervention in the reshaping process.

Notes

1. Why this happened is a mystery to me and to the Kapinga. It is possibly connected to a series of red tides between 1957 and 1968, but this is pure conjecture.

2. By the same token, there is no such thing as an unintentional slip of the tongue. Personal *faux pas* that anger or embarrass others are thought to be unconstrained reflections of what one truely thinks or feels. People are held responsible for such acts, unlike the individual in western societies, which recognize failure of personal integration legally as degrees of "diminished capacity," and, therefore, recognize degrees of legal and moral responsibility for individuals' acts. Kapinga, who do not expect integration of the self, demand only control of it and recognize what we might think of as

diminished capcity only in cases of insanity and possession by a spirit. But even insanity is the result of a person's own acts and is, ultimately, the fault of the victim (see, for example, Lieber 1991).

3. See Lieber (1990) for a comparison of the Kapinga conception of power with that of Pohnpeians, who, like Kapinga, expect power to come from powerful agents outside the community, but who also expect those agents and their power to become incorporated into the social order.

4. I need to tell you here that my characterization of the *tomono* as an underling of the high priest is my interpretation, and that some of the older men with whom I worked would and did disagree with it. All of them were clear in their view of the king being more powerful than the high priest; this was what they saw with their own eyes, as they put it. Indeed, when these men were in their teens and younger, the king was indeed the dominant political figure on the atoll. They remember him as he was at the turn of the century, at the zenith of his power. But when I asked these people to tell me what he did before he became king, what I got were his men's house and cult house functions. While Kapinga were able to list high priests' names from the last one in 1917 back to Utamatua, the island founder, no one could remember the name of a *tomono* any earlier than 1850 or so, even though genealogical memory and land histories extended back about a century earlier than that.

5. David went to great lengths during Emory's stay in 1947 to choose his informants and to monitor all of his interviews. Emory was aware of this but could do little about it. I think that David wanted to make sure that Emory never found out about the masters, and in this, he was successful.

6. The traditional Kapinga canoe, with a few modifications, continued to be built in Porakied into the 1960s because of its suitability for negotiating the shallow, craggy lagoon on Pohnpei.

11

The Americans: Institutionalizing Differentiation and Uncertainty

Compared with the transformation of their social and political order, the organization and conduct of fishing activity changed very little after World War II. The trend toward increasing frequency of fishing by individual fishermen and small angling crews at the expense of group netting, well established by the 1930s, continued unabated after the war, accelerated somewhat by the introduction of the spear gun in 1963. Imported fishing gear--nylon fishing line and nets, fish hooks, lures, leaders, snoods, sinkers, goggles, and spear guns--had replaced gear of native manufacture by 1975. Kapinga purchased the items on Pohnpei and sent them to the atoll or acquired them through mail order, just as they had before the war. Only coir and purse nets, hand nets, and traps were still being made locally. Periodic needs for large amounts of fish for celebrations and funerals are still most efficiently satisfied through netting expeditions organized through the men's house. The availability of cheap nylon nets has permitted some kinds of netting, such as garfish netting and plugging the channel, to be organized on an *ad hoc* basis.

Other than the spear gun, the most dramatic technological change in fishing activity has been the use of the six horsepower outboard motor mounted on an outrigger boom, making sails all but obsolete. Aside from decreasing the time spent getting to and from fishing grounds and increasing the cost of fishing, the outboard engine has had little effect on the conduct or organization of angling and netting activity. Except for the spear gun, one is hard put to find any qualitative change in how fishing is done, by whom, and with what that would distinguish pre- and post-war fishing activity. Even the spear gun, as a technological device, has had far less in the way of organizational ramifications than the throwing net, which rendered several netting and pole and line techniques obsolete while opening up previously unexploited opportunities, e.g., netting flying fish as they enter the lagoon. Yet the continuity of fishing techniques, the use of gear, and organizational trends contrasts sharply with the discontinuities of overfishing, of local perceptions of the deteriorating relationship between fishermen and the community, and of the emergence of fishing activity as a metaphor for community disintegration.

There is nothing mysterious about these discontinuities. The constraints on traditional fishing activities had been embedded in a hierarchically ordered social and ritual system that formed their context. When that system fell apart, fishing activity was recontextualized as part of a new social order formed through recombination of old with new institutions resulting in fishing activity being much more integrated into community decision making than it had been in the past. Just as the events of the Japanese colonial period served to recontextualize fishing activity, so the American colonial administration and its policies, Kapinga perceptions of them, and the relationship that developed between the administration and the atoll formed a new and radically different context of fishing activity. Its form is that of differentiated sets of activities, none of which was constituted with enough authority to coordinate or control the others. The social order, in other words, becomes atomized, part of that atomization process including a shift in consensus building from the men's house to a new, specifically political institution. This left the men's house as a single purpose institution that was not only marginal to community decision making, but also marginal to fishing activity as its range and frequency of activities continued to shrink. In this way, fishing activity became every bit as atomized as its context, making it such an appropriate metaphor for that larger context. That is what happened. Now I'm going to tell you how it happened and what Kapinga people have tried to do about it.

The Process of Atomization

The last two years of World War II left Kapingamarangi relatively isolated as Allied bombing and Japanese preparations for a possible invasion of Pohnpei cut off shipping to the atoll. Because of a Japanese sea plane base on Hale islet, the atoll did get some attention from the allies, including bombings, dog fights, and shelling from a battleship. The Japanese rifle vollies of 1914 paled by comparison. Assured that the Japanese would win the war and that Americans would treat them badly, a terrified populace watched the evacuation of the Japanese pilots and received American naval personnel.

If the Japanese administration took a benign disinterest in atoll organization, the United States colonial administration that followed was intimately concerned with it. The Naval administration (1946-1951) and the civilian Trust Territory of the Pacific Islands (1951-1987), whatever their differences, saw their role in Micronesian societies as agents of change. The name of the game was community development--political, economic, and social change in the American image of the democratically organized, entrepeneureal, self-reliant individuals. The Naval administration wasted no time implementing these goals, setting up schools--their lynch pin of change--dispensaries, and retail cooperatives and undermining the authority of local chiefs wherever and whenever possible.

By 1947, Kapingamarangi had a school, a dispensary, and a local branch of a cooperative selling handicrafts and copra to Naval personnel and consumer goods to atoll residents. The school teachers were two men with six months of training on Truk. Another young man trained on Pohnpei was the atoll nurse, and another was the co-op agent. While Naval personnel dealt with King David and his brother on all policy matters, patiently explaining their programs to secure their cooperation, they also spent time with younger men deriding these two leaders as backward autocrats. One of their proteges openly challenged David's successor (his half-brother), Duiai, in a monthly meeting. But when asked what alternative organization he would institute, the young man responded only with slogans (and an eventual apology). Duiai continued on as king until his death in 1954.

Meanwhile, the most promising of the elementary students went on to High School on Truk by 1950 for instruction in English, arithmetic, history, and training in teaching and clerical skills. They were indoctrinated in the ideology of democratic, American style political institutions. One of these students was Duiai's son, a very unusual man with a bright, quick mind and with what (to me) is an uncanny ability to perceive and understand not only "the other fellow's point of view," but also the implicit premises that underlie it, all of which he articulates clearly in any of five languages in which he is fluent. He went to work for the weather service on Pohnpei after graduating from high school in 1954, but returned to the atoll on the news of his father's death. Although he was elected to succeed his father, he saw nothing but trouble ahead should he occupy that position.

Only 25 years of age, his authority was tenuous, and he would have to deal with an administration that was at best manipulative and at worst hostile to the idea of traditional leadership. Working through men's house discussions, he floated the idea of abandoning the kingship in favor of a chief magistrate and an elective legislative council. He managed to convince his elders that (1) there was nothing a king could do that a chief magistrate could not, and (2) community policy ought to come directly from the people who have to live with it rather from one man, a young one at that. After months of discussion, he formally renounced the kingship, accepted the position of chief magistrate, and organized the election of a ten man legislative council. He then began training its members in making and drafting ordinances. Elderly men, respected as heads of families and church leaders comprised the membership of the early councils. These men were interested mainly in regulating personal behavior in accordance with church standards. The district administrator on Pohnpei vetoed almost all of their ordinances, leaving the young chief magistrate in the position of having to explain the separation of church and state that was Trust Territory law to men who did not want to hear it.

Regardless of the council's early legislative record, the structural change it represented was permanent. Political discussion had moved from informal consensus in the men's houses to formal discussion with majority rule in the council and community meetings. Even here, however, council discussions tend to be oriented toward achieving consensus before a vote. That these discussions encoded overt rather than subtle political manipulation and influence left the men's houses in the position of being ancillary institutions. Someone with a proposal to float could get his council representative to introduce it or discuss it informally with one or more councilmen, who might then present it formally. Alternatively, one could bring up issues needing ordinances with the chief magistrate or at a community meeting, and either could then refer it to the council. The men's houses became contexts for grumbling about the chief magistrate and the council, but their political clout was gone forever. It is one of many ironies of post-war change that the very cogency of the men's house in building consensus was its undoing as a viable political institution.

By the time that the new political order of chief magistrate, council and two municipal judges was formalized as a chartered municipality of the Pohnpei District of the Trust Territory in 1960, the men's houses were not only politically flaccid, but increasingly a social refuge for a politically impotent older generation of men. As it became clear that men with little or no experience with Americans, no command of English, and no formal schooling could not easily produce workable policies, younger men gradually replaced them on the council. These men all had at least an elementary education with some reading and speaking knowledge of English. They dealt more readily with American administrators (who favored younger men in any case) than did their elders. Some of these men were involved in the church and others not. By the mid-1960s, the political empowerment of the generation born in the mid-1930s and educated by Americans had entirely replaced the generation reared under Japanese hegemony. The individuation of political activity, which had already become well established in Porakied, emerged from this new community organization as competition between leaders for positions of influence on the council--chair, secretary, and treasurer--and for leadership in formulating policy became overt in face to face debate.[1] If consensus was impossible, then one might win or lose in a majority vote in the council or in the community meeting.

The structure of the new political order and at least the outlines of its *modus operandi* were clear enough by 1960. But the sorts of activities that constituted its regulatory domain and its relationship with the American colonial administration, to the extent that they ever became clear, emerged gradually through trial and error--issue by issue. Some issues, such as control of chickens and pigs or the construction of public facilities, such as a bridge between Touhou and Weelua, were obvious. Other issues, such as dealing with official misconduct of Kapinga employed by the administration or tracking a proposal through the administrative approval process, were not obvious. As the boundaries of municipal control *vis-a-vis* the school, the coop, the dispensary, and private businesses (such as retail stores) became clearer through trial and error, the relationship between the atoll and the administration became ever less so. To understand why this was the case, you need to understand two salient properties of the American colonial administration as they manifested themselves on the atoll: the administrative structure and the contradictory premises of its policies and programs.

Unlike the Japanese colonial administration, which presented itself as a single entity to atoll Kapinga, the American administration has always presented itself piecemeal as an often bewildering collection of departments, offices, agencies, and programs. Instead of a single supercargo doing company and administrative business with the king and/or his assistant, any number of department and agency representatives come ashore on a ship visit, sometimes to deal with atoll leaders, sometimes to deal only with local agency employees. The ship's supercargo, or "field trip officer," deals mainly with ship scheduling, passenger lists, delivering mail, and delivering whatever administrative notices are given to him. He is usually accompanied by a variety of other administrative personnel. These include health workers, educators, agency representatives, agricultural station employees, State senator, congressmen (or candidates for those offices), Peace Corps personnel, Maritime Authority and or State Marine Resources representatives, Pohnpei Federation of Cooperatives employees, and special programs directors, to name a few. Each of them contact their local employees or agents--teachers, school principal, nurses, director of a construction project, land owners, patients, trainees, and, if necessary, the chief magistrate and council or the entire community (usually when a new program is being initiated and needs to be explained). Thereafter, administrators deal directly with the local person responsible for running the program. The result is that legitimate authority, as Kapinga understand it, has become dispersed through the community rather than concentrated in one office or official body, roughly matching the dispersion of authority through the Pohnpei bureaucracy.

An American ideology of self-help and self-reliance has rationalized the introduction and structure of most development programs for which the atoll has been a target. The school, the dispensary, the co-op, the local court, the council, etc., were organized with the idea that the Kapinga--individuals all--would run them and be responsible for day-to-day decisions for them, albeit with "guidelines" established by whichever agency or department was charged with training, supervision, and funding for them. That the Kapinga had no choice as to whether or not to adopt most of the development programs (nor as to how they were to be organized and implemented) forms only one part of the paradoxical structure of "community development" on this atoll. The chief magistrate and council, charged with regulating local social order through enactment of ordinances approved by community vote, quickly found self-reliance did not really mean community autonomy, as they had been led to believe. Municipal ordinances did not become law until approved by the district administrator (or, since 1979, by the Governor of Pohnpei State). The fact that many of the council's earliest ordinances were vetoed by the district administrator despite overwhelming majority votes of approval by the community was sufficient to reinforce the Kapinga view that authority still lay outside the community.

The idea of self-reliance was further ambiguated by the fact that ordinances that were not vetoed were not always approved, either. Some of the ordinances submitted to the district administrator were ignored, some forgotten about, some lost in the bureaucratic machinery, and others approved only after long delays and repeated inquiries. Occasionally, a community proposal was granted with lightening efficiency even when it should not have been. For example, in 1966, after some months of council discussion about constructing a municipal office, one of the two local court judges went to Pohnpei, requested plans and materials for the building from the district administrator, and got the approval, the plans, and the materials within three days. This despite the fact that the council, not the judge, had the authority to make the request, and that the district administrator knew that he was bypassing "proper" channels, all to the consternation of council members.

By way of contrast, Kapinga leaders both on the atoll and in Porakied, requested and were promised a new lease on Porakied land in 1961. When the lease still had not been granted by the district administrator in 1966, they appealed to the High Commissioner of the Trust Territory. He instructed them to form a corporation to hold the land, but their incorporation papers were not even acknowledged on receipt. When new attempts at legal incorporation reached the High Commissioner's desk in 1977, the deputy High Commissioner sent the incorporation papers back to the district administrator suggesting that a rebellion was in progress and should be stopped.[2]

At the other extreme, the atoll occasionally has a program dropped on it with little prior consultation or assessment of need, e.g., a shipment of U. S. D. A. food in 1967 after a taro patch was flooded and the abrupt arrival of housing materials for "the aged" in 1976. Bureaucratic largess was more a justification for the existence of a program and its budget than a response to a crisis. The apparent mindlessness of administrative largesse, at least with regard to needs of its clients, is less important than the metamessage it encodes about where the Kapinga should look for the wherewithal to meet their needs and who it is that defines their needs.

The submission of ordinances and proposals have become, for Kapinga leaders, an appeal to higher authority for approval. Given the mixed success of these appeals, the council could never be certain whether or not their ordinances, no matter how carefully written, would become law. It was never clear when self-reliance, with which Kapinga have never been comfortable, or dependency, with which Kapinga are comfortable, would shape a government proposal or response to a Kapinga proposal. The paradox has generated what I have called elsewhere the community's "unrequited dependency" (Lieber 1990), which falls most heavily on the chief and council. Given the amount of work it takes to assess and garner public support for its ordinances, the council's mixed success has made community consensus ever harder to put together.

The bureaucratizing of authority and the self-reliance/dependency paradox sometimes dovetail. Although Kapinga are expected to run their own development programs, the community has no authority over them. When the community voted in a meeting to fire one of its teachers in the 1950s, the educational administrator on Pohnpei quickly intervened, reinstating the teacher and informing the chief magistrate and council that only the department of education that employed the teacher had the right to fire him. There was a similar incident involving a nurse that had the same result. Kapinga have learned that running a government program does not mean controlling it.

The bureaucratic dispersal of authority within the community has resulted in a differentiation of the community into semi-autonomous subsystems, each with its own locus of authority outside the community. The school, the dispensary, the court, the co-op, the council, etc., are each accountable to a different department or agency, and each is organized by status relations, e.g., teacher-student, customer-clerk, rather than by knowledge of personal biographies. The district administrator and, more recently, the Pohnpei State governor, theoretically the place where the buck stops, have rarely intervened in a situation involving decisions of an agency or department. Thus none of these separate local institutions coheres with the others in a single hierarchy of control.

The Protestant church became part of the differentiation process by the early 1960s. The district administrator's early vetoes of church sponsored ordinances, citing separation of church and state provisions of the Trust Territory Code, was only the first step toward a sacred-secular division that King David had so skillfully bridged in the Japanese era. Even as younger councilmen replaced their churchmen-elders, the church maintained its influence in proposals of ordinances, putting pressure on councilmen and garnering votes in community meetings. Tension between church elders and councilmen was apparent by 1960, as much an intergenerational as a sacred-secular struggle for control. Two issues in particular profoundly altered conception of their community-- alcohol and the funding of church projects.

The Japanese had prohibited alcohol consumption by Micronesians. When beer and liquor sales were legalized on Pohnpei in the early 1950s, only local ordinances could ban them on the atolls. But banning imports was only part of the problem, since homemade coconut toddy and a ghastly brew of sugar, water, and yeast could keep revelers at least lightheaded, if not totally hammered for days. The increasing frequency of drunken comportment, complete with song, dance, and an occasional brawl, was debated in meeting after meeting until church pressure produced a council ordinance banning all forms of alcohol and its consumption in 1963. Although the chief magistrate, himself a church member, protested that the ordinance would be unenforceable, the ordinance passed by majority vote in a bitter meeting. It was an empty victory, since the law has indeed been unenforceable.

The inability of the designated agents of the community on the atoll (and in Porakied) to control personal acts by decree was, for the first time, made all too apparent by this issue. Drinking, moreover, is different from getting a teacher fired or having ordinances vetoed by the district administrator, because the community has the legal and moral authority to outlaw drinking and to enforce its ordinance. It is, simply, unable to do so consistently.

Funding of church projects by the community has been every bit as volatile an issue as alcohol. In 1966, church leaders decided to replace the thatch roof on the Souhou church with corrugated metal. They got a councilman to propose an ordinance assessing each household so many metal sheets. That the few Roman Catholic families on the atoll would bear the burden equally with Protestant households was less important to councilmen than the now secularized political apparatus being used for purely religious purposes. The council voted down the proposal, citing separation of church and state in the Trust Territory Code. The minister then attempted to persuade the Porakied community to vote assessments, communicating his request on municipal stationery, but with the same result (Lieber 1984).

It is a differentiated community in a differentiated universe of supra-community authority that has ambiguated the locus of authority on this atoll community (and its resettled enclaves). In a community that has depended on swift and certain retribution for violations of its sanctified norms--and the word for sanctified or sacred is *hagamadago*, literally, 'causing fear'--the pervasive uncertainty about the locus of authority, its forms and applications could only promote a sense of disintegration of the social order.

This bleak picture of a community coming unglued belies, masks, and trivializes other observable realities of everyday life on this atoll. People go about the daily business of making a living, which comes mainly from local resources that they manage with care. There is, in fact, a surplus of resources that Kapinga no longer conserve, e.g., pandanus fruit and tuna. The council continues to meet, plan projects, and run them reasonably well. The church continues to command the loyalty and efforts of a majority of the adult population and, in fact, has expanded its programs over the years. Families continue to control land ownership and use, exercising their authority to regulate actions of their members. The school has expanded its programs to include literacy in Kapinga, preschool, and a curriculum in traditional lore and crafts, graduating ever larger classes and sending an ever growing contingent on to high school each year. The co-op operates with reasonable efficiency, and the growth of the handicraft market has at least partially offset falling copra prices. Even the natural disasters I described at the beginning evoke only momentary panic.

One of the many ironies of post-war atoll life has been the growing sense of chaos along with a corresponding growth and vigor of group organization of activities below the community level. Cooperative endeavor includes not only traditional, kin-group activities such as land management (Lieber 1974), canoe and house construction, wedding and first birthday feasts, and funerals, but also many other activities, some new and some old ones formerly organized by individual people. Kin groups became increasingly important after the war as the population grew rapidly, requiring land owners to will their plots to their children as a group. The small size of land plots has made further division unfeasible and group ownership and management necessary.

By the late 1960s activities formerly undertaken by single persons, organized by single persons, or done by *ad hoc* groups began to be issues around which permanent groups crystallized. Single focus cooperative groups seem to have originated in Japanese times and were reinvigorated at the urging of a Peace Corpsman in 1970. A group pools money, local resources, labor, or all three depending on its function. The idea quickly spread to encompass water catchment construction, roof thatching, digging new taro patches, purchase of outboard engines, preparation of sleeping and floor mats (for local use or for mail orders), and preparation of feast foods such as taro and breadfruit puddings. For example, a woman joins a taro pudding group, preparing a prescribed number of taro puddings for another member on demand and expecting that her own feast will eventually be similarly and dependably provisioned. She joins with the understanding that she cannot quit until all current members have completed at least one round of service. An outboard engine group meets periodically, each member contributing a cash assessment sufficient to achieve the total amount necessary for one outboard engine. A name is drawn from a hat, and that person gets the cash. One joins with the understanding of a full round of tenure before he or she can quit. Group organization employs the traditional kin group and men's house model of dual leadership--a headman who organizes the specific activity and an assistant who serves as secretary and messenger.

Besides these groups, council committees and church committees have proliferated through the 1970s and 1980s, each one serving some special purpose or project. These groups organize such things as bridge repair, outhouse construction and repair, sports competitions, song competitions, missionary activity, and visits and prayer services for the aged and ill.

Kapinga seem always to have been able to form groups on the spot for just about any purpose, and they enjoy the fellowship of group endeavor. They have been particularly creative in using group organization to confront new problems and needs arising from a changing social and economic environment. These new groups have served to fill in the seams wherein individual effort, family resources, or council intervention have been either insufficient or inappropriate. Kapinga, moreover, find nothing particularly remarkable about any of this. They take no noticeable pride in the unqualified successes of their organizational efforts in meeting common needs. Their successes seem not to have allayed their pessimistic perceptions of impending chaos.

What Kapinga do find remarkable is inconsistency in the operation of authority in those contexts where the locus of and the application of authority ought to be certain and unambiguous. Because the community and its authority continue to be symbolically charged with sanctity, certainty as to who is in charge and about the capability of those in charge to take charge are issues that matter to people. Periodic or consistent failures of expected constraints on personal activities in communal contexts are, therefore, bound to be highly visible. People respond to these failures much more emotionally than, say, to managerial problems in the school or the cooperative. People in their 40s and older speak nostalgically about kings David and Tuiai, while acknowledging that both had opponents and that not everyone was happy with particular decisions of either. But people say that they felt secure in the knowledge that their king would render an unambiguous decision and implement it on any public issue. It is not a matter of people yearning for an erstwhile authoritarian social order so much as a stated need for people to be certain that the community and its agents have the wherewithal to constrain personal activities when it has to do so. Alcohol consumption is a constant reminder that this may no longer be possible. The uncertainties that result are that much more frustrating when it is not clear to people whether particular leaders, particular categories of people, or the general populace are to blame (cf., Lieber 1977a, Silverman 1977).

Because fishing activity was part of the organization of the pre-colonial polity, the social constraints on fishing activity were imbued with the same sanctity as other activities constrained by priestly taboo. As is typical of rapid social change, the social organization of fishing on the atoll has changed while its symbolic associations of authority between categories of fishermen and groups of fishermen has not changed. The decoupling of fishing activity and political activity has not been accompanied by a corresponding differentiation of expectations of personal accountability to traditionally recognized authority and to other fishermen as a category. Thus, people's expectations are continually violated. Fishermen returning from angling no longer consistently share fish with those returning with empty canoes. People are upset by this trend because those with a good catch "are not acting like fishermen." That is, sharing of this sort is a categorical expectation, not of an interpersonal relation, but of a relationship between fishermen. People continue to decry the fact that a coconut leaf netting group distributes its catch only to the participants rather than to each household on the islet. Even fifty years after discontinuing the distribution of fish to all households, people still identify the men's house with the islet that it served. Use of the spear gun illustrates this decoupling process--indeed the spear gun has been to fishing activity what alcohol has been to political activity.

Spear fishing began as a sport of young men on the atoll in the 1920s with the introduction of the hand held wooden spear from Nukuoro. In 1963, young Kapinga men began to make and use a spear gun, again on the Nukuoro model. Consisting of a three foot metal rod propelled by surgical tubing mounted on a wood stock along with a metal trigger and a long string from rod to stock, the spear gun was a fancy slingshot. Although crude compared with today's western models, it was very effective. Deployed around coral heads, the outer reef slope, and in the channel, a single fisherman could come home with over 100 fish for a morning's work. By 1966, however, it was apparent to older fishermen that the spear gun was not an unmixed blessing. For one thing, after three years of intensive use, spear fishing no longer brought in the large catches that it had at the outset. Spear fishermen, mostly younger men, argued that the fish had become accustomed to the sound of the spear mechanism and ran when they heard it. Older fishermen argued that if this were true, then other methods used in the same areas should be productive, but they were not. Reduction in spear fish catches was accompanied by much smaller catches with every other method deployed. Certain that spear fishing was causing the depletion of fish in the lagoon and outer reef slope, older fishermen sought to persuade spear fishermen to give up the spear gun, to no avail. A few of the more respected fishermen then importuned council members to pass an ordinance banning the spear gun from the island, again without success. Older fishermen learned to live with this symbol of the erosion of their authority just as others have learned to live with drinking. They simply have stopped angling and trapping at coral heads and in the channel. More significantly, however, the intrusion of the spear gun into coconut leaf netting, the old stand-by, has served to erode what little authority was left to the men's house headman.

The critical moment in any surround employing a coir and/or purse net is that point at which the fish have been driven into a large, tight cluster in a space small enough to allow the two ends of the net to be brought together, closing off any possibility of their escape. At this point, the twenty to forty people that form the surround group are also brought together in a small, excited cluster. The men holding the net ends have to manipulate them rapidly on the commands of both the headman, who is standing shoreward of the net, and his assistants, who are seaward of it watching the fish and the manipulation of a net end. It is very noisy at this point, and those not holding the net need to be clear of it and quiet, allowing those manipulating the net to hear commands. But since acquiring lightweight, aluminum spear guns, young men have brought them along, spearing fish once they had clustered near the purse net. With one set of fishermen trying to close the net and another trying to spear fish, the noise and confusion consistently resulted in a large proportion of the catch escaping. The headman's prohibition of spear guns on netting expeditions was ignored, both in Porakied and on the atoll. The headmen's response to the erosion of their authority was to cease leading group expeditions for any occasions other than for provisioning all island feasts.

The decoupling of political and fishing activity that accompanied what we might call a deinstitutionalization of the men's house left fishing activity unconnected with institutional constraints, but not for long. The rapid adoption of outboard engines served to reconnect fishing activity to existing institutions on and outside the atoll: the local branch of the Pohnpei Federation of Cooperatives, the municipal council, and Pohnpei District (later State) legislature, all of which controlled the flow of cash necessary to get the engines and keep them running.

Kapinga fishermen on Pohnpei and Nukuoro began using six horsepower outboard engines on their canoes in the early 1970s. A minor modification of an outrigger boom allows it to be used as a transom for the engine mount. By the late 1970s, outboard engines had largely replaced sails, the few holdouts being those too stubborn or too poor to buy engines. These unfortunates were objects of ridicule in a "keep up with the Jones's" sort of scenario.

Outboard engines have several advantages over sails. Getting to fishing grounds is faster and easier, precluding the need to cover the long distances necessitated by tacking. This eliminates the need for anglers to go out, say, to Bumadahadi islet to sleep overnight in order to get to the channel early in the morning. Sails are bulky and heavy, particularly when they get wet. They are useless when the wind dies down. The outboard engine takes less space, and lack of wind is not a constraint. Another advantage of the engines is the ability to maintain precise control over the speed of the canoe, which is particularly important for trolling.

Although outboard engines require more work in maintenance than sails, they are reasonably reliable with proper care--flushing the engine, keeping the moving parts and bearings well lubricated, and occasionally replacing gaskets. When they do break down, they require more skills for repair than sails, and replacement parts may take months to arrive on the atoll. Engines are much more expensive to repair than sails, and not every fisherman has the requisite skills. This means compensating someone else to repair one's engine. Far more important than these considerations, however, is the fact that fishing has become the only subsistence activity that requires constant cash expenditure.

The gas-oil mixture that fuels an outboard engine is expensive--$1.90 per gallon in 1982 and going up. That gallon is sufficient for two long round trips beyond the channel or three or four shorter trips, say to the channel and a bit beyond. The supply of gas for the atoll, moreover, is limited to three 55-gallon drums brought to the Kapinga Co-op on each ship visit. Not all the gas is used for fishing, however, since people also use canoes to transport vegetable foods, lumber, and leaves from outer islets. In other words, it now costs money to harvest crops. When one takes into account the cost of the engine ($750), parts ($5 and up), the gas, and compensating a repairman for his labor, fishing has become a relatively expensive activity. This would constitute less of a problem if it were not for other expenses that people regularly have to meet with cash.

Besides a nominal municipal head tax, people make occasional and regular purchases at the island Co-op and by mail order. Regular purchases include rice, flour, sugar, soap, yeast, baking powder, coffee, tea, and cigarettes. Occasional purchases include cloth, tinned fish and meat, needles, thread, small knives, machetes, perfume, soy sauce, curry powder, salt, sandals, reading glasses, and sundries. Fishing line, hooks, sinkers, leaders, lures, adze blades, abrasives, glue, nails, screws, paint, and other tools are obtained by mail order. Church tithes, and collections for special projects require cash, as do trips to Pohnpei on the field trip ship.

With an expanding set of needs for cash, the avenues for obtaining it are few. There are salaried positions for five teachers and the island nurse paying about $200 per month. The chief magistrate's salary is about $100 per month. Two school lunch aides receive $25 per month, and a historic preservation curriculum coordinator receives about $150 per month. One young man gets $50 per month for collecting and mailing off measurements of daily tide levels. Two weathermen split a $150 per month salary. Other than these positions, cash income is secured by making copra and selling handicrafts. The municipal office uses a public works fund to pay laborers on public projects, such as pier construction or clearing the two small channels in the reef mentioned previously. With the decline in the world copra market, the present price fluctuating between four and seven cents per pound, real income from copra has declined in the past fifteen years. The handicrafts industry has also declined over the last ten years for several reasons, most importantly dependence on local tourist trade rather than developing export markets.

Against this background, continual cash expenditures for subsistence activities represent significant pressure on limited cash resources. Fishermen have adapted to the cash squeeze by conserving gas. This they do by carefully selecting their expeditions based on their calculations of probable catch sizes. Fishermen are particularly loathe to use gas for group netting expeditions, since the division of the catch means that a fisherman comes home with fewer fish than he could get by angling. If he decides that he wants to catch reef fish, he could do better spearing in the channel. These considerations have resulted in an overall reduction of fishing activity over a year, with fishing concentrated in the deep sea and in the channel. While I cannot demonstrate it, I strongly suspect that the sequence of conversion to to outboard engines and the subsequent overfishing of spinefoot and sea bass in the channel is not coincidental. Some spear fishing is done (increasingly) in the lagoon and on the seaward reef. When tuna are in season, fishermen are out every day trolling and angling. During these times men continue to fish until they run short of gas. During July, 1982, for example, there was a flurry of fishing activity for about three weeks until gas supplies were exhausted. Thereafter, young men went spear fishing at the outer reef. When tuna are not in season, angling and spear fishing are spread out over the month to six weeks between ship visits.

The conversion from sails to outboard motors and the consequent reduction in frequency and type of fishing activity in response to cash shortage has effectively narrowed the range of fishing activities being practiced. Given that it is the practice of fishing activities that communicates technical knowledge between generations, the emergence of cash as a major constraint on fishing activity had, by 1982, produced a another curious irony whereby more is ultimately less.

Kapinga fishermen in 1982 had a range of catch techniques that was literally unthinkable for their forebears. Besides traditional techniques, they also imported new ones from the Nukuoro, Japanese, Pohnpeians, and Americans. These included trolling, spear fishing, use of the throwing net, use of baited hooks tied to rocks on the outer reef slope, catching crayfish on the outer reef slope, and bottom fishing with multiple hooks on a single line. The throwing net replaced most in-shore pole-and-line fishing and opened up new possibilities, such as catching flying fish in the early evenings as they entered the lagoon. Spear fishing has replaced many netting techniques while opening up new possibilities, e.g., the acquisition of waterproof flashlights allows night fishing in previously unexploited habitats. Looked at from the Western point of view of a cumulative body of knowledge about fish and fishing, to which everyone has equal access, the Kapinga repertoire is truely impressive in its richness and variety (cf. Johannes 1981). But we know that Kapinga do not conceive of knowledge in this way.

One's knowledge is personal knowledge acquired by practice. Netting activity requires groups, and groups require knowledgeable leaders willing and able to take responsibility for organizing an expedition. The fishermen most knowledgeable in traditional techniques had all retired by 1982, and those in their sixties with some experience in many of them were busy angling and unwilling to mount netting and other sorts of expeditions. Few have actually led such expeditions; getting a group together is difficult; keeping young men from spearing fish during the final phase of the surround is bothersome (if not futile); and poor results will bring on a good deal of gossip and ridicule. Young men, the backbone of most group expeditions, would prefer to go spear fishing or angling with friends rather than taking orders from men with whom they rarely interact otherwise. Older men in a position to to teach the younger men are, thus, faced with more risks than profit. Angling will bring home more food than netting and with much less aggravation.

For these reasons, of the eighty-four traditional techniques, less than fifteen remain in use. Aside from moray eel trapping, diving for clams, netting flying fish, plugging the channel, and coconut leaf netting, all of the other traditional techniques in use are angling methods. From a cybernetic perspective, this is a social system that is losing much of its variety of subsistence strategies. As catch techniques disappear through disuse, fishermen become more dependent on those requiring cash expenditure, which in turn assures an accelerating loss of remaining techniques.

Searching for Solutions: Looking Outward, Looking Inward

Kapinga on the atoll have responded to their altered subsistence context in two diametrically opposed ways. One has been to look outward to the political contexts wherein possible alternatives for cash income might be generated. Another has been to look inward to adaptive alternatives generated locally, independent of outside control.

There is an increasing interest in council activity for generating new public works projects and in electing magistrates with political connections on Pohnpei. This necessitates an increasing involvement in interisland politics and economics. Aside from lobbying for more public works money, fishermen have also been active in pressuring both the district administrator and the district legislature and old Congress of Micronesia representatives for a pet project since the 1960s, lobbying to get a field trip ship equipped with a walk-in quick freezer for transporting fresh fish to Pohnpei. Local fishermen could sell their fresh catch at wholesale prices to the ship's supercargo. By the 1970s, the plan was expanded to include a large, gas powered freezer on the atoll that could be started when the ship was about to leave Pohnpei. This would give local fishermen about five days of fishing before the ship departed the atoll for

Pohnpei. This made economic sense to the fishermen, given the high prices for fresh fish on Pohnpei (three times the world market price for yellow fin tuna, for example) and the high demand for fish on Pohnpei. Getting freezers for the ship and the atoll was a campaign promise that every candidate for the Pohnpei District Legislature and for the Congress of Micronesia had to make to get atoll votes. All this despite the fact that it was clear as early as 1966 that the cost of modification and maintenance of the ship and/or the purchase of a freezer ship could not possibly be covered by the returns on fish sales from what were only two atolls that could supply deep sea fish--Kapingamarangi and Mokil.

In 1977, some Kapinga and Nukuoro fishermen on Pohnpei saw another commercial opportunity with the collapse of the Ponape Fishermen's Cooperative. Originally organized in the early 1950s, the coop bought fish from local fishermen and retailed them in Kolonia Town. The coop went bankrupt in 1975 through a combination of mismanagement and (alleged) embezzlement.

In 1977, a small group of Kapinga and Nukuoro fishermen began to explore the possibility of forming their own coop. They hoped to set up freezer and office facilities on the shoreline of Porakied village. Fishermen on Pohnpei urged the organizers to include atoll fishermen in their plans, and a young Nukuoro man travelled to Nukuoro and Kapingamarangi in July of 1977 to discuss the proposal with fishermen there. The proposal was welcomed by fishermen on both atolls, who expected that at last there would be a possibility of commercial fishing on the atolls. Fishermen joined the coop at $20 per share, and within a year, the fledgling company, incorporated in 1978 as the K and N Fishing Company, had $2500 in starting capital and a Board of Directors.

The directors had hoped for grant money to purchase a freezer, but the Economic Development Officer believed that fishermen committed to the project ought to build their own freezer (at less than one-tenth the cost of a purchased one) and refused to support a large grant request. Neither the directors nor the local fishermen were interested in organizing a freezer construction project. They hit on the idea of organizing a dried, salted fish business by early 1978. This had the advantage of involving atoll fishermen, who would catch and prepare the salt fish for sale to the coop, which would market the fish on Pohnpei and beyond. There was a market on Pohnpei for the fish, and there was some interest expressed by commercial concerns in Guam and Hawaii in 1978.

There were two major problems with this effort. One was the inevitable mold that quickly grows on the fish. The other, more serious problem was the unwillingness of the cooperative's elected leaders to manage the project. All of the leaders were men who were wage workers or businessmen, none of whom could spend the time to make the arrangements for processing the fish for distribution, making contacts and contracts with retailers, and the like. It has been very difficult in the past for Kapinga to manage a viable cooperative, and the fishing venture was no exception. Like modern fishing, the most successful business ventures in this community are ones that are run by individual people for personal profit. A microwave oven could have solved the mold problem. The management problem could not be solved, however, and the company ceased operation by mid-1978.

All of these economic and political issues were being played out amidst rapid change in the larger governmental structures that formed the context of the atoll's relationship with the outside world. The Federated States of Micronesia was created through a constitutional convention in 1975. It consisted of what had been the Yap district, Truk district, Ponape district, and Kosrae Island as its constituent states. The Federated States of Micronesia (hereafter FSM) constitution was the subject of a ratification vote in 1978. Atoll residents found the issue ambiguous and frightening, for it proposed an independent nation whose very independence Kapinga feared and mistrusted. To be ruled by islanders like themselves was not a prospect that anyone much relished. What Kapinga were most concerned about was the role of the United States in any new island government. People overwhelmingly favored continuation of the Trust Territory, so that the separation of the issues of nationhood and relationship of the FSM with the United States in separate referenda was unsettling. A last minute attempt in 1978 by a vocal Pohnpeian minority to defeat the ratification of the FSM constitution, based on expressed fears of out-islanders taking Pohnpeian land, did little to calm Kapinga's misapprehension. Indeed, this movement, broadcast on the government radio station, probably helped to insure a unanimous vote for ratification on the atoll.

By 1978, the Pohnpei District and its legislature had already been reorganized as a state government with a Pohnpei State legislature in anticipation of the ratification of the FSM constitution. Kapinga prepared to vote for their first governor and lieutenant governor, their representative to the new State legislature, and their FSM congressman the next year. It was clear that the Trust Territory government was phasing out its operations but unclear what would happen thereafter other than a (poorly understood) referendum on a Compact of Free Association with the United States.

The atoll's representative to the present Pohnpei State legislature has become a far more important position than the former representative to the Pohnpei District Legislature. The position is salaried, and the representative is under pressure to lobby for the freezer ship, public works projects, and other pork barrel goodies that will bring cash to the atoll.

Elections have become very competitive since 1978, with candidates campaigning vigorously. The Pohnpei State legislature generates and approves municipal budgets, so State level politics and the atoll's representation have become much more immediate concerns than in the past. Significantly, the men elected to represent the atoll have all been Porakied residents with bureaucratic experience and a command of spoken and written English.

I strongly suspect that the anxieties people expressed about the organization of their community were exacerbated by the ambiguities and uncertainties about their rapidly changing political context. My suspicion is strengthened by a set of events in July and August of 1982, an unprecedented social and ideological break in the pattern of change on the atoll since 1877, one that proposed rethinking the community from the inside out.

As the majority of Kapinga looked warily outward for solutions to their economic and political difficulties, a small but significant minority banded together to look inward to their past as a model for living together. There was, as I left the atoll in 1982, the beginning of a kind of "back to our roots" movement among some Kapinga families that was starting to gain adherents. The movement was led by a man who had been a church leader in his day, a man who was instrumental in bringing about many of the modern practices that are commonplace today. This man, now in his 70s, was a canoe and boat builder. He introduced modern western-style song composition on the atoll as a young man, and he had been a staunch supporter of the church. With advancing arthritis, he decided to leave his house on Touhou and move to Hale, the largest and mostly uninhabited islet on the atoll. He and his wife and several adopted children moved to his land there, rebuilding the dilapidated houses, clearing the ground, and replanting the groves. They were determined to subsist only on what they produced and to cook only traditional foods. Other people, curious about what the couple was doing, began to visit, and before long, younger couples began constructing houses of their own on the islet. A chapel was built on his land for evening and Sunday services, and he began to instruct the younger men in traditional fishing methods and to teach interested people traditional chants, which he had been collecting on tape for several years. By the time I left the atoll, the group on Hale had decided to stay there permanently, keeping their school age children there and demanding that the elementary school send a teacher to Hale if the islet children were to be educated. With six families with school age children, this presented a challenge indeed.

Although this movement did not survive the death of its leader in 1984, it represented an unprecedented response to social change on this island. Never before had Kapinga people chosen to view their own traditions as having an intrinsic value preferable to Western models of life style, subsistence techniques, and western models of social order. Without a clearly defined ideology at the outset, these people shared a distaste for what they saw as a rat race that enveloped them. They saw money and what was needed to get it as a waste of time and emotional energy. They were sick of the noise of outboard engines being flushed and of the chain saw recently imported from Pohnpei. They were disgusted with the political intrigues in the council and weary of worrying about whether the United States or other Micronesians would rule them. They spoke of being fed up with what people had to do to obtain rice, gasoline, cigarettes, and flour. They were unanimous in being sick of feeling driven. They saw themselves as forming a community with resources capable of producing what they needed to live well. Central to the idea of community was the church. This was a developing religious community. Thus, the group had no intention of abandoning the assumption that legitimate authority originates from outside the community, but only that of ignoring an administrative structure that was vague and unreliable. Nor did they think of rejecting all western goods and techniques. No one wanted to make fish hooks from shell or to discard steel adzes and the like. But there was a good deal of interest in old fishing methods, in making various kinds of ropes and traps, basketry, and reviving the use of preserved pandanus fruit to replace wheat flour. As I left the atoll, these were seen as some of the many possibilities for reconstituting their way of living together, and the people on Hale were very enthusiastic about the possibilities. These fifty or so men, women, and children were engaged in a heady experiment of rethinking a community by doing (cf. Silverman 1971). What distinguished them so sharply from their fellows back on Souhou was the constant expression of hope.

The Hale group was not the only one interested in reviving older fishing methods, however. Discussions were underway about the content of a curriculum on traditional island lore as part of the regular school curriculum. The Pohnpei Department of Education had hired a young man to assemble and coordinate a curriculum on the atoll, selecting curriculum items with a committee of older people. The program stipulated that elder knowledgeable people would be employed to give the classroom instruction. Discussions were full of controversy, e.g., what traditional lore could be included without offending the church hierarchy, who would be chosen to instruct and how, whether or not to include local medicine, and the like. Instructing children in traditional fishing methods was one of the least controversial and the most enthusiasticly received items of discussion. Although there was some disagreement about which methods to teach and who would lead expeditions, instruction in traditional fishing appeared to be one of the few certainties of the new curriculum as I left the atoll.

There were also signs that some men were hedging their bets on outboard motors. My host on the atoll had gotten synthetic sailcloth and was busily sewing when I left. Three more men planned to take advantage of the Pohnpei State Economic Development Office's programs to order synthetic sailcloth at cost from Taiwan. Their reasons were the same as those of my host. The cost of gas, its small supply on the atoll, and the unreliability of ship schedules made sails a wise investment, particularly sails with the obvious advantages of new synthetics. One of my mentors remarked to me that people had laughed at one diehard fisherman who eschewed the outboard engine, but after ten weeks with no ship visit, no gas at the co-op, and hardly anyone out fishing other than him, no one was laughing now.

In the summer of 1982, an uncertain political future, an early windy season, another breakdown of the field trip ship, and the depletion of the gas supply brought home to people their vulnerability in depending on outside resources they could not control. The ideological conservatism of the Hale group, the pragmatism of the fishermen wanting new sails, the local historic preservation committee's plans for traditional fishing as part of the school curriculum, and the enthusiasm of young men embarking on a new experiment in night spear fishing were very different responses to their situations. Yet all proceeded from a common premis that is universal in this part of the world--"maximize your options" (Silverman 1969, Lieber 1984a). So it appeared that the trend toward the loss of variety in the technological repertoire was being at least temporarily reversed in 1982. The different strategies may have had a common theme, but they also had a common problem--how to organize each of them.

The problem of reintegrating traditional subsistence techniques with modern practices is no different from the problem of setting up a fishing business on Pohnpei or getting a salt fishing industry going or forming a new committee or forming coalitions with other outer islands in the State legislature. It is the same problem that has confronted Kapinga people since the collapse of the ancient social order in 1917--selecting or inventing organizational modes that are adequate to meet people's needs and reasonably compatible with one another. I turn now to consider the context that constrains Kapinga choices of organized responses to an altered and uncertain environment.

Notes

1. In Porakied, leadership positions are, similarly, those of church, a men's house headman, and a ten man council, which worked with a village headman. Since 1970, the council chairman has functioned as village headman.

2. There are variations on this theme of paradox. One is the occasions when Kapinga efforts at self-help are interpreted as subversive, as with the incorporation papers for Porakied. Another instance of this sort was the Kapinga homestead program in the 1950's, in which Kapinga settlers on Pohnpei land were given rations for six months while they worked on producing their own food on their land. Unfortunately, their land was almost barren of food producing trees, so that when the rations ran out, they were forced into finding expedients to feed themselves. The district administrator labelled these expedients a "passive resistance movement" (Emerich 1960).

3. The chief magistrate formally renounced any political authority over Porakied in 1963 (Lieber 1968).

PART FOUR

How It Is, How It Was, How It Might Be

12

Stable Premises in a Changing World

This report began with a problem--getting lots of relevant data about traditional fishing very quickly. The solution to that problem was to choose *activity* as the analytical unit of description and explanation. Explanation consisted in delineating the variables that Kapingamarangi fishermen saw as constraining fishing activity and then describing and/or inferring the relationship among the constraints. The details of the techniques used by Kapinga fishermen before conversion to Christianity make it clear that fishing activity was organized in a hierarchy of constraints. At the top of the hierarchy of constraints was the relationship between wind-wave action-tide pattern and gods, determining access to fish habitats. Ritual position (including age stratification) determines a fisherman's access to particular techniques. The particular technique used, say angling or group netting, in turn determines which environmental variables a fisherman must attend to, e.g., availability of certain kinds of bait for angling or tide pattern variations to determine which fish are likely to be available and where.

This description of hierarchical ordering of constraints on fishing activity is, of course, a model abstracted from data on specific kinds of fishing expeditions. Its usefulness depends on its explanatory power and its predictive inferences, the most obvious of which is that any change in the higher levels of constraint would change the organization of fishing activity at the lower levels. This inference is confirmed by the changes in fishing activity that follow the demise of the cult house and conversion to Christianity, particularly the equalization of access to canoe construction wood. This results in a rapid increase in the number of individually owned canoes, whose outcome is a rapid increase in the frequency of angling. As the frequency of angling increases, that of group organized fishing decreases.[1] Equalizing access to canoes and, thus, to deep sea fishing results in a trend toward individuation of fishing activity and away from group organization of fishing activity.

Using the same analytical approach to fishing practices on Onotoa atoll, Ward Goodenough found the same process of change following increased access to wood for canoe construction. While the specific institutional outcomes of change for these two islands' hierarchy of constraints on fishing activity are different because of their structural differences, the *process* of change in both are identical. In both cases, single purpose institutions disappear when the activities they organize are obviated or reorganized. Multi-purpose institutions take on activities they had not previously organized, and these are combined with new institutions, particularly the church, in a transformed social order by a process of recombination. In both cases, recombination (rather than directed change employing alien models) is made possible by minimal interference from the colonial regimes controlling these islands.

The individuation of fishing activity on Kapingamarangi develops during the Japanese period, but it only becomes problematic for Kapinga people during the American colonial administration with the reorganization of the atoll's social order. Instead of a single hierarchical social order, the present social organization is a set of hierarchies, each with its own domain of activity and agency of outside control. Fishing activity has come to emblemize this partition of the community into separate, unintegrated institutions. All well and good, but the careful reader will have noticed a major gap in the argument I have constructed to explain the difference between the several contexts of traditional and modern fishing activity. My argument has not addressed or tried to explain the fact (or the implications that follow from it) that central to the traditional organization of fishing activity and to its reorganization in the colonial period is a single piece of hardware. The importance of the wind-wave-tide patterns, the panel of priests, of men's houses and their organization, of age stratification, of ritual classes, and of specific environmental variables in constraining the choice and procedure of fishing activity all converge on access or lack of access to the canoe.

Depending on one's theoretical preferences, one could emphasize the technological aspect or the economic aspect or the religious aspect of this complex set of relations around canoes as structuring the other two. My objections to any such approach are two: (1) the implication that Western cultural assumptions about the categorical compartmentalization of human social life are universally applicable (cf. Wagner 1971), and (2) the necessary reductionism that any such argument entails, i.e., explaining the organization of a whole by the operation of one of its parts. So, for example, one could take a sort of Marxist stance and focus on the control of the canoe--the means of production--by a privileged class, manipulating ritual regulations to maintain that privilege for a small set of people.

There is no question that this is true. The question is why it is true. Is it because there is a universal order of substructure-superstructure in which productive relations drive the rest of the social order (rendering the Kapinga ritual order economics in religious dress)? If this is true, then why doesn't the sacred class attempt to maintain its privileged position by gaining control of the church, the kingship, and the men's house and continue to restrict access to canoes instead of disappearing without a trace? Or are the facts of class privilege, like those of conservation of fish species before the 1970s, an outcome of other sorts of causal constraints on fishing activity and latent within that set of constraints?

The position I have taken here is cultural and systemic, and I intend to apply it to the centrality of the canoe. Kapinga people, in the organization of their community and its regulation of fishing activity, had developed a systematic set of responses to what they *knew* about their environment and about their own capacities to respond to it. This point would appear to be simple and straightforward on its face, but its implications for the Kapinga community and its historical transformations are anything but simple. This is because human knowing--from what it *means* to know anything to what can be known and how one knows to how the known is represented in thought, speech, and action--is a human construction whose meaning, shape, and content depends on how people in particular communities define and communicate these things. Because of this arbitrariness, human social systems have organizational possibilities that are not found in, say, biological systems. No viable organism, for example, organizes its systemic operations around its most dangerous variable. Bateson (1972: 442, 500) uses the example of breathing, which is designed primarily to get rid of carbon dioxide (relatively harmless even at high levels) rather than to take in oxygen, which is highly flammable and lethal at much lower levels than CO_2. Similarly, forest ecosystems are not organized around the potential for forest fires or volcanic eruptions. Because human ecosystems are culturally constituted and their variables culturally defined, human social systems can be and commonly are organized around precisely their most dangerous variables. In the pre-Christian Kapinga case, the gods are clearly the most dangerous component of their environment. It is around what Kapinga know about the gods and about how to deal with them that their social hierarchy is organized. Although data already presented should be clear enough on this point, it is very easy to overlook the obvious danger inherent in canoe use in favor of the privilege such use represents.

Canoes not only afford fishermen access to the far lagoon, the channel, and the deep sea, but also bring them into contact with powerful, unpredictable spirits who could be vengeful and gratuitously malevolent. Canoe use in these areas, particularly the deep sea that constituted one of the few available options for fishing during windy season, had the form of a near-perfect double bind from which there was no escape. For the population to feed itself, some of its members must expose themselves to contexts wherein their prey were controlled by agents who prey on people. To complicate matters, the signals of a spirit's presence are ambiguous, since they take the forms of sharks, rays, dolphins, and porpoises--it was not always clear when a shark was only a shark. There are four possible outcomes of such an encounter: a fisherman could decide that the it was only an animal and be right or wrong or decide that the animal was really a spirit and be right or wrong. Of these four, only a correct guess that it was an animal did not involve punishment of some sort. In the other three cases, at best the fishermen lost several days of fishing either because of the priest's taboo or because the spirit withheld the fish. At worst, the fisherman who guessed wrongly that the animal was only an animal would die, and the gods might withhold the fish for an extended period, resulting in a starving population.

Kapinga responses to this double bind have striking parallels to those of schizophrenics in double bind situations (Bateson 1972: 201-227)--ambiguating their own signals with verbal camouflages and using rote, formulaic sequences in dealing with the spirits. These responses are widely disseminated through the male population through rote memory.

If routine recitations of prayer and lexical camouflages were sufficient to pacify the gods, then age and class distinctions would be too artificial to be tolerated by people who, in most respects, are egalitarian in their dealings with one another. It is the unpredictability of the gods and the ambiguity of their representations that require every canoe crew to have workable contingency plans on an expedition. Minimal necessities are men who know (a) the difference between ordinary and extraordinary appearances of sharks, dolphins, whales, and rays, (b) when their least expected appearances are most likely to be spirit representations, and (c) the appropriate chant. For the six deep sea gods, it is necessary to have a man aboard with whom the gods he importunes are familiar. They should know him and 'like' him. A crew member who is both knowledgeable and of the sacred class is a further advantage, given that some of the cult house gods are former high priests, and it can't hurt if the man addressing them is one of their relatives. The importance of familiarity extends to the canoes themselves, many of which were named. Thus, a tuna crew would never use a brand new canoe with which the deep sea gods were unfamiliar.

Organizing this sort of reliable response to unpredictable and ambiguous danger is a matter of instituting social distinctions that allocate responsibility and authority for dealing with the danger to those most likely to have experience with and/or pre-established relationships with the dangerous agents in the environment. Age stratification and the sacred-secular class distinction accomplish this organizational task, if not perfectly, then at least well enough. The fact that these two categories cross-cut each other lends redundancy to a system whose major components--spirits and people--are more or less inherently chaotic and, therefore, unreliable.[2]

From this point of view, canoe ownership poses a special problem that other sorts of hardware (and technique) do not. Having one's own canoe presupposes personal autonomy in choosing the uses to which the canoe will be put. This freedom of choice always implies the possibility of a costly mistake on the water. Once a man has his own canoe, people hope that he chose his crew and conducted himself judiciously, but this was never guaranteed. As close as Kapinga could get to guaranteeing wisdom of canoe owners was to limit their numbers through careful selection.

Both the high priest and the *tomoono* had veto power over canoe construction, since both men had to participate in the ritual that initiated the work. Now, this power may have been a sacred-secular dialectic or an exercise in economic and political manipulation. But given the palpable danger implicit in canoe ownership and use, it is also clear that with a combination of the priest's ritual expertise and the experience a *tomono* had with the applicant on fishing expeditions, having them both sign off on the project constituted a fail-safe procedure for controlling potential loose cannons.

The prestige that Kapinga traditionally placed on deep sea fishing was a function of its inherent dangers. For the canoe owner, prestige derived from the ability to make autonomous choices, facing the danger of the ocean being one of them. His very ownership was a confirmation of a consensus of trust in his skill, courage, and prudence. For the crew member chosen from among his fellows, prestige came from the explicit recognition of his skill, experience, and courage. Being chosen was a commission, like being chosen to direct house or canoe construction. The prestige of deep sea fishermen was proportional to the dangers they faced and to the responsibilities they carried for the livelihood of others, much like the prestige of the descent group steward and the men's house headman.

If the precolonial social order was an organized response to what Kapinga people knew about their environment, then it follows that any major change in what people knew about their universe should have occasioned changes in their responses to their changed conditions (as they perceived them). While contact with Euroamericans and Melanesian and Polynesian crewmen and western goods represent major changes in what Kapinga knew about their world, it is significant that Kapinga responses were novel in their specifics but not in their patterns. The conversion of pandanus groves to coconut plantations for making copra, the rapid adoption of *Cyrtosperma* taro as a staple and the 40% increase in taro plantations, the rapid adoption of cloth, of metal tools and utensils, tobacco, tea, and sugar are clearly specific sorts of responses. But even with a universe containing two very different sources of power--one human and one non-human--Kapinga patterns of response change little if at all. Kapinga experience with Europeans and Americans told them very little about outside agents that they did not already know. These outsiders were capable of producing both abundant goods and sudden violence (including whippings and homicide), neither of which was very predictable. The same techniques that Kapinga used for dealing with the gods worked equally well with the colonialists--unstinting flattery of the outsiders coupled with self-deprecation, a continual flow of gifts and labor, and a local liaison to handle the bulk of dealings with them. Indeed, the only major structural change during the early contact period was the elaboration of the liaison position to that of island representative, a 'king' whose source of legitimacy, like that of priests, was powerful outsiders. Even the ten men who formed a competing copra producer's association organized their trading activity through a European liaison.

Kapinga's experiences of the structural identity of unpredictable Europeans and unpredictable gods vary with the sort of relationship they have with each. For many, if not most Kapinga, the danger of the gods is augmented by dangerous colonialists, whose almost continual presence on the atoll makes the land as dangerous as the deep sea. Those most closely associated with the colonialists were skeptical about the power of the gods. While some attributed the drought to the gods' vengeance for skeptics' many ritual violations, others construe it as evidence of the impotence of native ritual. The Nukuoro missionaries provide a third alternative (made legitimate by the gift of food), but this in itself does not necessarily preclude substituting a new double bind for an old one.

It is the nature of the Japanese administration and a Protestant church to which a reordered community adapts that obviates paradox in the relationship between the community and the outside powers that control it. The Japanese, to be sure, were capable of willful violence directed to both islanders and to one another. But the physical danger the Japanese represented was predictable, not whimsical. Japanese administrators' and employers' demands were clear and explicit, and violence was one result of disregarding them. Rewards were as predictable as punishments. Jehovah was similarly clear in what He expected from people, one of his demands being *aloho*, empathy and personal concern, aid and comfort. Giving up dancing, polygamy, cousin marriage, native ritual, and work on Sundays was little enough in return for protection from the spirits (now defined as embodiments of Satan) and from an eternity in the fires of Hell. Even if the levels of danger do not significantly decrease during this period, they are much more focussed and predictable. Japanese personnel and Jehovah might have seemed stringent in their demands, but neither was gratuitously malevolent.

That physical danger from powerful outside agents had come to be clearly contingent on how people responded to reasonably clear directives represented a simplification of the Kapinga universe. One Kapinga response was a reconstituted social hierarchy that was much less complex at its highest level than the panel of priests it replaced. The fact that the hierarchy was made legitimate by two distinct sources of authority was blurred by the king and his assistant being pastors in the church and by church rules of personal conduct being represented as civil law. The organizational model for the new hierarchy was the dual leadership typical of cult house, men's house, descent and work groups. The lines of authority developed under King David were clear, as were expected responses to non-compliance with or defiance of civil law and kingly edicts. Fines, community work details, jail terms, exclusion from church membership, and, as a last resort, facing criminal charges before a Japanese magistrate on Pohnpei were all options at the king's disposal. The complexity of this reorganized social system was located in the relationships among its institutional components--the church, the men's houses, descent groups, and community meetings. It is this reconstituted community hierarchy that forms the context of the individuation of fishing activity.

If the contrast between an individuated organization of fishing activity and a hierarchical organization of the community strikes us as an obvious one, it appears to have been unremarkable to Kapinga. This may be partly because the decreasing frequency of group fishing was gradual. Certainly the increasing autonomy of choice that fishermen enjoyed was contextualized by a scheduling of options constrained both by church rules (a seven day week) and household needs determined by female household heads. But this still does not explain why the reorganization of fishing activity posed no problem for anyone before 1956. What is clear is that the organization of fishing activity becomes a metaphor for social disintegration only when it becomes *recontextualized* as part of a transformed social order. That transformation, like the one before it, is the outcome of Kapinga attempts to adapt themselves to powerful new outside agents. It is how Kapinga construe this process of adaptation that explains why the individuation of fishing activity becomes problematic during the American administration.

Throughout the pre-colonial, early colonial, and Japanese periods, fishing activity is regulated by the larger community, whatever its institutional form. Fishing activity is integrated into the community organization through the men's houses, which are controlled by the cult house in the pre-Christian era and which are part of the community policy making apparatus during the Japanese and early American periods. The cult house embodies the community before 1917, and the king embodies it thereafter. These different embodiments, however, share a common assumption that is affected neither by Kapinga's changing perceptions of their environment nor by the changing forms that their community takes. Kapinga assume that 'community' is that institution which is organized to respond to danger from outside the island. This cultural premis--an arbitrarily constituted and shared proposition that unconsciously shapes the conclusions people draw about their experiences--remains stable and unquestioned to the present. As Kapinga's understandings about what constituted their universe have changed, they have adapted their activities and the institutions that organized them to fit their changed situations, always on the assumption that the powerful agents that controlled the universe outside their island represented palpable physical danger.

When it is powerful spirits that represent outside danger, it is the priesthood, embodying the community, that is organized to cope with it. Fishing activity both exploits environmental abundance and confronts environmental danger, the latter being encoded on the general term for fishing, *dabu ae*, 'surfacing (of the) sacred, of the ritually charged.' Community control of fishing activity serves to minimize its dangers and to regulate those dangerous encounters that cannot be avoided. Regulation focusses especially on the possession and use of canoes that connect danger from inside the community consequent on autonomous choice with danger from outside, i.e., the spirits. Both are assumed to be inherently chaotic, but only people are subject to constraint, specifically by limiting the autonomous choices they can make. Priestly control of canoe construction and of fishing areas are designed to do precisely this.

When it is the Japanese administration and Jehovah that represent physical danger, the form of the Kapinga community changes to adapt to those conditions. The church, the men's house, and the community meeting all serve to constrain the autonomy of the king and the populace. Fishing activity continues to be constrained by the men's houses--despite the fact that deep sea fishing no longer implies the dangers of spirits--because of the integration of fishing activity with political consensus organized through the men's house.

Given 'community' as Kapinga understand it, what happens if the powerful outside agents constituting the source of internal authority present no physical danger whatever? This is precisely the case with the American administration, although it takes Kapinga a while to realize it. Their initial encounters with Americans literally reeked danger with the strafing, bombing, dogfights, and shelling in 1944 and 1945. Kapinga were terrified of what they were led to believe would be inevitable atrocities by the American military. Since Americans' image of themselves in the international arena is of the Smokey the Bear variety, it is easy to dismiss the islanders fears for their lives and their readiness to do whatever was necessary to save themselves. Although their worst fears were quickly allayed by the gregarious, personable sailors who rapidly made goods available to Kapinga cut off from shipping for over eighteen months, the administrative personnel with whom Kapinga dealt from 1946 to 1951 were military men or civilians working for them.

Given Kapinga premises of relationship between the community and powerful outsiders, the transition from the Naval administration to the Department of the Interior control of the Trust Territory of the Pacific Islands constituted a cultural bait-and-switch. The big ships with guns and goods, free spending enlisted men, and bemedaled officers were replaced by a quieter, bureaucratized administration with a miniscule budget. This was an administration that, unable to control illegal imports of liquor or local production of toddy and "yeast," simply legalized liquor imports and licenced bars. The near-routine violence of weekend drinking in Kolonia town, with its frequent brawls, stabbings, and a rare shooting, sometimes resulted in a short jail sentence (when a perpetrator was actually arrested and tried) or, when a policeman was murdered in a bar in 1967, temporary closure of the bars. This was an administration that, finding it embarrassing to admit publicly that its personnel were embezzling funds, quietly fired them and let it go at that. Between 1971 and 1984, six Kapinga men were murdered by Micronesians. Of these only one was brought to trial, and he was given a two year work-release jail sentence. These are but a few instances of what, for Kapinga, has been a major organizational dilemma. The unquestioned power of the American administration has been embodied in a bureaucracy that has been every bit as unpredictable as the old gods while posing no physical danger whatever to anyone. By the time the latter becomes clear to Kapinga, they had already transformed the organization of their community to its present tri-partite structure and severed its operation from the church. In fact, the American administration employed mostly rewards, depending (unpredictably) on the form of the group for which rewards were intended and the form of the activities used by the group to secure them. Administrative rewards--development programs, jobs, grants-in-aid, budgets, and per diem--were filtered through separate departments agencies, and organizations, none accountable to the others and only the chief magistrate, the council and local judges being accountable to the community. Indeed, it was the latter whose organizational efforts were least predictably rewarded. Yet Kapinga continue to assume that the organization of the community is designed to deal with danger. For example, when the disastrous dimensions of the 1979 tidal wave became apparent, people expected the chief magistrate and council to act, although no one had any idea what they should do. But if the colonial administration was not a source of danger, then people had to look elsewhere for danger signals.

The inevitable place to look for danger signals in the Kapinga social order is the person, whose inherently chaotic self is constrained by his or her social relationships, failure of which results in disaster both for oneself and for others. American administrative policy has made the individual the target of its programs, with the development of personal autonomy as their goal. The relation between the community and the administration, thus, has the form of a double bind, but of a different sort than the pre-colonial bind. In order to cope with the perceived danger of powerful outside agents, Kapinga had to organize activities that promoted the autonomy of the most dangerous internal component of their social system. That those outside agents turn out to present unpredictable rewards rather than danger does not resolve the paradoxical structure of this bind. Only the signs--dangerous to not dangerous-- at the community-to-administration level of relationship are reversed. Like any human double bind, this one is perpetuated by high degrees of ambiguity at every systemic level from the relationship between the commuity and the administration to that of interaction between people. It is never clear when a council proposal will be accepted by the administration or rejected as representing too much or too little community autonomy. The boundaries of community control over people's activities are never clear, and the boundaries are made and kept fuzzy by the compartmentalization of atoll institutions under the control of bureaucratic fiefdoms on Pohnpei. This institutional fragmentation keeps the locus of authority and the legitimacy of its exercise on the atoll ambiguous. With little supervision, a teacher, a nurse, or a co-op manager are encouraged by their supervisors to use personal initiative in dealing with the day to day details of their jobs, e.g., dealing with a truant or disruptive student, recommending some students but not others for high school on Pohnpei, dealing with a co-op customer with bad credit, sending a pregnant woman to Pohnpei to be delivered against her family's wishes, etc..

When guidelines for making such decisions are opaque to those not familiar with them, it is often unclear whether an actor is "doing his job" or abusing his authority in arrogant disregard for the other. Accusations of the latter are common complaints on the atoll.

It is the ambiguities of the specific contexts of relationship at all levels of the Kapinga social system that mask its paradoxical nature. In this damned-if-you-do, damned-if-you-don't sort of contextual structure, victims of double binds ordinarily blame themselves for their pain, and Kapinga are no exception. It is persons, not the organization of their relationships, that are at fault for the disintegration of their community.

> Before, the community was sacred. Now each person has is own knowledge and his own truth, and the community is nothing.

And what could be a clearer illustration of unconstrained personal autonomy than fishing activity, *dabu ae*, a quintessential symbol of community integration and its sanctity, whose most important connection to a higher level of constraint is now with the co-op that controls the gas supply?

Understandably enough, the people that Kapinga most often blame for the failure of the community to constrain personal autonomy are their leaders. Leadership of any group, whether by consensus, vote, or appointment, is still considered a commission. As Kapinga talk about it, the success or failure of any group endeavor depends on how well the leader does his job, not on whether the group's organization is the most efficient one for the task at hand. If their leaders were competent, wise, and committed to the community rather than to their own aggrandizement, then people would listen to them and follow them, as they did Kings David and Tuiai.

People assume that one who seeks or accepts a position of leadership has the knowledge, skills, and personal contacts to (a) acquire all requisite materials and information about their use to perform the task at hand and (b) authority sufficient to compel minimal compliance of others with the demands of the particular project, ordinance, or plan for which he or she is responsible. Such assumptions are based on biographical information people have about the leader's past performance, friends on other islands, contacts in the Pohnpei bureaucracy, etc.. No one questions the leader's authority until he or she makes a mistake or antagonizes the people whom he leads. The leader of a construction project, for example, has a good deal of latitude to choose people to whom to delegate tasks and in the timing of tasks. He may take liberties with design, e.g., of a building, a bridge, the content and order of presentation of a Sunday school class, and the like. His decisions may occasion discussion, criticism, and gossip, but no one questions his right to do these things. A commission to direct anything assumes the necessity for autonomous decisions, but it precisely those decisions which people point to when the project founders, not as specific errors but as evidence of personal inadequacy--laziness and arrogance being the most frequent charges. People do not see any particular pattern in these phenomena and their timing; they see instead only a series of instances of people whose personal ambitions got the better of them. Personal autonomy for people in leadership positions has come to mean having enough rope to hang oneself, as exemplified by the fact that no chief magistrate since the early 1970s has served more than a single term.

Double binds never resolve themselves. The way out of a double bind is either through a sudden insight wherein one of the parties involved sees the paradox for what it is, as is common with Zen students (Herrigel 1989) or when a person (or persons) involved sees that there is an alternative configuration to the sort of relationship in which they have been trapped.[3] The Japanese colonial period resolves the pre-colonial bind with a differently structured alternative. With the termination of the Trust Territory, Kapinga experience both insight into and an alternative configuration of their relationship to powerful outsiders. The Hale group's "back to our roots" movement turns on the explicit recognition of people's dependency on powerful outsiders as the cause of their difficulties and the cultivation of their own environmental and human resources as its solution. Identifying the dependency relation is not the same as identifying the premis that shapes it or the double bind that maintains it, but the detrmination of these people to test the truth of their proposition through practice provides the necessary condition for taking that next logical step. For other Kapinga, the impending termination of the United States trusteeship, the ratification of the FSM constitution, and the incorporation of Pohnpei district as Pohnpei State, pose an (unavoidable) alternative way of ordering the relationship between community and administration. This is a relationship to which the assumption of dependency is inapplicable. It is not Europeans, Asians, or Americans who exercise power from vast continents far away. It is other islanders like themselves who now constitute the outside agents of authority, goods, and danger. In order to understand why vesting of authority in fellow islanders obviates the double bind and the dependency relation on which it depends, we need to push the cultural argument one more logical step, taking the premis of the relationship between the community and powerful outsiders as a variable rather than a given. The premis is one of a number of ways that Kapinga could have viewed their universe. Why this one and not some other? Pohnpeians, for example, see power as emanating from agents outside the island who become incorporated into the island social order (Lieber 1990). Rather than speculating about the origin of this premis, we can use available data to understand the context that makes it possible.

This premis and the traditional social order in which it was expressed is itself the outcome of a historical process that combined the organizational model of the Kapinga's Ellice Island ancestral population with several hundred years of isolation from other islands. Traditional history and an occasional castaway told people of a world in which other islands existed, but none of them had any relevance to the Kapinga community. The occasional landfall of a castaway canoe was considered the work of the gods taking pity on the unfortunates, or, as in the case of the Marshallese castaways who slaughtered over half the Kapinga population in 1865, as punishment for ritual infractions (Emory 1965: 53-55). Indeed, castaways were called only 'castaway' until they either left the island or underwent a ritual that cleansed them of supernatural power of their home islands. Only then were they given Kapinga names and allowed to marry. Geographically and ritually, Kapinga maintained their isolation.

I find it difficult to conceive of evolving a premis of the sort Kapinga held about community dependency on outside, non-human agents in a world including other islands with whom Kapinga were in regular contact, as is the case in atoll clusters and complexes such as the Marshall Islands, the Western Caroline atolls, the Tokelau islands, etc.. The assumption of interdependence with other island peoples, whether peaceful or warlike, presupposes alternative resources and strategies for dealing with the vagaries of abundance and disaster by locating their potential outcomes in relations with people on other islands (cf. Alkire 1978). In other words, the the premise of dependency of the sort that Kapinga have developed is inconceivable in a multicultural milieu.

It has become fashionable to talk about multiculturalism as if it were some recent discovery instead of what it really is--a condition of human life that is as old as the human species. With only rare exceptions, the human communities that we know of in the prehistoric and historic records typically developed and maintained themselves as parts of a larger social universe of other communities, separate from and different from themselves, but connected to themselves by the many and varied sorts of relationships--economic, political, religious, etc.--that typically connect regions. Typical of these societies--the vast majority that we know about--is their interdependence (and a community's integrity may be as dependent on its enemies as on its allies), and the flow of goods, people and knowledge across ethnic boundaries. Even when a community does not borrow the technology or the ritual or the practices of another, the people in that community more often than not know about them, at the very least as those tangible tokens of difference distinguishing "us" from "them." More importantly, the world views of these communities always include "us," our supernaturals, and those other communities with whom we have to deal. This has two important implications: one is that when the crunch comes, even a supernaturally induced cruch, there are those other communities to whom we can turn for help. The second is that for this to work, there must be reasonably consistent interpretation of cultural difference built into the world view (see, for example, Flinn 1992).

In a monocultural community, one without those "others" separate from and distinct from "us," the only thing that unites us, that makes us a community, is whatever common fate befalls us at the behest of the powers that be, however these are defined. Nothing stands between us and these agents of power and control--usually deities--other than the (usually ritual) techniques by which these agents can be influenced. The relation between us and the outside world is a vertical relation between the agents of the commuity and the agents of power. When people's techniques of influencing these agents fail (as in a drought, a typhoon, etc.), there is nothing left to do but panic or suffer quietly. The result is a kind of fatalism, a frustrated acceptance of adversity sequentially blaming it on us and later on the whimsey of the gods. This relation of dependency on powerful outside agents is typical of monocultural societies.[4]

But the end of isolation rarely, if ever, ends the vertical relation between us and agents of power. Imperial colonial powers typically replace the home grown variety on Kapingamarangi, Bikini, Nukuoro, the Marquesas, and a very few other monocultural islands. Contact with other communities comes with the imperial power's needs for mobile labor and markets, but the erstwhile isolates always experience these contacts as a function of their relationship with the imperial power.

This precolonial pattern of powerful outside agents mediating Kapinga contacts with other islanders holds unchanged from 1877 to 1979. Early colonial contacts on the atoll with Melanesian and Polynesian ships' crew are mediated by ship captains and first mates. Regular contacts with resident Nukuoro and Samoan depend on their relationship to the resident Europeans whom they serve (or to whom they were married). The few Kapinga who travelled elsewhere did so as ship's crewmen or as spouses of Europeans, bringing back tales of Melanesian cannibals and rebellious Pohnpeians controlled only by German might. The geographical shape of Kapinga's known world was reordered during this early colonial period with inclusion of Nukuoro, Pohnpei, Samoa, New Britain, New Guinea, and with such places as

England, Germany, America, and Denmark: vague in location but clear in their embodiment of abundance and danger. The pattern of relationships between the atoll and these places is identical to that of the pre-colonial period, however: contact with other islanders is an outcome of control by powerful outside agents.

During the Japanese colonial period, Kapinga experience their first regular emigration and daily face-to-face contacts with Micronesians. It is the administration's need for labor that initially determines emigration patterns. A resident Kapinga population on Pohnpei is assured not only by Porakied village, but by their reputation as deep sea fishermen and the constant need of Japanese restaurants and Japanese and Micronesian residents. The settings of contacts with Micronesians are work crews (on plantations, construction sites, factories, the Kolonia docks, and road projects), church participation, and commercial ones (as customers in Japanese and Belgian businesses). Work contacts are mediated by Japanese foremen and commercial ones by business owners. The Protestant and Catholic churches, controlled by American and European pastors and priests, were the safe houses for inter-ethnic contact. Other than four marriages between Kapinga women and Micronesian men, trade partnerships between Kapinga fishermen and Micronesian land owners constituted the only intimate one-to-one or family-to-family relationships that were not mediated by colonial institutions. Despite any danger it may have posed, The Japanese administration also represented sponsorship (e.g., the land grant in Kolonia) and protection, not only for Kapinga but for other out-islanders whose presence on Pohnpei was also at the administration's behest.[5]

Sponsorship and protection were important to Kapinga because the danger inherent in relations with Micronesians was less predictable than that with Japanese. Pohnpeians in particular, with their acute sensitivity to rank differences, were easily offended by perceived insults, and fist fights with Pohnpeians were common in the early days on Pohnpei. More frightening was Pohnpeian sorcery and magic, whose victims could as easily be friends as enemies. These dangers were avoidable by keeping one's close contacts within church membership and by choosing one's trading partners carefully and by being scrupulously generous. Kapinga, through these several contexts of contact, come to see Micronesians as people much like themselves, dependent on the will of colonial personnel and constrained by their authority. This pattern of contact in an expanding world hardly challenges the premis of Kapinga's dependency on powerful outsiders or the (more abstract) assumption of isolation that makes that premis possible. Even as these formerly isolated populations begin to travel elsewhere and to form personal relations with people of other communities, such as trade partnerships and "fellow congregants" in Christian churches, these relations are adaptive expedients, contingent on the relationsips between the "monoculturals" and the imperial agents. So, for example, the American administration's policy of ethnic integration in a kind of Pohnpeian citizenship has succeeded only in intensifying interethnic isolation of populations in their enclaves. The expansion of Trust Territory funding through the 1960s and 1970s created a rapidly expanding bureaucracy and a spate of agencies. Increasing income from fishing, wage work, and especially handicrafts and private businesses in Porakied allowed Kapinga residents to transform their village economy from a cash-subsistence mix to a full cash economy and to withdraw from trade partnerships into a self-made ghetto. Even the Congregationalist church gave up its role as a central focus of interethnic contact 1979. Church contacts with Micronesians both on the atoll and in Porakied are organized on an ethnic congregation-to-ethnic congregation basis (Lieber 1984).

It was in this social milieu that Ponape District was reorganized as Pohnpei State and the FSM constitution offered for ratification. That Kapinga on the atoll and on Pohnpei should have been uneasy about the prospect of political independence from the United States is hardly surprising. Positions of political power such as the governor and lieutenant-governor, department heads, agency chiefs, congressmen and their staffs are all occupied by Micronesians, islanders like themselves. This poses a peculiar dilemma for Kapinga on the atoll and in Porakied.

Micronesians may have the political and economic power that colonial rulers used to have, but certainly not the sort of (cultural) legitimacy as rulers that Europeans, Japanese, and Americans had, at least in Kapinga thinking. Unless Kapinga can assimilate them perceptually to colonial ruler status, their only other alternative is to establish some sort of interdependence with other island polities. But quick conversion from a premis of authority rooted in isolation to one that assumes island interdependence is as likely a perceptual gymnastic as assimilating Micronesians to colonial ruler status.

The Kapinga dilemma is an outcome of another crucial feature of the monocultural community, one that is only partially replicated in large scale, modern nations with a dominant subgroup exercising political hegemony--that is the way that US is defined. In most of the world's societies where diverse communities have been in contact for a long time, identities of these communities are mutually definitive, and us comes to be defined in contrast to specific others. Thus, a community's sense of itself comes to be reasonably specific. The monocultural community, on the other hand, tends to see itself as "just plain folks" and everyone else as "the ethnics" (cf. Kirkpatrick n. d.). Differences between itself and other communities (after imperial contact) are reckoned on a case-by-case basis. We are fishermen, unlike all those others except the Mokil people, who are also fishermen, etc., etc.. With no vision of "us" as anything other than just plain folks, there can be no vision of "our" place in a set of interacting communities other than one of equal dependency on and domination by the same imperial power. Such a view can work for only as long as the monocultural community enjoys the protection of the imperial power. But as colonial powers are succeeded by emerging nations, monocultural communities face a series of political crises attendant precisely on their places in these emerging nations.

From this perspective, the Hale movement, as remarkable as it may have been, was just the flip side of the same old coin. If you can't look outward (read upward) with any degree of certainty, then the only other place to look is inward.[6] A truely radical shift in people's thinking would have been to pose the alternative of forming alliances with other islands, but this option did not enter into any of the discussions I heard during the transition period of the early 1980s. Community interdependence, which has been standard operating procedure in the multicultural Micronesian islands from time immemorial, must be negotiated if it cannot be assumed, and the avenues of such negotiation are few enough to allow for some prediction of its most likely outcomes.

Kapingamarangi municipal funding no longer comes from chief magistrate requests to the district administrator or to agency heads. The municipal budget is now funded through the state legislature and is the state legislator's responsibility to push. As is true of any such body, getting one's budget items approved is as much a matter of political leverage as it is of need. Outisland legislators appear to be learning the value of coalition politics, swing votes, and old fashioned horse trading. Interdependency, in other words, is likely to take the form of island coalitions negotiated by legislators.[7] This places the Kapingamarangi representative in a unique position, since he resides in Porakied with constituents both on the atoll and in Porakied. His position in Porakied, however, also affords him some political leverage in Kolonia Town politics, since about half of the Porakied residents are registered to vote in Kolonia Town, and the prospect of a bloc vote is sufficient for office holders and office seekers to seek his support. Every legislator elected since 1979 has been a man with bureaucratic experience and connections in various departments, enabling him to use his contacts to speed up actions on requests, release funds, and the like. The state representative, in other words, occupies a position that has the potential for finally integrating the separate hierarchies on the atoll and for reintegrating the atoll with Porakied. If this is what in fact happens, as is likely, then I expect that church membership will become a more important part of a representative's qualifications than it has been for chief magistrate or councilmen, a tacit symbol of integration.

Another possible avenue of interdependence is coalition of municipalities in the same congressional district. For example, a proposal from the Pingelapese state legislator to redraw congressional districts in Pohnpei State elicited an instant response from the chief magistrate of Sokes municipality and the Kolonia Town council, who opposed any change in their district, which includes Sahpwafik, Nukuoro, and Kapingamarangi atolls. A delegation representing Sokes municipality and the Kolonia Town council, after securing the Kapinga legislator's signature of support, came to the atoll in 1986 to secure the support of the chief magistrate and municipal council. Their suggestion to convene a conference of district chief magistrates the next year met with approval, but also with some skepticism as to whether it would really happen.[8] Indeed, this sort of attempt at coalition would depend on requisite funding, at least some of which would have to come from the State legislature, requiring the support of state representatives. While this avenue remains open, I suspect that it will be used for particular issues rather than as a permanent standing group. Even so, the identification of these municipalities as a group sharing common interests (and, for the most part, common identity as being comprised largely of outislanders) proposes an interdependence with political power at both the state and congressional levels. It is an option that can be tapped as needed, but it does not have the integrative potential for Kapinga that the legislator's position has.

The state legislator will inherit his constituents' demand to provide freezers on the field trip ship and the atoll to market fresh fish. The cost of this project will continue to be prohibitive, and he will have to come up with some viable alternative as a political necessity. I suspect that dried salt fish will continue to be the most feasible alternative and that organizing its packaging and marketing will continue to be the major problem he will have to solve. He will need to use his connections either to get start up funds for a private business or to integrate atoll fishermen into an established business, of which there is one in Kolonia Town at present.

If the legislator can avoid the kind of comingling of public with private business concerns that has discredited leaders in the past, we should not see the turnover in state representatives that we have in chief magistrates. The incumbent will share more attributes with the old king than with the chief magistrate, save for the inconvenience of election campaigns. My argument thus ends the way it began--with a testable hypothesis and, if I may be permitted a little luxury, a bit of hope.

Notes

1. That the change we observe is in frequencies in deployment of particular techniques rather than in the organization of the techniques themselves is to say simply that constraints are hierarchically ordered. Characteristic of any hierarchy is what Simon (1973: 9-11) calls the "near decomposability" of hierarchical structures. This means that the components of any hierarchical system are more stable than the relations between the components.

2. See Singh (1976) for an account of different organizational models for constructing reliable systems from unreliable components. The models used are of nervous systems, but they could be applied equally to genetic control systems and social systems.

3. See Bateson's (1961) *Percival's Narrative* for 19th century autobiographical account of how a schizophrenic patient conducted his own ethnographic investigation of how normal families operate, comparing his findings with his own experiences to understand his paradoxical family relations and how they led him to madness.

4. Kurt Godel demonstrated long ago that any closed system of axioms inevitably generates paradoxes (Nagel and Newman 1958). The cultural isolation of Kapingamarangi and other commuities like it fulfill this crucial condition of the closed system.

5. The Japanese administration, for example, made it very clear to the paramount chief of Nett 'state' that Porakied and its people were not part of his political domain when he attempted to control the village in the late 1920s.

6. The inward looking self-sufficiency of the Hale group contains within its premises its own inevitable paradox. Where and to whom does the community turn to cope with the next disaster?

7. Moves in this direction began in 1983, initiated by the Nukuoro and Ngatik (now Sahpwafik) legislators, who proposed a land boundary survey for these two atolls, inviting the Kapinga legislator to join.

8. I am indebted for these data to Eve Pinsker, who was present at this meeting.

Epilogue

I got to test these predictions after this last chapter had been written, spending parts of November and December, 1990, on Pohnpei. I'm right about the position of the legislator, but I underestimated what he could do, so I'm wrong about the likely trend toward renewed interest in sails and traditional techniques. The interest in teaching traditional fishing to school children disappeared when the funding for historic preservation in the school curriculum ended. People's anxiety about their community and their future, at least to the degree I saw it from 1977 to 1982, was a phase contingent on perceived crisis. What helped to allay their fears was the emergence of a strong, consciencious, politically astute legislator in 1983, whose track record since then is unparalleled by any previous representative (including the FSM senator). The son of the atoll's first ordained minister and an active church elder with years of experience at various levels of the Pohnpei bureaucracy, this man's quiet, dignified demeanor, subtle sense of humor, and ability clearly and firmly to articulate his views exudes authority. He has managed to get the field trip ship equipped with a "quick" freezer ideal for storing fresh fish for transfer to larger freezers for long-term storage. Because of the short period of the ship's stay and the time and manpower needed for unloading and loading goods, fishermen have had little time to collect fish for sale. The legislator then managed to get a $50,000 budget line for a freezer, thermostatically controlled compressor, and a generator large enough to run them approved by the legislature.

Public works money has expanded under his direction, as has the handicraft market. He also helped to broker a project in commercial seaweed farming on the atoll, although market conditions have made the future of this labor intensive farming uncertain. With more money available on the atoll, there are more outboard engines augmented by three fiberglass boats with 80 horsepower motors, despite the rise in gas prices.

There are indications that his position is indeed approaching that of the old king, somewhat to his chagrin. The atoll magistrate and council, who are responsible for preparing the municipal budget, have left the matter to him for several years. Although budget items are discussed in council meetings, the decisions about what the municipality needs are now his. He is not happy about the extra work of having to meet last minute deadlines for budget submission, and he is considering not running for reelection.

That the form of atoll leadership has changed in the predicted direction and that fishing activity is one of its most visible emblems serves to illustrate the *systemic* nature of social change. Although the organization of the Pohnpei State Legislature differs little from the Ponape District Legislature that preceeded it, the control that the State legislature has over budgetary and other resources (e.g., public land) differ radically from the advisory role of its predecessor. The atoll, through its legislator, has the authority to negotiate for and to control its own flow of resources. The relationship between the state legislator and the governor has also changed, with each having a legally defined sphere of authority and interdependence. If the *structure* of these political institutions has not changed, their activities and, consequently, their relationships most certainly have. The context of Kapingamarangi's relationship with the State is very different from that with the former Ponape District. The same process of recombination of activities with institutions that characterized the changes described for Onotoa and Kapingamarangi atolls in the early 1900s can be seen to organize the pattern of change in Pohnpei State today. The strategies by which the atoll's representative adapts to a recontextualized political order have changed from appeals to higher authority to negotiation, political alliances, vote trading, block voting, and the like.

The activities of the atoll's legislator have changed as the political context has changed. The form of his collegial relations, however, replicates the trade partnerships of earlier years. It is clear that people's expectations of this man and their deference to his authority both on the atoll and in Porakied differ little from those of the former kings. The municipal council's abdication of its budgetary authority to the legislator is but one example of this reconstituting of an older institution. Another is the absence of Kapinga other than the legislator at the many sessions of the Pohnpei State Constitutional Convention held to formulate policy on issues affecting municipalities. These meetings, according to Eve Pinkser, who was present at most of them, drew large audiences of municipal officials and other local leaders from the atolls and Pohnpei municipalities. While Kapingamarangi's larger political context may have changed, the local premise of its relationship to that context--the contextual structure--has not, nor is it likely to change any time soon.

The realities of political and economic interdependence between island municipalities directly challenge Kapinga people's traditional monocultural premis if and only if they become a conscious part of ordinary people's experience. But one of the most important features of the old kingship replicated in the legislator's position is precisely that his political strategies remain matters of private, elite communication. Ordinary people are interested only in results, not the processes by

Epilogue

which they are attained. Thus, old patterns of elite communication ensure that the *practice* of interisland interdependence is a prerogative of leadership rather than a shared recognition of the conditions of living in a multicultural universe. The maintenance of the contextual structure of atoll-to-outside relations leaves the Kapinga community vulnerable to the inevitable variability in the competence of its elected legislators, but this is true of any of Pohnpei State's municipalities. This potential cost is balanced by the reintegration of an atomized Kapinga community.

I can think of no more appropriate way to end my account than this one--a discussion of the communication processes that make a human community a social system.

Appendix 1:
List of Catch Techniques

I list the catch techniques described in Part Two following the same order of presentation of the chapters, i.e., netting, pole and line, etc.. But the organization of the list is different from that of the chapters, where my major concern is to show how a single method, e.g., surround, varies with the particular fish sought, the area fish fished, and the environmental conditions of timing. In this listing, I follow the order that I used to collect the data. Each catch technique is organized by calm season, year-round, and windy season methods. These are subdivided by day and night fishing, and, where appropriate, by techniques targeting an area and techniques that target a species. Each major subcategory has a two letter code, and each member of the category, that is each particular technique in the coded category, has a number just to its left. To the right of each catch method in parentheses is the page number or numbers in Part Two where you will find the description of that technique. So, the number to the left is the code number that identifies it, while the numbers to the right indexes it in the text. I arrange the listing in this way for two purposes. One is to provide anyone interested in comparing Kapinga traditional fishing with that of some other community. This list can be used as a handy check-list for comparison with published work (e.g., Catala 1954, Black 1981) and/or by anyone contemplating doing field research on traditional fishing elsewhere, an activity that I cannot encourage strongly enough.

The second purpose of this arrangement is to help to contextualize the list of named species given in Appendix 2. Because this list is alphabetized, it is randomized from a Kapinga poitn of view. It would be useful only to comparative linguists and specialists in Oceanic fisheries but for two features of the list. One is the evidence it provides of an obviously detailed knowledge of local varieties of fish. You can see this, for example, in those varieties of fish, e.g., triggerfish where the genus is distinguished and the specific varieties are indicated by color or habitat

213

differences. The second feature to note is the fourth column in the list. For each fish, all of the techniques used to catch it are listed in the column, each one being listed using the codes from Appendix 1. The addition of the catch technique codes in the fourth column of the list not only shows how each one of these fish was caught, but gives you an idea of the variety environmental contexts--the sort of ecological niche--in which these fish operate. You have only to scan this list to get a good idea of the extent to which Kapinga exploited their marine resources. Specifically, even a casual glance at the list gives substance to the assertion in Chapter 9 that traditional fishing activities distributed catch pressure over a wide variety of fish species.

NETTING

Netting expeditions conducted during calm season: daylight (NC)

techniques designed to exploit an area

1	*gubenge hoologi hagabae*	'netting (by) pushing (toward) rock piles' (70-72)
2	*gubenge hohoologi aga i dai*	'netting (by) pushing up to the lagoon beach' (65-66)
3	*gubenge holoholo aga i dai*	'netting (by) spreading out toward the lagoon beach' (64)
4	*gubenge taile laa dua*	'netting (while) strolling seaward' (62)
5	*gubenge tila aga*	'netting (while) glancing up' (62-63)
6	*heehee agau*	'walking the reef' (61)
7	*bono ae hanga*	'plugging the channel' (58-59)

techniques designed for particular species

8	*gubenge donu*	'netting coral trout' (60)
9	*gubenge baua*	'netting rabbit faced spinefish' (59-60)
10	*gubenge bongongo*	'netting vermiculated spinefish' (60)
11	*gubenge manu*	'netting birds' (rainbow runners) (69-70)
12	*gubenge abi*	'netting spotted surgeonfish' (69)
13	*gubenge gala i dai*	'netting goatfish lagoonward' (63)
14	*gubenge ngadala agau*	'netting Waigeu drummers' (74)
15	*gubenge tawe*	'netting flying fish' (74)
16	*gubenge manini*	'netting striped surgeonfish' (69)
17	*gubenge humu*	'netting triggerfish' (also windy season) (76)

hand netting for bait

18	*di waga llama*	'the torch canoe' (for flying fish) (74-75)
19	*gubenge gube*	'netting small Apogon' (75-76)

Netting during the calm and windy season: evening or night (NY)

1	*gubenge dunga lloo*	'netting soldierfish' (64-65)
2	*gubenge haadolo*	'netting squirrelfish' (68-69)
3	*gubenge buu awa*	'netting (at) the end of the surge channel' (61)
4	*modoholo*	'on the reef flat' (64)

Netting done during the windy season (NW)

1	*gubenge lou niu*	'coconut leaf netting' (66-67)
2	*gubenge tebu*	'netting (by) diving' (72-73)
3	*gubenge gala i tua*	'netting goatfish seaward' (68)
4	*gubenge iha*	'netting garfish' (58)

POLE AND LINE

young boys' techniques (PK)

1	*i tongo tai*	'at the beach and channel shore' (79)
2	*i ni madapua*	'at the tide pools' (79)

Calm season fishing during the day (PC)

technique designed for an area

1	*hihi nia dogo*	'pole and line (at) coral heads'* (79-80)
2	*hihi leduge*	'pole and line (for) handfish' (80)

technique designed for particular species

3	*hihi humu*	'pole and line for triggerfish'* (80)
4	*di waga diu*	'the dipped canoe (bonito)' (80-81)
5	*hihi ngadala agau*	'pole and line (for) Waigeu drummers' (81)

Calm season fishing at night

technique designed for particular species

6	*hihi dangau*	'pole and line (for) snapper' (82)
7	*hihi dalinga*	'pole and line (for) mullet' (82)
8	*hihi malau pungu*	'pole and line for crimson squirrelfish' (82-83)

Windy season fishing (PW)

technique used at seaward beaches

1	*hihi madu*	'pole and line (for) goatfish (variety)' (83)
2	*hihi dangau kila*	'pole and line (for) snapper (variety)' (83)
3	*hihi iha gaa*	'pole and line (for) garfish' (83-84)

technique used at lagoon beaches

4	*hihi gala*	'pole and line (for) goatfish' (84)
5	*hihi ganae*	'pole and line (for) blue spot mullet' (84)

WEIRS (WR)

1	*awa daueni*	'minnow weir' (87-88)
2	*awa gala*	'goatfish weir' (88-89)
3	*awa iha*	'garfish weir' (89)

----

* Can be done during windy season when conditions permit.

TRAPS (T)

1 *uu daa*   'red squirrelfish trap' (93)
2 *uu hagabilau*   'stinky trap' (93-94)
3 *uu dagabe*   'sea perch trap' (94-95)
4 *uu baabaa*   'flat trap' (reef eels) (94)
5 *uu haganiga*   'rounded trap' (moray eels) (95-96)
6 *ulu dahi*   'enter once' (young boys' coconut shell net) (96)

ANGLING
Lagoon angling (LD) during daylight

techniques designed for an area

1 *aangoli ni daula*   'angling at anchorages' (103-104)
2 *di uga danudanu i dai*   'the buried line lagoonward' (101)
3 *aangoli i di awa*   'angling in the main pass' (101)

techniques designed for a particular species

4 *aangoli gelu*   'angling (for) Vlaming's unicornfish' (103)
5 *aangoli ngadala agau*   'angling for Waigeu drummer' (103)
6 *aangoli uli*   'angling for gold band fusilier' (102-103)
7 *aangoli muu*   'angling for large eyed sea bream' (100)
8 *aangoli kau*   'angling for Black Jack' (103)
9 *angoli dagabe*   'angling for sea perch' (103-104)
10 *aangoli dalinga*   'angling for mullet' (104)

Lagoon angling done at night (LN)

techniques designed for a particular area

1 *dabu ae dono di ae hanga*   'fishing at the base of the channel' (101-102)
2 *dili duu langa*   'invent steps on a coconut tree' (101-102)
3 *aangoli a di awa boo*   'night angling in the main pass' (102)

techniques designed for a particular species

4 *aangoli daa*   'angling for red squirrelfish' (100)

Deep sea angling done during calm season (DC)

technique designed to exploit an area

1 *uga hagalala*   'deep (water) fishing line' (105)
2 *gadigadi laa nua*   'biting in the shallows' (110)
3 *danudanu i dua*   'burying the line seaward' (109)
4 *hagalulu bongoo*   'chumming the hole' (107)

technique designed for a particular species

    5 *aangoli kau*   angling for black jack' (106)
    6 *aangoli malianga*   'angling for fusilier' (110)
    7 *di waga madaligi*   'the canoe of the Pleides' (tuna canoes) (107-108)

Evening and night angling (calm season)

technique designed to exploit an area

    8 *dabu ae hagalewelewe*   'fishing (that) causes (something) to fall freely' (110)
    9 *lullulu nia hadu*   'jerking the stones' (107)
   10 *dabu ae hetau*   'fishing to fit (one another)' (111-112)

Daytime angling done throughout the year (DY)

technique designed to exploit an area

    1 *dabu ae tagihagi*   'fishing (by) picking' (108-109)

technique designed for a particular species

    2 *di waga hogoulu*   'the shark canoe' (110-111)
    3 *di waga hoologi*   'the pushing canoe' (111)
    4 *aangoli gina*   'angling for rainbow runners' (108)
    5 *aangoli gelu*   'angling for Vlaming's unicornfish' (106-107)

Appendix 2: Native Fishes of Kapingamarangi Atoll

I present here a list of Kapingamarangi names for fish in four columns: the first column lists the Kapinga name, the second one the scientific name, the third one the common name, and the fourth one lists the methods used to catch the fish (using codes from Appendix 1). I have attempted to make this list exhaustive, but a note of explanation is in order. The core of this list was generated as part of the research for the *Kapingamarangi Lexicon* (Lieber and Dikepa 1974). Our aim was an exhaustive list of root words, so our identifications were not very accurate. The list of fish names did give a basis on which to begin to ask specific questions about fish and fishing when the research began in 1980.

I began my work by asking a number of men to look at photographs of Oceanic fish in several books (Bagnis et. al. 1972, Hobson and Chave 1979, Marshall 1965, Tinker 1978). Each man was asked the Kapinga name for every fish recognized in a picture (with a separate list of responses kept for each). When several people viewed a book simultaneously, I kept a record of responses for each picture, noting both those on which there was agreement and those on which there was disagreement. When people disagreed, I tried to find out what the basis of disagreement was. This information was supplemented by Foss Leach's collection and accurate identification of 100 fish species. I have the most confidence in his identifications, and I have marked each one in the listing with an asterisk (*). I also use the tilde (~) to mean "similar to," and NI to mean no information available.

For comparative purposes, it is worth noting that fishermen commonly distinguish juvenile from adult forms of some species, especially deep water jack fish. This was important ritually, since fishermen commonly used the juvenile form as a euphemism for the adult fish. They do not appear to distinguish gender variations, however. Kapinga use several different principles for classifying fish, including form (particularly head form), color, size, habitat, strength, or habits.

KAPINGA NAME	SCIENTIFIC NAME	COMMON NAME	CATCH METHOD
abi	Acanthurus ~guttatus	spotted surgeonfish	NC12
adu*	Katsuwanus pelamis	skipjack	PC4
adu balebale	Katsuwanus ~pelamis	skipjack/bonito	PC4
adule	Selar sp.	scad	LD1, LD6
agu	Tylosaurus crocodilis	crocodile needlefish	NC18, LN1
agu moana*	Tylosaurus indicus	needlefish sp.	NC18, LN1
agu gau woo	Tylosaurus sp.	needlefish	NC18
ahulu (see maduailau)	Parupeneus ~pleurostigma, ~trifasciatus	goatfish sp.	
alaala*	Caranx melampygus	blue finned trevally	NC2, NC4, NW1, LD2
alawa	Carcharhinus ~longimanus	Oceanic white-tipped shark	DY2, DY3
baaheni*	Bolbometopon bicolor	two color parrotfish	T1, NY 1
baaheni uli*	Cetscarus pulchellus	red speckled parrotfish	T1, NY1
baba	NI	squirrelfish sp.	DC1, DC9
bakau lloo	NI	goby sp.	
baibai*	Arnoglossus ~interinedius	flounder	LD2
balaawa	Pomacentrus sp.	damselfish sp.	
balagia*	Chlorurus microhinus/[Scarus gibbus - Ruppell]	blunt-headed parrotfish	NC2, NC12, NW1, T2
balangi*	Acanthurus xanthopterus	black-barred surgeonfish	NC4, NC12, NW1, T1, LD3, LD4
balai	Abedefduf, Pomacentrus, Plectroglyphidion sp.	damselfish	
balai gamugamu	Pomacentrus sp.	damselfish (coral dweller)	
balu (i)haganga	Aphareus ~fureatus	small toothed job fish	DC1, DC5
balu hogoulu	NI	shark sp.	
baua*	Siganus rostratus	rabbit-faced spinefoot	NC1, NC9, NW1, LD4
belubelu	Selar sp.	scad	DY1, DY4, DY5
bihomale	~Pseudobalistes sp.	NI	PC2, PC6
bologoiee	Gobiidea	goby	T6
bono	Conger sp.	white eel	NY4, T4, DC3
bonono (see Ilahi)	Cheilinus sp.	wrasse sp.	

bongoia		red soldierfish	NY1, NY2
bongongo*	Adioryx rubra or cornutus	vermiculated spinefoot	NC1, NC10, T1, LD7
bongongo loobuge	Siganus ~vermiculatus	rabbitfish	NC7, NC10, LD7, NY4
bongongo luuli*	Siganus sp.	gold spotted spinefoot	NC7, NY4, T1, LD7
bulu ngaa mee*	Siganus chryospilos	flower cod	LD3, LN1, LN3
	Epinephelus fuscog		
panipani	Corphaena sp.	dolphinfish	PC4
daa*	Holocentrus ruber	red squirrelfish	LN4, DC8, DC10
daadiwa	Naso sp.	unicornfish	PC 6
daaea*	Lutjanus sebae	red emperor	DC9, NC3, NC5, NY3, PW2, T1, DY1, LD7, LD9, LN4
daaea uli*	Aethaloperca rogea	blue-flushed rock cod	DY1
daahudi	NI	sleeper#PW1	
dabaduu*	Sphyraena jello	slender sea pike	DC6, DC8, DY5
dada*	Lutjanus coatesi	red bass	PW2, T2, LN2, LN3, DC1, DC3, DC5, DC8, DC9
dagabe	Lutjanus sp.	sea perch	T3, LD9
dagabe agau	Lutjanus ~kasmira	blue-lined sea perch	T3, LD9
dagee	Caranx sp.	large blue jack	LD2, DC8
dagua*	Thunnus albacares	yellow fin tuna	DC1, DC7
dagugu	Abedefduf sp.	blue banded damselfish	NW1, PC1, T6
daiawa*	Acctopoma maculatum	large coral trout	LD3, DC3, DC8, DC9
dalahala*	Pygoplites diacanthus	blue-banded angelfish	NW1
dalinga	Mugil sp.	mullet	NY4, PC7, LD10
dalinga mee*	Cheilinus fasciatus	scarlet-breated Maori wrasse	PC1, PC7
dama datada	NI	NI	LD2, LN1, LN5, LN8, LN9
dama n(i) di mogomogo	Amphirion sp., Apogon sp.	cardinalfish, clownfish	
damedaneauli	Echeneis sp.	remora	
dangau	Lutjanus sp.	parrotfish	NC1, NC3, NY2, NY3, T1, LD9, LN1
dangau bulabula*	Lutjanus semicintus	half-banded parrotfish	NC2, NC3, NY3, LN1, PC1

KAPINGA NAME	SCIENTIFIC NAME	COMMON NAME	CATCH METHOD
dangau podo*	*Lutjanus janthinuropterus*	yellow-streaked parrotfish	NC2, NC3
dangau podo*	*Lutjanus rivulatus*	blue spotted parrotfish	NC2, NC3
dangau gaa*	*Lutjanus monostigma*	one-spot parrotfish	NC2, NC3, NY2, PW2, LN1, DC9
dangau kila	*Lutjanus sp.*	snapper	NC2, NC3
daudahi	*Zanclus sp.*	Moorish idol	NC2, NC3, NY3
daueni	NI	minnow	W1
dauiohi	NI	minnow size reef fish	PK1
debedaa	*Futularia or Aulostoma sp*	trumpetfish	NW4
debedaa gamugamu	*Aulostomus sp.*	trumpetfish	NW4
deedee*	*Arothron stellatus*	starry toad fish	NW1
degemoomoo*	*Ostracion tuberculatum (and other O. sp.)*	(black spotted) boxfish	NC2, NW1
delemanga	*Gnathandon speciosis*	golden jack	LD1
didiadolo	*Chromis sp.* (several)	puller sp.	PC1
dihidihi*	*Chaetodon sp., Heniochus sp.,*	butterfly fishes	NC1, NW1
dilibai*	*Epibulus insidiator*	telescope fish (sling paw)	NW1
dodohai	Gobiidae	goby	
doholaa	NI	whale	NW1
dolobani	*Saurida sp.*	lizardfish	NC8, T1, LD3
donu*	*Plectropoma maculatum*	coral trout/cod	LD3
donu agau	*Plectropoma sp.*	cod	LD3
donu bakau	*Plectropoma sp.*	cod	LD3
donu madaahale*	*Plectropoma melanoleucus*	footballer trout	NC2
dooligi*	*Hemigymnus melapterus*	thick lipped wrasse	
doudu*	*Didion sp.*	porcupine fish	NC1, PC2, PC6
dulu	*Thalassoma sp.*	fire wrasse	NC1, PC2, PC6
dulu golo lenge	*Thalassoma sp.*	wrasse	NC2, PC1
duluhale	*Cheilinus sp.*	wrasse	NY1
dunga lloo	*Flammeo sp., Adioryx sp.*	soldierfish sp., squirrelfish	

tangi di walu	Monotaxis sp.	sea bream sp.	NC5, LD7
tawe	Cypselurus sp.	flying fish	NC15, NC18
tawe hua	Cypselurus sp.	flying fish sp.	NC18
tuigolo	NI	squirrelfish sp.	PC1
tiladee	NI	small reef fish	PK1
gabigabi	NI	jellyfish	NW1, LN2, DC8, DC9
gada*	Caranx sexfasciatus	great trevally	NW1, LN2, LN3
gada alaala	Caranx sp.	trevally	NW1, LN2, LN3
gada llehu*	Caranx ~ignobilis/elacate	lowly trevally	DC3
gada moana	NI	NI	NC3, NC13, NY2, NY4, PW1, PW4, WR2, LN1
gala*	Parupeneus ~janseni	goatfish	NW1
galili	Labroides ~dimidatus	paradise fish	NY3, PW5
galili moana	Labroides sp.	paradise fish	NC2, NW1, LD5, LD7
ganae*	Valamugil seheli	blue spot mullet	NC17, PW5, LD3, LD4, DC6, DY5
ganigani hadu	Platax obicularis	narrow-banded batfish	NC1
gelu*	Cyphomycter vlamingi	Vlaming's unicornfish	T5
gelu agau*	Naso unicornis	long-snouted unicornfish	T5
gihaa bungaa hadu	NI	eel sp.	NC6, DC9, T4
gihaa dongo pada	NI	eel sp. (large spots)	T4
gihaa kene	NI	eel sp. (white)	T4
gihaa hagamadago	Echidna nebulosa	reef eel	NC 1, NW1
gihaa luuli	Gymnothorax javanicus	Javanese moray eel	LD2
gili bege	Cantherhines dumerili	green file fish	NC11, LD1, DC8, DY4
gili uu	Zebrasoma sp.	tang	PC1, NC2
gina*	Elegatis bipinnulata	rainbow runner	PK1
golohedunga	Thalassoma hardwicki (Bennett)	six-barred wrasse	
gololaagi	NI	minnow size reef fish	
goonau	NI	Dolphin	
gube	Apogon sp.	cardinalfish	NC19
gube pada	Apogon sp.	cardinalfish	NC19

KAPINGA NAME	SCIENTIFIC NAME	COMMON NAME	CATCH METHOD
gube huu lloo	Apogon sp.	cardinalfish	NC19
gugu*	Macolor sp.	black sea perch	LD3, DC8, DC9
kau	Caranx lugubris Poey	black jack	NC17, LD8, DC1, DC6, DC8, DC10, DY1, DY5
haabodo	Lutjanus rivulatus or Lethrinus	sea perch or emperor	PW2, T2, LD3, LN3, DC1, DC5, DC9
haadolo	Flammeo sp., Adioryx sp., Holocentrus sp.	soldierfish, squirrelfish	NC7, NC12, NY3, NY4
hagulaa duagua	Makaira sp.	marlin	DC1, DC5, DC7
hagulaa hagulaa	Istiopharus sp.	sailfish	DC1, DC5
hai*	Amphotistuis kuhli	blue spotted stingray	
hai bongoo	Carcharhinus ~menisorrah	grey reef shark	
hai dahadaha	Pastinachus, Dasiatus, or Manta sp.	ray (general for ocean rays)	
hai lodo gelegele	Taeniura sp. or Himantura sp.	ray (sand dweller)	
hai manu	Aetobatis sp.	eagle ray	
halaha	NI	small reef fish	PK1
hau(t)hau	Pterois sp. (several)	zebrafish	NW1
hau gili awa	Gymnothorax fluvimarginatus	dark hatched moray eel	T5
hiba	NI	flying fish sp.	NC18
hiiloo	NI	unicornfish sp.	DC8, DY5
hina*	Macolor niger	black and white sea perch	NW1, LD9
hingala	NI	NI	NW1
hoale	Kuhlia sp.	bream	NC5, PC2, PC6
hogoulu*	Carcharhinus spallan zani	black tip shark	DY2, DY3
hogoulu hongo baba	Carcharhinus ~melanopterus	black-tipped shark	
hogoulu hogoulu	NI	shark sp.	
hugu agau	NI	tang sp.	DY2, DY3
			NW1
hugu laba	NI	tang sp.	LD1, LN3, DC1

hugu manga	Trachinotus bailloni	swallow tail	NW1
hugu manuu	Upeneus sp.	goatfish sp.	NY1, NY2, LD2
hugu mee*	Callicanthus lituratus	Poll unicornfish	NC6, NW1
huhu*	Scarops jordani, Callyodon ~niger, Scarus sp	Jordan's, Dusky, parrotfish sp.	NC2, NW1, T1, T2, LD3
huhu balagia	Scarops rubroviolaceus (Bleaker), Scarus sp.	meadow parrotfish	NC2, NW1, T1
huhu bobo	Scaops sp., Scaus sp.	parrotfish	NC2, NW1, T1, LD3
huhu dee	Scarus ~Forsteri	parrotfish	NC2, NW1, T1
huhu gonoehe	Scarus or Scaops sp.	big belly parrotfish	NC2, NW1, T1
huhu mee	Scarus ~chlorodon Jenys or ~Forserti	green beak parrotfish	NC2, NW1, T1
huhu modu lua	Scarus or Scaops sp.	parrotfish	NC2, NW1, T1
humu	Sufflamen sp.	triggerfish	NC17, PC3, DC5, DY5
humu agau	Balistoides sp. or Sufflamen sp.	triggerfish	NC17, PC3, DC5, DY5
humu daalo	NI	~clear finned triggerfish	NC17, PC3, DC5, DY5
humu dee	NI	triggerfish sp.	NC17, PC3, DC5, DY5
humu habula*	Sufflamen sp. or xanthicthys sp.	triggerfish	NC17, PC3, DC5, DY5
humu hagabegebege*	Melichthys buniva	black triggerfish	NC17, PC3, DC5, DY5
humu hagalala	Sufflamen sp. or Xanthicthys sp.	triggerfish (deep water)	DC1
humu hole	Amanses sp.	file fish	NW1
humu hongo agau	NI	triggerfish	NW1
humu laagau hangehange	NI	triggerfish	NC17, PC3
humu lenge	Melichthys sp.	triggerfish	NC17, PC3, DC5, DY5
humu uli	NI	triggerfish	NC17, PC3, DC5, DY5
huoua	NI	mullet	NC18
huubaga*	Acanthurus sp.	surgeonfish sp.	NC5, LD4, DC5, DC6, DY5
iga bou*	Grammatorcynus bicarinatus	salmon mackerel	LD1, LD4, LD6, DY4
iga buhi*	Pranesus sp.	common hardyhead	
igaa tuu	Ruvettus ~pretiosus cocco	oilfish	LD3, DY5
iga hebu*	Naso brevirostris	short-nosed unicornfish	NC1, LD1
iga mahi	Caranx sp.	jack	NW4, WR3
iha*	Rhynchorhamphus georgi	long billed garfish	PW3
iha gaa	Rhynchorhampus sp.	garfish sp.	

KAPINGA NAME	SCIENTIFIC NAME	COMMON NAME	CATCH METHOD
imu*	*Pseudobalistes flavimarginatus*	queen triggerfish	LD2, LD4
imu walu*	*Naso annulatus*	ring-tailed unicornfish	LD2, LD4
imu ulitimu mmee	*Pseudobalistes fuscus*	marbled triggerfish	LD1, LD2
labelabe	*Coris sp., Hemipteronotus sp.*	combfish, bar-checked wrasse	NC2
labelabe hau baa	*Coris sp.*	combfish	NC2, NW2
labiaa*	*Naso sp.*	unicornfish	DY5
lalaia	*Carcharhinus sp.*	reef shark	
lali*	*Thalassoma lunare*	moon wrasse	PC1
latihoe	*Cheilinus trilobatus*	triple-tail Maori wrasse	NC12, PC2
laloale*	*Carangoides oblongus, Caranx melampigus*	blue jack	NC4, NW1, LD1, LD3, DC6, DY5
laloale bitibiti	*Alectis indicus*	thread fish	NC4, NW1, LD1, LD3
laloale modumodu*	*Carangoides ~laticordis, ~gilberti*	~blue trevally, ~striped jack	NC2, NW1
leduge	*Para sp., Cirrhites ~pinnulatus*	striped handfish	PC2, NY3
leilei	*Chorinemus sp.*	slender leatherskin	DC8, DC9
liba*	*Acanthurus pyroferus*	orange-gilled surgeonfish	NC2, NC5, NW1
liba daa*	*Acanthurus olivaceus*	orange epaullet surgeonfish	NC1, NC2, NC5, NC6, NW1
liba gonoehe*	*Acanthurus gahmon*	black-barred surgeonfish	NC5, NW1
liba habula	*Acanthurus achilles Shaw*	red-spotted surgeonfish	NC2, NC5, NW1
liba hai ono tau	*Acanthurus lineatus*	zebra-striped surgeonfish	NC2, NC5, NW1
liba loobuge dono hiwahiwa	*Acanthurus sp.*	surgeonfish	
liba luuli	*Acanthur / Ctenochaetus sp.*	surgeonfish (thick lipped)	NC2, NC5, NW1
liba maadolo dono ngudu	*Acanthurus sp.*	surgeonfish	NC2, NC5, NW1
liba uu	*Acanthurus sp.*	surgeonfish	NC5
lihaliha	*Caes / Pterocaesio sp.*	cleaner wrasse	T3
Ilahi	*Cheilinus undulatus*	napoleonfish	NC2, LD2
llanga mala	NI	NI	
lolebe (see dagee)	*Caranx sp.*	small jackfish, (juvenile)	PK1
lugulugu	*Lethrinus ~variegatus*	emperor (~variegated emperor)	DC9, DC10, T3

maadau dalinga	Sphyrna lewini	hammerhead shark	LD3, LD9, PC1, DC4
madabagu*	Cephalopholis cyanostigma	blue-spotted rock cod	DC1, DC4, DC5
madabiabia	Cephalopholis urodelus	flagtail	DC8, DC9
madaele*	Cephalopholis miniatus	coral cod	NC3, LD2
madagaladi*	Chanos chanos	milkfish	NC1, NC3, NY2
madagiwi	Scolopsis / Pentapodus sp.	spinecheek or bream	T5
madalili	Gymnothorax ~ undulatus	moray eel	DC8, DC9
madamada*	Apareus ~rutilans	small toothed jobfish	NC3, NY3, PW1
madu	Parupeneus macronemus	goatfish sp.	NC7, NC13, NY4
maduailau*	NI	long-barbled goatfish	PK1
mataligau	Corphaena hippurus	small reef fish	DC1, DC5
mahimahi	Acanthocybium solandri	dolphin fish	DC7, DC8, DC99
mala*	Hococentrus sp.	wahoo	NC1, NC3, NW1
malali	Holocentrus tiereoides	ornated wrasse	DC4
malau (malau hadu)*	Ostichthys murdjan	pink spotted squirrelfish	PC8, DC10
malau pungu*	Ostichthys adustus	Crimson squirrelfish	DC10
malau pungu luuli*	Adioryx sp. / Holocentrus sp.	blue squirrelfish	LN4, DC4, LN10
malau daa	Caesio xanthonotus	squirrelfish	NC17, DC6
malianga	NI	fusilier	
malili	Acanthurus ~sandvicensis	NI	NC1, NC12, NY3
manini	Epinephelus damelii	surgeonfish	DC4, DC8, DC9
manu guoua*	Parahemistictus sp. / Paracirrhites sp.	saddled rock cod	PC2
maulungu	Bolbometopan muraticus	multicolored handfish/hawkfish	NC2, NW1
melenge*	NI	double-headed parrotfish	
moe aa	NI	shark sp.	
moe hoeho	Saurida sp.	whale or porpoise sp.	PK1
mogo	Triaenodon apicalus	lizardfish	DY2
mogo lewe*	Carcharhinus menisorah	white-tip shark	DC1
mongohenua	NI	grey shark	LN2, LN3, T2, DC1
muiha	Monotaxis granoculis	large grouper	NC6, LD2, LD4, LN1
muu*	Lethrinus fletus	large-eyed sea bream	NC6, NY2, LD4, LD9, LN1, LN4
muu gaa*		red-finned emperor	

KAPINGA NAME	SCIENTIFIC NAME	COMMON NAME	CATCH METHOD
muu madawai	*Lethrinus sp.*	emperor	NC6, LD4, LN1
nanua	*Kyphosus sp.*	topsail drummer	NW1
nohu*	*Scorpaena cardinalis, Antennaruis sp., Synaneeja*	scorpionfish/toadfish/stonef.	NW1
nonu	*Lethrinus sp.*	emperor	DC1, DC5, DY1
ngaa*	*Megalops cyprinoides*	ox-eye herring	NC1, LN4, DC4
ngadala	*Epinephelus sp.*	sea bass	NC4, NC6, NC14, NY2, PC5
ngadala agau*	*Kyphosus ~vaigensis*	Waigeu drummer (rudderfish)	LD3, LD9, DC4
ngadala baabaa	*Epinephelus ~socialis*	leopard sea bass	NC1, NC2, NW1, PW2, LD2, LN1
ngadala bahi dua	*Epinephelus sp.*	sea bass	NC2, NW1
ngadala daalo*	*Epinephelus ~taurina*	estuary rock cod	LD3, LD9, LN2, LN3, LN4, T1, DC1, DC9, DY1
ngadala dee*	*Epinephelus sp.*	sea bass	NC1, NC2, NW1, LN1
ngadala dongo lligi	*Epinephelus melanostigma*	sea bass	DC8, DC10
ngadala e tau	*Epinephelus sp.*	sea bass	T2, LN2, LN3
ngadala mee	*Epinephelus sp.*	sea bass	NC1, NC3, NC5, T1, DC4
ngadala mogo dee*	*Epinephelidae*	small reef fish	PK1, LD1
ngadule	NI	long nosed emperor	LD1, DC1, DC2, DC3, DC5
ngudu looloo	*Lethrinus ~miniatus*	sea bass	NC1, NC2, DC3, NY3, PC2, PC6
ngudungudu	NI		
ogoogo	*Lethrinus ~xonthocheilus*	short-nosed emperor	NC1, NC5, NW1, LD2, LN1
ono	*Ariosphyraena barracuda*	barracuda	DC1, DC7, DC8
udu*	*Aprion virescens*	green jobfish	LD1, LN2, LN3, DC2, DC8, DY1
ulahi*	*Hipposcarus longiceps*	long-nosed parrotfish	NC1, NC2, NW1, T1, LD1, LD2, LD4, LD7
uli*	*Caesio coerulaureus*	gold banded fusilier	LD2

ulua	*Caranx ignobilis*	large big headed jack	LN2, LN3, DC8, DC9
uu nauna	NI	NI	NC1, DC5
wale*	*Arothron hispidus*	broad barred toadfish	NC1, NW1, DC5
wale dongo kene	*Arothron sp.*	toadfish (white spotted)	NC1, NW1, DC5
wale gimoo	*Arothron nigropunctatus / A. canthigaster*	yellow pufferfish	NC1, NC2, NW1
wale tawe	*Arothron sp.*	pufferfish	NC2, NW1
walu	*Gymnosarda sp.*	dog-toothed tuna	NC18
wede	*Parupeneus sp.*	goatfish	NC3, NC13
wede mee	*Mulloidichthys sp.*	goatfish	LD1, LD3
wele	*Variola louti*	chameleon sea bass	LD3, DY1

References

Alkire, W. 1978. *Coral Islanders*. Arlington Heights, Illinois: AHM Publishing.
Ashby, R. 1953. *Design for a Brain*. New York: Wiley.
———. 1956. *Introduction to Cybernetics*. New York: Wiley
Bagnis, R and P. Mazellier, J. Bennett, and E. Christian. 1972. *Fishes of Polynesia*. Papeete, Tahiti: Editions du Pacific.
Barnett, Homer G. 1953. *Innovation: the Basis of Culture Change*. New York: McGraw-Hill.
———. 1983. *Qualitative Science*. New York: Vantage Press.
Barnett, Steven and Martin G. Silvernman. 1979. *Ideology and Everyday Life: Anthropology, Neomarxist Thought, and the problem of Ideology and the Social Whole*. Ann Arbor: University of Michigan Press.
Bateson, Gregory (editor). 1961. *Percival's Narrative: a patient's account of his psychosis, 1830-1832*. Stanford: Stanford University Press.
———. 1972. *Steps to an Ecology of Mind*. New York: Ballantine Books.
———. 1983. *Mind and Nature*. New York: Bantam Books.
Bateson, Gregory and Mary Catherina Bateson. 1987. *Angels Fear: towards an Epistemology of the Sacred*. New York: MacMillan and Co.
Becker, Carl L. 1958. *The Declaration of Independence: a history of political ideas*. New York: Vintage Books.
Benedict, Ruth. 1934. *Patterns of Culture*. Boston: Houghton Mifflin.
Berrien, Kenneth. 1968. *General and Social Systems*. New York: Wiley.
Bidney, David. 1967. *Theoretical Anthropology*. New York: Schocken Books.
Bryan, E. H. Jr. 1972. *Guide to Islands in the Tropical Pacific (Polynesia, Micronesia, Melanesia)*. Honolulu: Pacific Science Center, Bernice P. Bishop Museum.
Buck, Peter (Te Rangi Hiroa). 1930. *Samoan Material Culture*. Bernice P. Bishop Museum Bulletin no. 75. Honolulu: Bernice Bishop Museum Press.
———. 1950. *Material culture of Kapingamarangi*. Bernice P. Bishop Museum Bulletin 200. Honolulu: Bernice Bishop Museum Press.
Carroll, Raymonde. 1988. *Cultural Misunderstandings: the French/American Experience*. Chicago: University of Chicago Press.
Carroll, Vern. 1970. Adoption on Nukuoro. In *Adoption in Eastern Oceania*, edited by Vern Carroll. ASAO Monograph Series no. 1. Honolulu: University Press of Hawaii.

_____. 1975. The population of Nukuoro in historical perspective. In *Pacific Atoll Populations*, edited by Vern Caroroll. A.S.A.O. Monograph Series no. 3. Honolulu: University Press of Hawaii.

_____. 1977. Communities and non-communities: the Nukuoro on Ponape. In *Exiles and Migrants in Oceania*, edited by Michael D. Lieber. A.S.A.O. Monograph Series no. 5. Honolulu: University Press of Hawaii.

Chapple, Eliot D. and Cartlon Coon. 1942. *Principles of Anthropology*. New York: Holt.

Chowning, Ann and Goodenough, Ward H. 1966. Lakalai political organization. *Anthropological Forum* 1: 412-473.

Comaroff, J. L. 1982. Dialectical systems, history and anthropology: units of study and questions of theory. *The Journal of Southern African Studies* 8: 143-172.

Conklin, Harold C. 1957. *Hanunoo Agriculture: a Report on an Integral System of Shifting Cultivation in the Philippines*. Rome: Food and Agriculture Organization of the United Nations.

Eilers, Anneliese. 1934. Inselm um Ponape. In *Ergebnisse der Sudsee-Expedition, 1908-1910*. Edited by Georg Thilenius. II Ethnographie; B Mikronesien. Vol. 8. Hamburg. (English translation by the Bishop Museum Library)

Emerick, Richard. 1960. Homesteading on Ponape: a study and analysis of a resettlement program of the United States Trust Territory government of Micronesia. Ph. D. dissertation, University of Pennsylvania. (Available from University Microfilms, Ann Arbor, Michigan).

Emory, Kenneth P. 1965. *Kapingamarangi: Social and Religious Life of a Polynesian Atoll*. Bernice P. Bishop Nuseum Bulletin 228. Honolulu: Bernice Bishop Museum Press.

Flinn, Juliana. 1992. *Diplomas and Thatch Houses: Asserting Tradition in a Changing Micronesia*. Ann Arbor: University of Michigan Press.

Goodenough, Ward. 1963. *Cooperation in Change*. New York: Russel Sage Foundation.

Herrigel, Eugen. 1964. l *Zen and the Art of Archery*. New York: Pantheon Books.

Herdt, Gilbert. 1987. *The Sambia: ritual and gender in New Guinea*. New York: Holt, Reinhart, and Winston.

Jerome, John. 1980. *The Sweet Spot in Time*. New York: Summit Books.

Johannes, Robert. 1981. *Words of the Lagoon: Fishing and Marine Lore of the Palau District of Micronesia*. Berkeley: University of California Press.

Kirkpatrick, John. n. d. Ethnicity in Marquesan ideology and practice. Prepared for the Association for Social Anthropology in Oceania symposium on Cultural Identity in Oceania, Salem, MA, 1985. (Available from the author.)

Kita, J. 1987. The sweet spot in cycling. In *Bicycling* 28, no 8, 44-46.

Lansing, J. S. 1991. *Priests and Programmers: Technologies of Power in the Engineered Landscape of Bali*. Princeton, New Jersey: Princeton University Press.

Levy, Robert. 1970. Tahitian adoption as a psychological message. In *Adoption in Eastern Oceania*. Edited by Vern Carroll. ASAO Monograph Series no. 1. Honolulu: University Press of Hawaii.

Lieber, Michael D. 1968. *Porakiet: a Kapingamarangi Colony on Ponape*. Eugene, Oregon: University of Oregon, Department of Anthropology.

———. 1970. Adoption on Kapingamarangi. In *Adoption in Eastern Oceania*, edited by Vern Carroll. Association for Social Anthropology in Oceania Monograph Series no. 1. Honolulu: University Press of Hawaii.

———. 1974. Land tenure on Kapingamarangi. In *Land Tenure in Oceania*, edited by Henry P. Lunsgaarde. ASAO Monograph Series no. 2. Honolulu: University Press of Hawaii.

———. 1976. Riddles, cultural categories, and world view. *Journal of American Folklore* 89:255-265.

———. 1977a. Change in two Kapingamarangi communities. In *Exiles and Migrants in Oceania*. Edited by Michael D. Lieber. ASAO Monograph Series no. 5. Honolulu: University Press of Hawaii.

———. 1977b. The resettled community and its context. In *Exiles and Migrants in Oceania*. Edited by Michael D. Lieber. ASAO Monograph Series no. 5. Honolulu: University Press of Hawaii.

———. 1984. Strange Feast; negotiating identities on Ponape. *Journal of the Polynesian Society* 93; 141-189.

———. 1990. Lamarckian identities on Kapingamarangi and Pohnpei. In *Cultural Identity in Oceania*. Edited by Jocelyn Linnekin and Lyn Poyer. Honolulu: University Press of Hawaii.

———. 1991. Cutting your losses: death and grieving in a Polynesian community. In *Coping with the Final Tragedy: Death and Grieving in Transcultural Perspective*, edited by Dorothy Counts and David Counts. New York: Baywood Press.

Lieber, Michael D. and Kalio H. Dikepa. 1974. *Kapingamarangi Lexicon*. Pacific and Asian Language Texts: Polynesia. Honolulu: University Press of Hawaii.

Macdonald, Barrie. 1982. *Cinderllas of the Empire: towards a history of Kiribati and Tuvalu*. Canberra: Australian National University Press.

Malinowski, Bronislaw. 1922. *Argonauts of the Western Pacific*. London: Routledge, Kegan, and Paul.

———. 1944. *A Scientific Theory of Culture and other Essays*. Chapel Hill: University of North Carolina Press.

———. 1945. *The Dynamics of Culture Change*. New Haven: Yale University Press.

Manolescu, Kathleen Marie. 1987. *An Approach to the Ethnography of Farming as a Culturally Structured Technical System*. Ph. D. dissertation, University of Pennsylvania, Philadelphia, PA. (Available from University Microfilms, Ann Arbor, MI.).

Marshall, T. C. 1965. *Fishes of the Great Barrier Reef and coastal waters of Queensland*. Sydny: Livingston Publishing.

McCorckle, Thomas. 1963. *A New Method of Community Analysis*. Harrisburg: Commonwealth of Pennsylvania, Department of Sanitation.

McCracken, J. M. 1979. Rethinking rural poverty. *Journal of African History 19*: 614-615.

McCulloch, W. 1965. *Embodiments of Mind*. Cambridge, Mass.:M. I. T. Press.

Maruyama, M. 1963. The second cybernetics: deviation-amplifying mutual causal processes. *American Scientist* 51: 164-179.

Mead, Margaret. 1978. *Culture and Commitment: the New Relations Between the Generations in the 1970s*. Revised edition. New York: Columbia University Press.

Miller, G. A. 1975. *The Psychology of Communication*. New York: Basic Books.

Nagel, E. and J. R. Newman. 1958. *Godel's Proof*. New York: New York University Press.

Opler, Morris E. 1946 Themes as dynamic forces in culture. *American Journal of Sociology* 51: 198-206.

Pattee, Howard H. (ed.) 1973. *Hierarchy Theory: the Challenge of Complex Systems*. New York: George Braziller.

Paul, Benjamin, editor. 1955. *Health, Culture, and Community*. New York: Russel Sage Foundation.

Poole, J. F. P. 1985. Coming into social being: cultural images of infants in Bimin-Kuskusian folk psychology. In *Person, Self, and Experience*, edited by Geoffrey M. White and John Kirkpatrick. Berkeley: University of California Press, pp. 183-242.

Rappaport, Roy. 1971 Ritual regulation of environmental relations. In *Melanesia: Readings on a Culture Area*, edited by L. L. Langness and J. C. Weschler. Scranton: Chandler.

———. 1986. The construction of time and eternity in ritual. Text of a lecture delivered for the David Skomp Distinguished Lecture Series, Indiana University, October, 1986. Bloomington: Indiana University, Department of Anthropology.

Reusch, J. and G. Bateson. 1951. *Communication: the Social Matrix of Psychiatry*. New York: W. W. Norton.

Riesenberg, Saul H. 1968. *The Poneapan Polity*. Washington, D. C.: Smithsonian Institution.

Royal Anthropological Institute. 1951. *Notes and Queries in Anthropology*. 6th edition, revied and rewritten, London: Routledge, Kegan, and Paul.

Schneider, D. 1968. *American Kinship: a Cultural Account*. Chicago: University of Chicago Press.

Schwartzman, Helen. 1981. Hidden agendas and formal organizations or how to dance at a meeting. *Social Analysis 9*: 77-88.

Shannan, C. E. and W. Weaver. 1949. *The Mathmatical Theory of Communnication.* Urbana: University of Illinois Press. Shore, Bradd. 1984. *Sala I'lua: a Samoan Mystery.* New York: Columbia University Press.

Silverman, M. G. 1969. Maximize your options: a study in symbols, values, and structure. In *Forms of Symbolic Action*, edited by Robert W. Spencer. Proceedings of the 1969 Annual Spring Meeting of the American Ethnological Society. Seattle: University of Washington Press.

Silverstein, M. 1976 Shifters, linguistic descriptions, and cultural catgories. In *Meaning in Anthropology*, edited by Keith Basso and Henry A. Selby. Albuquerque: University of New Mexico press, 11-56.

Simon, H. A. 1968. *The Sciences of the Artificial.* Cambridge, Mass.: M. I. T. Press.

Singh, Jagjit. 1966. *Great Ideas in Information Theory, Language, and Cybernetics.* New York: Dover Publications.

Spicer, Edward H., editor. 1952. *Human Problems in Technological Change: A Casebook.* New York: Russell Sage Foundation.

Tinker, S. W. 1978. *Fishes of Hawaii.* Honolulu: Hawaiian Services, Inc.

Viviani, Nancy. 1970. *Nauru: Phosphate and Political Progress.* Honolulu: University Press of Hawaii.

Wagner, Roy. 1971 Are there social groups in the New Guinea Highlands? In *Melanesia: Readings in a Culture Area*, edited by L. L. Langness and John C. Weschler. Scranton: Chandler and Sharp Publishers.

White, L. A. 1949. *The Science of Culture.* New York: Farrar Straus.

Whyte, L. L., A. G. Wilson, and D. Wilson (eds.) 1969. *Hierarchical Structures.* New York: American Elvesier Publishing Company.

Wiener, N. 1965. *Cybernetics, or Control and Communication in animals and machines.* Cambridge, Mass., M. I. T. Press.

Wiens, Harold. 1956. The geography of Kapingamarangi Atoll in the Eastern Carolines. *Atoll Research Bulletin* 48. Pacific Science Board, National Research Council.

———. 1962. *Atoll Environment and Ecology.* New Haven: Yale University Press.

Praise for **MORE THAN A LIVING**

"An accurate and most fascinating account of traditional fisheries in one of the most remote of the Caroline Islands."

—*Mike A. McCoy*
Fisheries Officer, Yap State
Federated States of Micronesia

"*More Than a Living* is more than a book about fishing on a remote Pacific atoll. It is a first-rate ethnography that makes innovative use of cybernetics and systems theory. Writing in a lively style, Lieber gives us a clear understanding of what it is like to be a Kapinga person in the 1990s following the myriad changes that have affected this community over the past century. ... Lieber sets a very high standard for others to follow."

—*Mac Marshall*
Professor of Anthropology, University of Iowa

Polynesians of Kapingamarangi refer to fishing as the "surfacing of the sacred." Shaped by the relationships between a coral reef ecosystem and a religion designed to appease powerful spirits, traditional fishing activity once signified the integration and sanctity of community. In *More Than a Living*, Michael Lieber compares changes in this traditional activity with those in the larger Kapinga community. Lieber's findings offer a lucid portrayal of how culture shapes a community's response to change.

Michael D. Lieber is associate professor of anthropology at the University of Illinois at Chicago.

For order and other information, please write to:
WESTVIEW PRESS
5500 Central Avenue • Boulder, Colorado 80301-2877
36 Lonsdale Road • Summertown • Oxford OX2 7EW

ISBN 0-8133-8780-9